Contents

Understanding Contractual and Tortious Obligations

Preface

An introduction to the law of obligations could adopt a number of approaches. A standard approach is to provide a comprehensive and readable summary of the rules of contract, tort and restitution; on the Continent the best of these – the works of the Natural Law School and the subsequent civil codes – have been described as 'elegant nutshells'. The chapters which follow will not adopt this approach, although one might continue to aim for elegance. The chapters will not set out to be fully comprehensive of contract, tort and restitution. Instead they will focus on topics that provide a structural and methodological insight into contractual and tortious obligations, with the object of guiding readers towards points of view that might be helpful in tackling not just the more imaginative essay question but also the more interesting hypothetical litigation problem. Thus some areas within the law of contractual and tortious obligations will be mentioned only in passing, the reader being left to research the detail in one of the many more comprehensive textbooks on the law of contract or tort. Equally, only very few cases and statutes will be examined in any detail; cases and materials books are, therefore, a vital supplement if what the professional bodies now call Obligations I and Obligations II are to be understood in their rich depth. This selective approach will allow this present, relatively brief, book to employ chapter topics that stress the structural aspects of contract and tort.

The relatively abstract level at which this book will operate will be reinforced to some extent by a willingness to look beyond positive English law. Several national and transnational codes such as the *Principles of European Contract Law* will be used to provide on occasions a background framework. Sometimes various articles in these codes can more or less reflect the legal position in England, but their real importance is that they offer particular models that can act as points of comparative reference for understanding the model adopted by the common law in respect of certain topics (or indeed whole areas) of liability. This approach can be of great value when it comes to analysing factual situations because different models can provide, if not always different solutions, at least alternative ways of conceptualising the problem. In addition, it may be that such codes represent the future; and so another aim of this book is to be forward-looking and to recognise that English law is now to be understood in the context of an ever-growing European Union (a point that does seem to be recognised by the UK judiciary, if not by the law faculties). Yet in being forward-looking it will stress *difference* – particularly with respect to methodology and legal *mentalité* – as much as similarity.

The form and substance of this book owes much to others, and the various debts are, it is hoped, acknowledged, at least in part, by the reference bibliography. A special debt is owed to Professor Stephen Waddams, not just for his encouragement, but also for his willingness to spend time sharing with me his vast depth of private law knowledge and his sophisticated understanding of the common law mind. In allowing me an early glimpse of his work on common law legal reasoning, it can truly be said that this present book is one of the first to benefit from his recent detailed research and reflection. Comments and observations over the years by Tony Weir, Bernard Rudden, John Bell and Pierre Legrand invariably stimulated me into reflection; and Kevin Gray's deep and thoughtful work on property concepts is a continual source of inspiration. Professor Nick Kasirer kindly sent me copies of his recent work on classification and the law of obligations, work which I found of great value. My colleague Dr Sophie Vigneron generously read the whole manuscript and made many invaluable comments and suggestions. Various anonymous readers also deserve mention, since their observations and criticisms proved extremely useful and the book has benefited as a result. Lastly, I must thank my wife Jennifer, who has been most tolerant about my absences in Europe and my late night working.

Geoffrey Samuel
Kent Law School
June 2005

Table of Cases

Table of Legislation

Statutes

Statutory Instruments

European Legislation

Abbreviations

BGB	*Bürgerliches Gesetzbuch* (German Civil Code)
C	*Code of Justinian*
CA	Court of Appeal
CC	*Code civil* (French Civil Code)
D	*Digest of Justinian* (also Dalloz)
G	*Institutes of Gaius*
HL	House of Lords
J	*Institutes of Justinian* (also Justice of the High Court)
JCP	*Jurisclasseur périodique* (La Semaine Juridique)
LJ	Lord Justice (Court of Appeal)
PC	Privy Council
PECL	*Principles of European Contract Law*
PETL	*Principles of European Tort Law*
UNIDROIT	*Unidroit Principles for International Commercial Contracts*

Introductory Remarks

The law of obligations is now a common term in English law, both in professional practice and in academic writing. It is an import from the civil (Roman) law tradition and thus represents a concrete link, at least at the level of language, between English and continental private law. Some, no doubt, see its adoption as an early step in a journey towards the complete harmonisation (whatever that might mean) of private law among the Member States of the European Union. Indeed, there are now codes for both the law of contractual and non-contractual obligations. These codes, in particular the *Principles of European Contract Law* (PECL) and the *Principles of European Tort Law* (PETL), will be important reference points in the chapters that follow since, even if they do not represent current English positive law, they can help foster an understanding of how a law of obligations is structured. Nevertheless, the use of the term 'obligations' in this present work, and the references to European codes, are not to be taken as implying that harmonisation of the common law and civil law is a foregone conclusion. In fact the adoption of the civilian category of a law of obligations does not come without a number of serious conceptual problems. Some of these problems will be dealt with in more depth in the chapters that follow.

In England the term 'law of obligations' is a generic category embracing three areas of law: contract, tort and restitution (unjust enrichment). It is not entirely clear if trusts belong within the law of obligations since they tend to be more closely associated with the law of property. However, they could have just as valid a claim to be included as, say, the law of restitution because trustees can be held liable for breach of a legal duty. Both the liability and the duty can be very similar to liabilities and duties within the law of obligations (see, eg, *Royal Brunei Airlines v Tan* (1995)); indeed certain trust liabilities are actually classed within the law of restitution. It should thus already be apparent that the category of the law of obligations is not necessarily one that fits easily into the contours of the common law. Common lawyers have historically used a classification model very different from the Roman one, even if both systems once thought in terms of a collection of forms of action (see Samuel, 2003; Kasirer, 2003).

This history of English law, among other things, will reveal that the present categories of contract and tort are a relatively recent way of classifying liability cases. This is not to say that contract was unknown to common lawyers before the 19th century, but it was often hidden behind a set of forms of action that had little or no connection with Roman law thinking. Trespass and debt were once more familiar categories than contract and tort. The modern categories emerged and were consolidated in their definitive forms only over the last two centuries, and restitution has gained its independence just very recently. The modern categories have, now, become detailed if not complex, yet the chapters that follow will not attempt to outline all the main principles of contract and tort (or restitution). Instead the emphasis will be on how English law approaches liability for breach of (or failure to perform) contractual and tortious obligations. In other words, the tendency will be to look at what happens when things go wrong between the parties to an obligation.

In truth the law of tort can be approached only from a liability point of view because, unlike contract, the subject is not one, even in the civil law, that thinks easily in terms of a pre-existing binding legal bond between persons. The obligation to compensate arises out of the accident or the wrongful act itself. Nevertheless, there are exceptions to this obligation point. Participating in certain activities, such as driving and manufacturing, or occupying land, can be seen to carry with it duties or obligations towards others affected by these activities; and the existence of such an obligation is recognised by the various actors (or in some situations imposed by public law) in the recourse to liability insurance (cf *Gwilliam v West Herts NHS Trust* (2002)). Given this idea that an obligation can attach to activities, where damage has been caused by a person or thing under the control of another, this will be presented in this work as a liability for persons and for things (**Chapter 9**). This is rather French in its approach in the way it echoes a liability arising out of art 1384 of the *Code civil*. Yet it is adopted here not so much to show harmonisation solidarity with civil law, but simply because it is a most valuable approach to problem analysis. Distinguishing between harm arising out of an individual act or omission and harm arising out of a thing is a factual distinction that is often useful to make when reflecting upon the legal concepts and rules that might be applicable. Indeed some things, like dangerous premises, products or animals, attract their own specific contract and (or) tort rules (partly statutory). Harm caused by one person connected by way of contract to another person can create causation and (or) duty problems, and thus the idea of a liability for people is another useful analytical tool.

This work will focus primarily on contract and tort since these are foundational subjects in the law schools. Yet the law of restitution cannot be completely ignored as its main principles form part of the Obligations I and II syllabus and, anyway, both contract and tort problems can give rise to restitution issues (see, eg, *Att-Gen v Blake* (2001)). Indeed, as Professor Waddams (2003) has shown, there are many cases that transgress the boundaries between contract, tort, restitution and property. The main structure underpinning liability arising out of the principle of unjust enrichment will thus be surveyed, but with reference to a draft Scottish statute which could act as something of an unofficial code (**Chapter 11**). However, this survey will be particularly brief and will by no means attempt to do the law of restitution justice, even in the context of a short book. The law of restitution is as detailed and rich as either contract or tort, but it tends to be studied in depth only at postgraduate level.

Lastly, an introductory comment must be made about legal method and reasoning, because this is an aspect of legal knowledge that is as vital to the understanding of liability in English law as any positive rules of law. The official view of legal method in the law of obligations is that judges apply pre-existing contract and tort rules to sets of litigation facts as they present themselves before the courts (see **6.3.2.2**, below). This view is not wrong, especially with respect to contract which is a subject that has many more rules than tort (see, eg, the *Code civil*). But such a view is only part of a larger methodological framework in which judges arrive at their solutions to cases using concepts, arguments and justifications drawn from sources not just from within the law but also from outside it (see **6.3.2.5–6.3.2.9**, below). This is an aspect of English law that has long history (see Lobban, 1991). Policy and morality have their role to play in judgments, and even where judges reason from within the law they might well draw some of their ideas and concepts, as has already been suggested, from areas beyond contract or tort (see on this Waddams, 2003; and see also the recent case of *Chester v Afshar* (2004)). If contract and tort are to be properly understood, the methodology of the judges cannot be ignored as something 'outside' legal knowledge.

1   Locating the Law of Obligations

The purpose of this first chapter is to attempt to give an overview of contractual and tortious obligations, and to place them in the more general scheme of what a continental lawyer sees as 'private law'.

1.1   Common law and civil law: general remarks

Lord Diplock once began a judgment by asserting that the 'law of contract is part of the law of obligations' and that the 'English law of obligations is about their sources and the remedies which the court can grant to the obligee for a failure by the obligor to perform his obligation voluntarily' (*Moschi v Lep Air Services* (1973), 346). For its time this comment was, and indeed remains, noteworthy. First, because he places contract within a larger generic category of 'obligations', and for anyone with a rudimentary knowledge of Roman law and (or) modern continental law (known as the civil law tradition) this has interesting comparative law implications. Secondly, although he mentions sources, he goes on to make it clear that the real focal point is the failure to perform. 'Obligations which are performed voluntarily', he goes on to state, 'require no intervention by a court of law' since they 'do not give rise to any cause of action'. This failure to perform is the key to understanding much (admittedly not all) of contract and tort, and it will be the main focal point of the following chapters. Thirdly, and associated with the last point, Lord Diplock links obligations to remedies. What remedy the claimant is seeking is another important, indeed often vital, means of understanding contract and tort cases.

A work on the law of obligations seems, then, to have to function at a number of different levels. Not only does it have to analyse this import from continental law and to set out its main characteristics, no doubt distinguishing obligations from other areas of the law; it equally has to marry obligations to the traditional common law notions of causes of action and legal remedies, which may respond, at least historically speaking, to patterns of thought that are rather different from the patterns of legal thought in Roman legal science. One should not be surprised, therefore, if a work on the English law of obligations proves to be rather complex, for one has to relate the notion to two, rather separate legal mentalities (English and continental), rooted in differing institutional histories and differing methodological approaches.

This difference of methodology ought perhaps not to be underestimated. In the civil law tradition on the Continent the development of law as a body of knowledge has largely been in the hands of university professors. The French law professors of the 16th century, seeing themselves as 'legal scientists' (from the Roman expression *scientia juris*), forged, through great effort, the modern rigorous research methods. And their successors in Europe, the Enlightenment jurists of the 17th and 18th centuries, believed that legal reasoning could be reduced to a hardened systems model axiomatic in nature, like those to be found in mathematics. Solutions to cases for many continental jurists were a matter of rational deduction from a set of normative axioms. As one legal historian has written, the 'distrust with regard to judges was in reality only one particular aspect of a more general conception, typical of the Enlightenment philosophers, but already present in the 17th century: that of society as a *regulated machine*'. That is to say, society 'was no longer conceived as a natural organism, but as a vast machine constructed piece by piece, from a founding contract, by the legislators'. Indeed, 'Frederick II, in a revealing text written at the beginning of his reign, compared society to a watch and the legislator as a watchmaker' (Carbasse, 1998, § 176).

One of the notable characteristics of the common law tradition, in contrast, is that for much of its history it never subscribed either to the continental deductive methodology, or indeed to the need for university faculties of law (Lobban, 1991). Common law faculties in England are largely a 20th-century phenomenon, and thus for much of its history the expounding of English law has been in the hands of judges. Nevertheless, some of the continental methods and theories crossed the Channel, especially during the 19th century, when English law was experiencing something of an identity crisis. In the new university law faculties Roman law was taught alongside English law subjects, and gradually a new 'scientific' spirit infected the teaching, and to some extent the procedure and practice, of law, whereby 'the law could be satisfactorily declared in isolation from particular facts' (Waddams, 2003, 36). This scientific attitude is still prevalent in the law faculties, with the result that many academic lawyers find it difficult to distinguish between 'the law' as a positive set of rules and 'thinking like a lawyer'. For 'thinking like a lawyer' is intimately bound up with knowledge of positive rules themselves; one applies the rules simply in as logical manner as possible. Thus one law professor has written that a better 'understanding of the law depends upon a sound taxonomy of the law'. And if scholars turn their back on this sound taxonomy, 'the common law will dissolve into incoherence' since information 'which cannot be sorted is not knowledge' (Birks, 2000, li).

Taxonomy is undoubtedly important to the understanding of contract and tort because it organises both the rules and concepts (to some extent at least) and the actual facts that go to make up cases. In addition these two categories make up a higher category, that of the law of obligations. In turn 'obligations' forms one of three categories (the others are 'persons' and 'property') which belong to the even higher category of 'private law'. This whole scheme then reflects itself back into the facts of social reality. There are social relations between people and things (property) and between person and person (obligation), while some intangible 'things', such as liberty, dignity and privacy, attach to each person in society not because of a relation, but because they are part of being human (persons). As a Cambridge examination paper once asserted (inviting candidates to discuss the assertion): 'before one can apply the law the facts must be categorised; but before the facts can be categorised the law must be applied'. Abstract legal thinking, in short, comes almost unconsciously into play when lawyers put their mind to a raw set of facts.

However, too rigid adherence to 'sound' taxonomical schemes can distort the understanding of contract and tort. This point has been convincingly illustrated in a work recently published by Stephen Waddams (*Dimensions of Private Law* (2003)), where he points out that overly schematic analysis of common law contract and tort cases is likely to inhibit understanding. For in many single decisions *a range of arguments rooted in a mass of differing categories and concepts is deployed by both counsel and judges*. Thus *Lumley v Gye* (1853) might formally be a 'tort' case to be classified, according to a 'sound' taxonomy, strictly in the tort books. Yet an analysis of the reasoning in the decision uncovers a very different situation; there are arguments, concepts and principles plundered (so to speak) from a range of legal fields, and as a result *Lumley v Gye* could equally be said to be an 'unjust enrichment' – or even a 'property' – case. As Waddams says, a 'desire for precision and order naturally leads to a search for clear categories and good maps, but such a search, if pressed too far, may be self-defeating, for material that is inherently complex is not better understood by concealing its complexity (Waddams, 2003, 2).

1.2 Law of obligations

Many of these valuable points made by Professor Waddams will be reiterated in subsequent chapters in the context of particular examples. However, an understanding of contract and tort, as has already been asserted, does require a knowledge of taxonomy, if only to make sense of Lord Diplock's comment about contract being part of the law of obligations. One must turn, then, to the law of obligations scheme itself.

1.2.1 Definition

The notion of a law of obligations comes from Roman law, where an obligation was defined as 'a legal bond (*vinculum iuris*) whereby we are constrained to do something according to the law of our state' (J.3.13). This definition is rather meaningless as a proposition. However, the metaphorical image of a *vinculum iuris* binding two persons has proved extraordinarily powerful and lies at the heart of all modern definitions of a law of obligations (Kasirer, 2003, 398–9). And so, for example, in French law an obligation is still defined as a *lien juridique*. In addition to this idea of a legal bond between two people, the law of obligations is to be understood as an area of law occupying a central part of what a continental jurist would call 'private law' (itself to be distinguished from public law). As we shall see, this central part can really be understood, like a map, only by its relationship with surrounding areas; for the law of obligations forms part of a system. This system, as a result of its origins in a Roman work called the *Institutiones*, has been called the 'institutional system', and the law of obligations forms a central part of its structure (Stein, 1984, 125–9). In other words, some knowledge of continental law is essential if one is properly to understand the law of obligations as a generic (higher) category.

1.2.2 Real and personal remedies

Another way of understanding the law of obligations is from the position of legal remedies and legal rights. In Roman law two fundamental types of remedy underpinned private law. An action *in rem* was a claim used to vindicate ownership or some lesser property right in a thing; it was a remedy aimed at the thing itself. The substantive area of law concerned with these real remedies was (and remains in modern continental law) the *law of property*. The other type of remedy was an action *in personam*; these personal actions were aimed not at things but at another person, and the substantive area of law dealing with these claims was the *law of obligations*. Accordingly the law of obligations is in part to be understood in contrast to the law of property. This contrast is today one of rights: real rights (*iura in rem*) are contrasted with personal rights (*iura in personam*) and the law of obligations is that area of law concerned with personal rights. This property and obligations dichotomy can be put another way. The law of obligations is about *owing*, while the law of property is about *owning* (and its associated lesser rights and interests). These two concepts of owing and owning dominate private law.

1.2.3 Institutional system

The first and main point that needs to be reiterated about this Roman definition of the law of obligations is that the category of obligations cannot be understood in isolation. It is part of a system called the 'institutional system', which takes its name from the Institutes (*institutiones*) of Gaius (published around AD 160) and of Justinian (AD 533). These books were elementary teaching manuals and differed from other texts on Roman law in that they treated law in a systematic and relatively abstract way. The system developed by Gaius, and adopted by Justinian, is focused around the three institutions of *persona, res* and *actio*. 'All our law', said Gaius, 'relates either to persons, to things or to actions' (G.1.8; J.1.1.12). Later civilians replaced *actio* with *obligatio* – for the two terms appeared synonymous – and their modified scheme has acted as the basis of all civilian legal thinking right up to the New Dutch Civil Code (1992).

Moreover, the institutional system of persons, things and actions is fundamental to the understanding of all private law in the whole of Europe, including the common law. The reason for this is not that common lawyers imported or transplanted wholeheartedly Gaius into their law. It is more subtle than that. Gaius had created a way of viewing not just law but the social world of fact which was equally made up of persons, things, and law courts and their procedures (actions). Gaius' scheme made sociological sense. Thus all rules, in any system, are centred around either a 'person' ('no person may ...'), or a 'thing' ('goods supplied under the contract are reasonable fit ...') or an 'action' ('damages may be awarded ...'). Yet Gaius was going further than this, because the law flowing between persons, things and actions could be reduced to *legal relations* such as the *vinculum juris* and *dominium* (ownership). Thus the institutional system was a constructed model of persons, things, legal remedies (actions) and legal relations that seemed to make complete sociological sense. Law, in other words, seemed to be a mirror image of the real world.

1.2.4 Non-consumable and consumable property

This interface between institutional system and fact can be illustrated with reference to the distinction between consumable and non-consumable goods. If A lends B a book and fails to return the object, A can recover the book by asserting his legal relation in the thing itself. In practical terms this could mean that should A find the book lying in the corridor outside B's room, he can simply retake possession of the object. If the book remained in the possession of B, and B refused to return it to A, the latter could bring a vindication action, that is to say an *actio in rem* (or in English law the tort of conversion) aimed at the book itself. In short, the book remains his in the strict sense of an actual and direct *dominion* between *persona* and *res*.

However, if A lends B a loaf of bread the *dominium* relationship must come to an end the moment when B eats the thing. In fact, Roman law took the view that the *dominium* relationship came to an end the moment A transferred consumable goods like wine, flour or oil to another (unless perhaps A did this only for their safe-keeping) (G.3.90). The only legal relation that existed from the moment of the disappearance of the ownership relationship was an obligation to return an equivalent amount of the property (D.12.1.3). If A therefore found a loaf of bread lying in the corridor outside B's room, he would not be entitled to take it.

This property distinction reflected itself equally in the law of obligations. If A lent B a book and the book was destroyed in some accident for which B was in no way responsible, B might well have a defence to any contractual claim brought by A against him (D.13.6.18pr). However, such a defence would never be available in the case of goods to be consumed: *genera non pereunt* (Jolowicz, 1957, 93). Thus if A lent B a loaf of bread which was then eaten, through no fault of B, by a hungry dog, B would still owe A a loaf of bread.

1.2.5 Money

What if A lent B a sum of money: is this property to be treated as consumable or non-consumable? The Romans gave a clear answer to this question: money was property to be consumed, and so when one person lent a sum of money to another it could be recovered only via an *actio in personam* (D.7.5.5.1). Thus if A lent B a sum of money for the weekend, and on Monday A found the sum lying on B's desk, A would not be entitled to retake it even if the sum consisted of the same coins or notes (unless again the notes and coins were transferred in a bag only for their safe-keeping). This is one reason why Roman lawyers found it necessary to develop a third category of obligations, alongside contract and delict, called quasi-contract (or unjust enrichment in later civil law) (cf **Chapter 11**). If A paid money to B by mistake, perhaps thinking B was C, the payment could not be recovered by an *actio in rem* since money, like flour or wine, was a consumable item; ownership passed to the payee on payment. However, the payee could not keep the value of the money since there was no cause to justify the payment; he would be obliged to re-convey an equivalent amount, on the basis that no one should be unjustly enriched at the expense of another.

As we shall see, English law more or less conforms to this pattern of legal relations at the level of fact. Nevertheless there are exceptions, one of the most important being the equitable remedy of tracing (see Hudson, 2001, 150–60). The Court of Chancery took the view that money might *not* be a consumable on occasions, and thus could be reclaimed from another's patrimony on the basis of an *in rem* relation.

1.2.6 Proprietary remedies in English law

Another complication when comparing English and Roman thinking is that the common law never developed a specific *in rem* property action for vindicating ownership. It uses the law of tort, and these tort remedies are based more on possession than on ownership. Thus real property (land) is protected from interference by others by the torts of trespass and nuisance, while personal (moveable) property is protected by the tort of conversion (cf **7.3.3.3**, below) (based on denial of title) and trespass to goods (based on interference with possession). This does not necessarily cause practical problems as such, but it does give rise to conceptual difficulties in that the law of tort is part of the law of obligations. Consequently, the common law could be said not to keep strictly separate the relation between person and thing (property) from the one between person and person (obligations).

This problem has been exacerbated recently, with the Court of Appeal allowing a person to use a proprietary remedy to repossess land belonging to another on the basis only of a contractual relationship with respect to the land (*Manchester Airport Plc v Dutton* (2000)). Again this is not necessarily problematic from a practical aspect; indeed the majority in the Court of Appeal took the view that their decision was particularly pragmatic. But it does raise a question about whether the notion of a law of obligations can really be imported into English law, for the English law of things turns out to be structurally complex in comparison with Romanist thinking.

1.2.7 Continental systematics and English methods

The fact that one can identify the law of obligations with continental legal systems suggests that there is a structural basis here that transcends the national state. But problems are immediately encountered once one turns from, say, German or French law to the common law tradition. The rigid systematics which underpin the German Civil Code and, to some extent, the French Civil Code are not to be found in the common law. Certainly the term 'law of obligations' is now widely used not just by academic lawyers but also by judges (see, besides Lord Diplock, Lord Goff in *Henderson v Merrett Syndicates* (1995), 184). Yet the transplanting of a law of obligations category from continental law into English law does not come without conceptual problems.

There is another point that needs to be made about the continental and the English approaches to the law of obligations. It is important to distinguish between the law of obligations in the early civil law period (Roman classical law, post-classical Roman law, medieval Roman law) and obligations in the later civil law (Humanist and Enlightenment influences, codification and post-codification). For one factor that underpins the early and later periods is the style of reasoning. Roman and medieval Roman law were uncodified systems in the modern sense of the term 'code', and thus the techniques were case-orientated (see Samuel, 2001, 5–7, 18–20). Modern civil law, thanks to the influence of the Enlightenment, is, as we have already mentioned, traditionally founded on an inference model (codes) where solutions are deduced via syllogistic logic from a major (code provision) and minor (facts of a case) premise. French cases in particular have a very distinctive formal style, even if beneath this style other factors may well be at work (Samuel, 2001, 31–3).

The common law method is very different in style. For a start, private law (if such a category exists in the common law) is rarely expressed through general principles (cf Samuel, 1998). This is partly due to the fact that the basis of civil liability has grown up around different types of forms of action and different species of remedy. Certainly, there are generalities; all contracts are governed by a general theory of contract, and one can probably say now that there is a general principle of fault liability. But the forms (causes) of action can still exert an influence, with the result that the alphabet remains one way of classifying the common law (Kasirer, 2003). Secondly, therefore, the idea of symmetry and classification is much less important to the common lawyer. Law, thanks to the forms of action, is seen as being located as much in fact as in any notion of an abstract rule, and this has resulted in reasoning methods that are more rooted in analogy and policy than in deduction (see **6.3.2.3**, below). Common law methods are much closer to those of the old Roman jurists. Thirdly, there are of course formal differences of method. Precedent is said to be central to the common law, while case law (*la jurisprudence*) is not a formal source of law in France. And precedent in turn requires knowledge about what binds and which court decisions are authoritative. Fourthly, there are the methodological issues surrounding interpretation of texts, especially legislation and written contracts. Common law interpretation is said to be more literal than in France, the judges often refusing to look beyond the text itself (cf **6.3.3**, below). These issues of style are important to an understanding of the law of obligations in Europe.

1.3 Internal structure of the law of obligations

When one turns to the internal structure of the law of obligations, it is tempting to think that, as far as the English lawyer is concerned, such structure ought to be analysed strictly from the common law position. However, contract and tort are two areas of English law that have been, and still are, influenced by continental systematics. Accordingly, attention needs to be focused on both civil and common law.

1.3.1 Civil law

As we have seen, the notion of a law of obligations goes back to Roman law, where it was a category that consisted of personal actions (*actiones in personam*) that could be brought by one person against another named person. The Roman sources themselves reveal a lack of interest in developing any general theory of obligations, the jurists concentrating almost entirely on the various species falling within this area of law. They mainly discussed the different kinds of contracts, delicts (torts) and actions (remedies) that made up the generic category of the law of obligations. Justinian subsequently (in the 6th century) defined an obligation as a *vinculum iuris* (legal chain), and this definition is retained in modern civil law. But between form (*vinculum iuris*) and substance (the details of contract, delict and quasi-contracts) there is little useful refection on theory. All that one can usefully say is, first, that an obligation arises out of either a legal act or a legal fact (see, eg, Quebec CC, art 1371); and, secondly, that in the civil law systems the law of obligations is dominated by the paradigm of a contract (see, eg, Polish CC, art 353).

This idea of contract as paradigm obligation goes back to Roman law (D.5.1.20), but it remains particularly important in the modern law because contract is a form of private 'legislation' (cf CC, art 1134) that is forward looking. It needs detailed provisions to set out the situations as to when and for what a person will be held responsible (UNIDROIT, art 1.3). Delictual liability and unjust enrichment liability are mainly backward-looking. They are categories of liability rather than legal acts, and although each source may result in textbooks as long as any on contract, they require many fewer facilitative rules. The *Code civil* has over 200 articles devoted to contracts in general (leaving aside the rules on the various named contracts), but only half a dozen dealing with delictual liability (although now somewhat extended by the new art 1386 on product liability). Non-contractual obligations tend to emphasise liability rather than formation.

1.3.2 Common law

The starting point for civil liability in the common law is to be found in the existence or non-existence of a cause of action. These causes of action were developed out of the old common law forms of action, which were 'not merely a choice between a number of queer technical terms' but 'a choice between methods of procedure adapted to cases of different kinds' (Maitland). As Van Caenegem has observed, these 'writs covering the various types of cases had not been based on substantive legal categories or any legal plan'. And if 'there was a plan behind it all, it was merely to create an adequate royal remedy for a number of very common wrongs, which upset society and with which the existing courts dealt in too slow, cumbersome and incalculable a way' (1971, § 22). When the forms of action were finally abolished in 1852, their ghosts remained as 'causes of action'. A cause of action has been described as 'simply a factual situation the existence of which entitles one person to obtain from the court a remedy against another person' which, historically, 'varied with the nature of the factual situation and causes of action were divided into categories according to the "form of action" by which the remedy was obtained in the particular kind of factual situation which constituted the cause of action'. However, 'it is essential to realise that when, since 1873, the name of a form of action is used to identify a cause of action, it is used as a convenient and succinct description of a particular category of factual situation which entitles one person to obtain from the court a remedy against another person' (Diplock LJ, in *Letang v Cooper* (1965), 242–3).

Despite the growth of ideas such as 'obligations', the causes of action remain the key to the factual situations, since a cause of action is the means by which one organises the facts in terms of the law and the law in terms of the facts. It is the means by which one discovers within the facts whether or not a remedy exists. However, the remedy may also have an independent role in that some remedies (eg, injunctions) can attract their own rules beyond those to be found in substantive textbooks on contract and tort. Remedies, in other words, bring their own dimensional structure in the legal equation (see, eg, *Miller v Jackson* (1977)).

The forms of action thought in terms of particular types of writ, of which the most important dichotomy was that between trespass and debt. Trespass was a compensation (damages) action based upon a 'wrong', while debt (together with detinue) was a claim for a specific sum of money founded upon a 'right'. In these latter claims the plaintiff was vindicating something that was 'his', and this strict liability aspect of debt (claim for a specific sum) and detinue (claim for a thing) is still to be found in the common law (although detinue has been abolished in form but preserved in substance). An action for debt is quite different from an action for damages (trespass) (*Jervis v Harris* (1996), *per* Millett LJ). Equally, an action in conversion (detinue) is quite different from a claim in negligence (*Moorgate Mercantile Ltd v Twitchings* (1977)). However, with the abolition of the forms of action, the common law adopted the civilian categories of contract and tort (delict).

1.3.3 Contract

The fundamental idea of a law of contract – or at least a law of contracts – is Roman in origin (see Weir, 1992). The Romans developed a sophisticated set of contractual ideas around a range of transactions, the most important amongst them being sale, hire, partnership, loan and deposit. In addition the Romans developed some more general ideas of contracting; thus formal promises (stipulations) were enforceable at law provided they were spoken in a particular form, and pacts and innominate (unnamed) contracts were also given legal enforceability where justice required (D.19.5.1). Each different kind of contract in Rome was given its own legal action, and these different legal actions were procedurally separate institutions. Thus there was no general theory of contract in Roman law.

However, the Roman jurists recognised that all the different contracts shared the common denominator of agreement (*conventio*) (D.2.14.1.3). Consequently they were able to categorise them within the single classification of actions *ex contractu*, and this helped pave the way for a general theory of contract. In the later civil law the medieval doctors of law and the canon lawyers developed the common denominator of *conventio* and *consensus* (also found in Roman law) into such a general theory. Thus by the 16th century lawyers on the Continent recognised a general common principle that all contracts should be kept (*pacta sunt servanda*). There was no longer, then, a law of contracts based on a set of empirical transactions and associated legal actions. There was a general theory of contract that was to find its most perfect expression in the French *Code civil* of 1804: 'Les conventions légalement formées tiennent lieu de loi à ceux qui les ont faits' (contracts legally formed have the force of law between those who have made them) (CC, art 1134).

To say that contract was unknown in England before the 18th century would be to misinterpret legal history. The Court of Chancery had been familiar with (Romanist) contractual notions long before the Industrial Revolution, and academic writing since the Middle Ages was well acquainted with Roman law and thus the law of contract (Gordley, 1991). But contract as a dominant legal institution is largely a creature of the 19th-century common law, and it is during this period that it reached its 'classical' form (Atiyah, 1979). The basic principles of offer and acceptance, consideration, terms and breach were all worked out during the period between the end of the 18th century and the beginning of the 20th century, often with the help of continental doctrine. And the result was that many of the older forms of liability founded on status, debt and bailment became completely submerged under the new general theory of contract.

Breach of contract is, accordingly, a cause of action in itself (historically based on breach of promise as a tort). Whether English contract can be seen as a form of private legislation as in France (CC, art 1134) is not easy to determine, since its basis is in promise rather than agreement (cf **3.2.5**, below). However, as an aspect of commercial law there is no doubt that contract is an instrument for businesses to establish their own rights and duties, and it is for the courts to enforce these terms without (as yet) regard to notions such as good faith. Only where consumers are concerned might the courts be willing to take a more interventionist approach. Contract, in short, is the foundational element of English commercial law, and it is often helpful to see the commercial contract as a form of private legislation, even if the same cannot now be said of private and consumer contracts (*The Chikuma* (1981), 322).

1.3.4 Delict

Roman lawyers also developed a number of legal actions for compensation for harm which were not based on *conventio* but upon ideas such as fault (*culpa*). As with contract, the Romans did not, however, develop a theory of non-contractual liability for harm based upon a single general principle. Such a general principle was a later civilian development. Instead they developed a number of different actions dealing with particular types of wrongdoing. The most important of these actions was the one based on an old statute called the *lex Aquilia*, which allowed a person to claim damages for damage done to his property as a result of the intentional or careless behaviour (*culpa*) of another (see generally Kolbert, 1979).

This idea of fault liability attracted a huge amount of case discussion in Roman law itself, and out of these discussions it became possible to induce some more specific ideas such as causation and foreseeability (D.9.2.31). Where there was fault (and of course cause and damage) there was, prima facie, liability (D.9.2.44pr). Moreover, in addition to this idea of *culpa* liability, the Romans went some way in developing certain kinds of liability based upon ideas other than fault, and some of these were classified as quasi-delicts (see **1.3.5**, below). The owner of a house was, for example, strictly liable (that is, without proof of fault) for things thrown or falling from his house onto the public way (see D.9.3.1). Roman law thus provided a model not just for a sophisticated law of contract, but also for a law of non-contractual liability; and these non-contractual delicts were all said to arise out of wrongs (*ex malificio*) (D.44.7.4pr).

Just as in contract the later civilians focused on *conventio* to develop a general principle of contract, so they used *culpa* to fashion a general theory of delict. In France this general theory, thanks to writers such as Domat (1625–96), was taken to a high level of abstraction, and in the *Code civil* any act which causes damage must be compensated by the person whose fault it was that caused the damage (art 1382). However, in German law, fault, damage and causation are not enough; the victim of the damage must also show invasion of a specific interest or right (life, body, health, freedom, property or other right) (BGB, § 823).

When one turns to English law there is no law of delict as such (cf Scotland). There is instead a law of 'tort'. If it is not contract it must be tort, said Bramwell LJ in *Bryant v Herbert* (1877, 390), referring to a statutory dichotomy between actions founded on contract and on tort. Damages claims that could not be accommodated under contract were put into a separate category of 'tort', a word simply meaning 'wrong'. Tort is seen as an equivalent category to contract, yet it is actually rather different in that it is not a normative obligation in itself. There is no such thing as a 'breach of tort obligation' (*Bradford*

Corporation v Pickles (1895)). In order to succeed in a tort claim, the claimant must establish a specific cause of action such as trespass, negligence, nuisance, defamation, conversion, interference with contract or whatever. Failure to plead and to prove a specific cause of action will result in failure of the claim for damages (*Esso Petroleum Co Ltd v Southport Corporation* (1956, HL)).

Despite this cause of action basis, it possible to identify some motivating general principles beneath the causes of action in tort, although whether all such actions can be conceptualised in terms of a pre-existing 'duty' is doubtful (*Stubbings v Webb* (1993), 508). Damage is usually the starting point of tort (but cf defamation), yet economic loss and nervous shock present problems with regard to the torts of negligence and breach of statutory duty. With respect to liability without fault (liability for people or things under one's control), it is by no means easy to establish any general principle similar to art 1384 of the *Code civil* (see **1.3.5**, below). The decision in *Rylands v Fletcher* (cf **9.3.5**, below) could have acted as the basis for such a general principle, but the House of Lords has consistently refused to develop any such strict liability idea (see now *Transco plc v Stockport MBC* (2004)). The result is that the UK law is rather out of line with some of its EU partners. Tort thus remains a rather fragmented subject protecting a whole range of different interests and, as a result, it is impossible to think in terms of a general theory.

1.3.5 Quasi-delict

The category of quasi-delict in Roman law included a number of actions dealing with particular liabilities (liability of occupiers to those on the street, together with the liability of judges, carriers, innkeepers and stablekeepers), and it is the most problematic of all the sub-divisions of the law of obligations because to 'find a common denominator for what has been lumped together here, is not at all easy' (Zimmermann, 1996, 16). One theory is that the category represents strict liability claims, and thus it is a useful heading under which one can state that the French jurists went further than the induction of a single principle based on *culpa*. They also continued to develop the forms of stricter liability established by the Romans with respect to slaves, buildings and animals. The French jurist Pothier (1699–1772) thus declared that a master was generally liable for delicts committed by his servant. However, it is probably true to say that these stricter forms of liability were not widely seen, before the 19th century, as harbouring some general principle of liability without fault, if only because *culpa* carried with it such a moral force, leading in turn to the principle of justice, especially in Germany, that there should be no liability without fault (another French theory is that delictual liability represents intentional damage, while quasi-delictual liability refers to unintentional harm).

Nevertheless, art 1384 of the *Code civil* declares that 'On est responsable non seulement du dommage que l'on cause par son propre fait, mais encore de celui qui est causé par le fait des personnes dont on doit répondre, ou des choses que l'on a sous sa garde' ('One is liable not only for the damage that one causes by one's own act, but also for that which is caused by the act of persons for whom one is responsible or by things which one has in one's keeping'). This principle was originally interpreted largely in terms of fault, but as the industrial and technological revolution progressed the French jurists liberated themselves from their preoccupation with *culpa* to develop a principle based on risk. *Ubi emolumentum ibi onus* (where there is profit there is liability) became the basis for making the employer liable for the delicts of his employees; and 'collective solidarity' based upon the widespread existence of insurance ensured an ever-increasing liability without fault for damage done by things. Whether this area of strict liability is rightly called 'quasi-delict' is a matter of debate. Indeed, the exact meaning of quasi-delict in Roman law itself is a matter of controversy and no theory fully explains its underlying principle (if any).

There are one or two references to quasi-delict in the 19th-century English law reports, but these references remain obscure and undeveloped. In short, the category of quasi-delict has no meaning to the common lawyer. However, with regard to the next category the position is very different.

1.3.6 Quasi-contract

The Romans never allowed an *actio in rem* to be used to recover money paid (cf **1.2.4**, above), and this forced them to develop a number of remedies to deal with claims for the repayment of money paid either under contracts that turned out to be defective, or where there had never been a contractual relationship. The two most important remedies were the *condictio*, an *actio in personam* for a sum of money paid, for example, to another under a mistake, and the *actio negotiorum gestorum contraria*, which was a restitution claim available to someone who had reasonably intervened into the affairs of another in the sole interests of that other (J.3.27.1).

These actions were independent of any contractual relationship, and the Romans hinted that they were motivated by the principle that no one should be allowed unjustly to enrich themselves at the expense of another (D.12.6.14; D.50.17.206). Such a general principle was seized upon by the later civil lawyers as the basis for all of the quasi-contractual actions, and this unjust enrichment norm found its place alongside *conventio* and *culpa* as an axiom of the law of obligations. In German law, therefore, a 'person who acquires something without any legal ground through an act performed by another or in any other manner at another's expense, is bound to render restitution' (BGB, § 812; see also Polish CC, art 405). This code principle stands in contrast to the *Code civil*, which simply keeps the specific Roman quasi-contractual claims together with a range of other specific instances where an enrichment cannot be retained (arts 1371–1381). Nevertheless, the *Cour de cassation* has recognised unjust enrichment as a general principle of law (Cass.req.15.6.1892).

If one had to look for a focal point that underpins quasi-contract and unjust enrichment, and distinguishes this area of the law of obligations from contract and delict, it is this. Whereas contractual and delictual liability look to the notion of damage wrongfully caused, unjust enrichment takes as its point of departure the idea of an enrichment, or benefit, that cannot be justified. In many ways, then, it is the other side of the coin to *responsabilité civile*; it looks to the gain in the defendant's patrimony and not to any loss in the claimant's patrimony, although if the enrichment is not at the expense of the claimant there can be difficulties (cf Proceeds of Crime Act 2002).

In English law the term 'quasi-contract' was used to cover those debt claims that could not be rationalised directly under contract. The most important of these claims was the action for money had and received, which was probably a common law version of the equitable remedy of account (itself originally a common law form of action), a claim whereby a Court of Equity decreed that an account be taken to see if money was owing to a claimant and, if so, that it be paid. The equitable remedy did not need a contractual relationship since the Court of Chancery had its own fiduciary obligation more or less related to, or developed out of, the trust. However, the common law did need a motivating obligation to act as the foundation of the debt claim. Accordingly, contract was called in to supply this normative dimension; the court would imply a contract between the parties (*Sinclair v Brougham* (1914)).

The implied contract theory has now been abandoned and replaced by the principle of unjust enrichment (*Kleinwort Benson v Glasgow CC* (1999); and see **1.3.7**, below). However, this principle is not capable *in itself* of generating a claim. One still needs to establish a cause of action in quasi-contract, or in some equitable claim. Another possible normative criterion is ownership; a claim in debt is, seemingly, a proprietary claim founded on the idea that a debt is a chose in action, that is to say a form of property (*Lipkin Gorman v Karpnale* (1991)). Quasi-contract seems, then, to have moved from being a question of *owing* (obligation) to one of *owning* (property). Yet the position remains unclear since the action for money had and received, along with the other quasi-contractual debt claims of the action for money paid and the action on a *quantum meruit*, is undoubtedly a personal (*in personam*) rather than a proprietary (*in rem*) claim.

1.3.7 Restitution (unjust enrichment)

The most striking inroad, then, into the contract and tort dichotomy has been the acceptance in recent years of what Lord Wright in 1943 called the 'third category of the common law which has been called quasi-contract or restitution' (*Fibrosa etc v Fairbairn etc* (1943), 32). Quasi-contract was recognised, as we have seen, but it was subsumed under the category of contract. Equally, many of the equitable remedies used in restitution cases, if they could not be squeezed within the contract and tort dichotomy, were classified under trusts. Today this has changed. The common law is in the process of adopting the independent category of restitution based upon the normative principle of unjust enrichment (no one should be unjustly enriched at the expense of another). It is, as has already been mentioned, probably true to say that there has not yet been a complete break with the law of causes of action and equitable remedies; that is to say, there is no general enrichment action based directly upon the unjust enrichment principle. In order to succeed in a restitution claim, the claimant must bring himself within an existing head of claim, such as money had and received, or within the scope of an established remedy, such as tracing or account. Nevertheless, the value of the unjust enrichment principle lies in the fact that it can act not just as a common denominator for a whole range of debt, damages and equitable remedy cases, but as a counterpoint both to the fault principle and to the promissory obligation. In civil law systems restitution is part of the law of obligations and thus stands in contrast to proprietary claims; in the common law, however, there is an intermixing within the category of restitution, of *in rem* and *in personam* remedies. This can cause confusion when comparison is made with Roman and continental law.

1.3.8 Property and bailment

This property and obligations confusion is not confined to restitution. Common lawyers rarely think in terms of a general category of property that encapsulates both personal and real property (but cf Lawson and Rudden, 2002). Property, as a category, tends to be confined to land law. This thinking is beginning to change, but one reason why personal property has until recently failed to attract its own category is because many of the remedies are classed as torts while some of its rights are associated with contract (bailment, debt, tracing and void contracts). The intermixing of property and obligations would be confusing to the civil lawyer because Roman learning traditionally keeps separate rights *in rem* (owning) and rights *in personam* (owing). Moreover, the English lawyer even uses proprietary remedies to further obligation ends. Equity (and to some extent the common law), for example, recognises the right of a beneficial owner to 'trace' money into the bank account of another and to claim this sum on the basis that the claimant is owner. Tracing (both at common law and in equity) has become an extremely complex remedy, and this is partly because it is in essence an *in rem* remedy attached to an *in personam* category (restitution) (see *Agip v Jackson* (1990, ChD), (1991, CA); Proceeds of Crime Act 2002, ss 304–306). In other words, the remedy belongs to the law of property, while the substantive area of law that supplies the motivating principle (unjust enrichment) belongs to the law of obligations.

Another area of confusion, for the obligations lawyer, is bailment. This is a relationship specific to common law systems based on the transfer of possession in a chattel, and the rights and duties arising out of bailment belong to the law of property rather than to the law of obligations (*Building and Civil Engineering Holidays Scheme Management v Post Office* (1966)). However, these duties can be modified by contract and the actual remedies protecting bailment are tortious (Torts (Interference with Goods) Act 1977). Some commercial cases, where tort, contract and bailment rights and remedies become intermixed, can thus be extremely complex, particularly when insurance is involved (see, eg, *The Albazero* (1977); *East West Corpn v DKBS A/S* (2003)). What must be stressed, however, is that property rights can be of importance in the way that they affect, or appear to affect, rules in contract and tort. Thus bailment can seemingly 'affect' the rules of vicarious liability and contract (*Morris v Martin* (1966)), as well as seemingly reversing the burden of proof (*Houghland v Low* (1962)).

1.3.9 Public and private law

Another dichotomy that is beginning to assume more importance in the common law is the one between public and private law (see **8.4**, below). This distinction, inherited from Roman law, is fundamental in continental legal systems, which see a conceptual difference between power based on sovereignty (*imperium*) and power arising out of ownership (*dominium*). In the common law world, however, the distinction has traditionally been rejected. Public bodies have been subject to the same contract and tort law as private persons and commercial enterprises (Taggart, 2003). Indeed many of the leading duty of care cases in the tort of negligence have been cases which, in French law, would have fallen outside of the *Code civil* and would have been heard only in the administrative courts. The major exception in English law was with respect to the liability of the Crown, but the general immunity in tort has been changed by statute (see now *Mulcahy v MOD* (1996)).

The absence of the distinction was considered by many public lawyers to be constitutionally healthy, and there is certainly a case for saying that all legal persons should be subject to the same legal regime. Nevertheless there are some situations where the absence of a distinction can be seen as creating difficulties. Public officials who humiliate citizens can be sued for damages only if the citizen can establish the existence of a specific tort or invasion of a human right (*Wainwright v Home Office* (2004)); yet it is arguable that such 'private law' thinking is inappropriate when it comes to constitutional rights. While it is perfectly defensible to assert that the law should ignore behaviour that merely humiliates when it occurs between private persons, when a public officer or body deliberately humiliates a member of the public it is arguable that this behaviour ought to be sanctioned by public law. A further difficulty arising out of the absence of a distinction is that the development of liability without fault might be said to have been prevented as a result of the absence of a formal set of public law principles. Had the facts of a case like *Read v J Lyons & Co* (1947) arisen in France, the plaintiff, injured by an unexplained explosion in a munitions factory, would have been able to claim damages without having to prove fault. The case would not have been regarded as a 'private law' action, but one in public law in which the principle either of public risk or of equality of burdens would have ensured the payment of compensation by the state.

In fact the common law has moved some way towards formalising the distinction between public and private law at the level of procedure (*O'Reilly v Mackman* (1983)). But this new formality did not at first make life any easier for claimants with respect to tort actions against public bodies. However, the position has been modified as a result of the Human Rights Act 1998 and the influence of Strasbourg. In the area of contract, *O'Reilly v Mackman* appears to have imported some confusion, while in restitution and defamation the distinction does go some way towards favouring the citizen against the state. The Human Rights Act 1998 is, however, having an important impact on all areas of the common law, and it is difficult as yet to assess the full effect on the law of obligations. It has been asserted, however, that the Act, although at first sight seemingly emphasising the distinction between public and private bodies, will (together with the help of EU law) probably end up by rendering the public–private distinction even more obsolete (Oliver, 2000).

1.3.10 Status and obligation

The Human Rights Act 1998 has also contributed to another institutional complication, namely, the relationship between the law of persons and the law of things. The law of obligations in Gaius' scheme formed part of the law of things; this broad category, focused around a 'thing' (*res*), was to be contrasted with the law that attached to the 'person' (*persona*). The law of persons was not concerned with patrimonial (wealth) 'rights' but with rules about the person as a person. In traditional civil law these 'law of persons' rules fell into two broad categories: there were rules dealing with personality (who has legal standing to sue and be sued) and rules dealing with status. This latter notion, not easy to define (Jolowicz, 1963, 374–80), was concerned with the position, or more realistically categorisation, of a person in the eyes of the law. Thus the difference between freemen and slaves, between citizens and aliens, and between adults and minors was a matter of status. Contemporary civil law has gone further and added what might be seen as a new dimension to the law of persons, rights that arise purely out of the nature of human personality itself. As the most basic of these rights are to be found in the European Convention for the Protection of Human Rights, it follows that the Human Rights Act 1998 has the effect of intermixing personality (law of persons) rights with patrimonial (property and obligation) rights.

Yet status and law of obligations rights can become intermingled even outside of the human rights arena. In the law of contract the distinction between 'consumer' and 'professional', like that between adult and minor, can be seen as a question of status (see, eg, *Stevenson v Beverley Bentinck Ltd* (1976)), and this status will often have dramatic effects on enforceability (Stone, 2002, 63). Similarly, in the law of tort, status can be important; the duty owed by an occupier of land to a 'visitor' is very different from the one owed to a 'trespasser'. In the law of personal property the expressions 'bailor' and 'bailee' also suggest status as much as proprietary relation.

Maine once famously said that 'we may say that the movement of the progressive societies has hitherto been a movement *from status to Contract*'. This invites the cynical response that the movement within contemporary Europe is a retreat from contract towards status: EU law looks to status groups such as 'consumers' rather than to legal relations like obligations. Such a response, as far as it is true, actually results from a failure within the law of persons itself, namely, that 'legal persons' (corporations treated as if they were people: D.50.16.16) are to be considered as economic equals to human persons. In terms of actual social and economic reality such a view is ridiculous. Yet what perhaps is unfortunate is that 'consumers' end up as incapables; that is to say, they are treated as if they are in the same category as children, the mentally retarded and drunks (Atias), and this in turn impacts upon the law of contract. General rules have to be increasingly modified by consumer protection provisions, which, although no doubt socially desirable, leads to increasing complexity as regulation and private law meet head-on. In fact, if there is one category where public and private law meet, it is the law of persons.

1.4 European developments

There are a number of European initiatives with respect to the law of obligations. These initiatives operate at a variety of levels. First, there are the positive laws emerging from the EU in the form of Directives, perhaps two of the most well known to date being the one on strict liability for dangerous products (Council Directive of 25 July 1985) and the one on unfair contract terms (Council Directive of 5 April 1993). In English law these two Directives resulted in the Consumer Protection Act 1987 (Pt I) and the Unfair Terms in Consumer Contract Regulations 1999.

At another level, however, there is the more ambitious project of a European Civil Code aimed at harmonising the private laws of all the Member States. This is a project that has generated much debate (see, eg, Legrand, 1996), but it has resulted in the drafting of a European code of contract law known as the *Principles of European Contract Law* (PECL). A similar project in the area of tort is being pursued by various groups of academics, of which perhaps the European Tort Law Group is of most interest to the common lawyer given the flavour of the code they have drawn up, namely, the *Principles of European Tort Law* (PETL). These two sets of principles (PECL and PETL), or 'unofficial' codes, are of value to the student of the law of obligations in the way they give insights into the concepts and structure of contract and tort law respectively. Neither code represents English law, but they do give expression to what might be called 'general principles' of the law of obligations. Moreover the PECL have received the backing of both the European Parliament and the European Commission (see Staudenmayer, 2002). If one adds to these two codes the Draft Rules on Unjustified Enrichment (Scottish Law Commission, DP No 99, Appendix), one has something like a draft code of general principles on the European law of obligations.

Thirdly, there are the more indirect influences. The judges themselves are not immune to European ideas and, indeed, the development of a general theory of contract during the 19th century was in part the result of a mini-reception of civil law (Samuel, 2001, 103–10). More recently the judges have sometimes looked to Europe when faced with particularly difficult cases and while foreign jurisprudence has not the status of precedent it can sometimes indicate where justice might lie (see, eg, *Fairchild v Glenhaven Funeral Services Ltd* (2003)). Moreover, a number of UK judges are proficient in European languages and some spend time not only mixing with French, German and other European colleagues but also contributing to academic life in continental universities.

2 Contractual Obligations: General Provisions

When one turns to look at the substantive detail of the law of obligations, it is difficult not to start with contractual obligations. The subject is central to the codes and to English commercial law, and it is contract that has been codified at an international and European level (see PECL and UNIDROIT). As these codes have a first chapter devoted to 'General Provisions', it would seem fitting to provide an overview of these provisions. In addition this chapter will set out a framework for understanding contract.

2.1 Historical and definitional considerations

Consideration has already been given in the last chapter to the historical and conceptual background to contract in both the civil law and the common law traditions, but contract requires a further chapter on generalities for several reasons. First, because it is underpinned by a number of general principles which are relevant to the subject in its entirety. Secondly, because although there is a general theory of contract both in the civilian and in the common law traditions, there are nevertheless different types of contract; these different types need to be identified and classified at an early stage. Thirdly, because the scope and limits of the contractual obligation have to be identified; such identification is necessary not just because it can be important, at a formal level, to know when one is moving from contractual to non-contractual rights, duties and (or) remedies, but also because identification of the domain of contract is of importance for conceptual and policy reasons. Fourthly, a general section can be useful for a number of other reasons; for example, it can contain some general definitions, some rules as to mandatory and non-mandatory provisions, articles about usage and custom, and so on and so forth (see generally Chapter 1 in the PECL and in UNIDROIT). Finally, a chapter on contract generalities is important for setting out the methodology by which contract as an area of law and as a conceptual and practical concept can be understood.

2.1.1 Definition of contract

Defining the law of contract is both simple and difficult depending on the scheme of analysis adopted. It is simple to the extent that it can be summed up, at the level of form, by expressions such as legally enforceable agreements or promises. Thus contract has been defined as 'a promise or set of promises that the law will enforce' (Pollock), or as 'an agreement that is freely entered into on terms that are freely negotiated' (Stuart-Smith LJ in *W v Essex* CC (1998), § 50). Difficulties arise when one tries to match these definitions with the mass of factual situations to be found in the cases. There are many factual situations displaying the essential requirements of a contract which turn out not to support a contract. Equally there are other facts which do not seemingly support a contract, yet the disappointed party still manages to secure a legal remedy, if not always an actual contractual remedy.

Another difficulty arises when one tries to approach contract and its definition from a functional perspective. What is the *purpose* of contract, or what does it *do*? This perspective is difficult not just because contract has a whole range of different functions. It is difficult, first, because these functions are shared by other areas of the law; and, secondly, because it is not always clear that the identified functions actually require, or fully correspond to, a law of contract. Indeed it has been said that the 'classical model of contract, notwithstanding its formal perpetuation to the present day as a body of general principles, was a failure' (Atiyah, 1979, 693). In short, contract theory on the one hand and social and commercial reality on the other are not always reconcilable.

Thus at the level of form it is by no means clear that terms such as 'promise' or 'agreement' adequately give expression to the substance of contract, whether this substance is seen as a set of rules or facts that make up contractual situations. Accordingly there is a range of cases where there are 'promises' and (or) 'agreement' but no contract or contractual liability (for example, liability in misrepresentation). Equally there are contractual situations where there are no promises or real agreements but there is nevertheless a contractual relationship or contractual liability (see, eg, *Blackpool & Fylde Aero Club v Blackpool BC* (1990)). Sometimes the courts are quite open about this mismatch; and so, for example, the judges have indicated on a number of occasions that liability in tort is being imposed to fill a gap in the law of contract (see, eg, *Hedley Bryne v Heller & Partners* (1964); *White v Jones* (1995)). Academics have talked of contract as a remedy.

2.1.2 Private legislation

Perhaps the most challenging theory is the one to be found in art 1134 of the French *Code civil*, which asserts that a contract has the force of legislation between the two parties. This is the starting point for the idea of contract as private legislation. There is no doubt that this thesis has some support in commercial reality, in as much as contractual relationships are often reduced to texts and that these texts attract the same methodological analysis as statutory interpretation (see, eg, *Staffs Area Health Authority v South Staffs Waterworks Co* (1978)). In civilian systems the role of the courts is to give expression to the will of the parties, just as it is to give expression to the will of the legislator when it is a matter of a statutory text. One way of understanding contracts, therefore, is to see them as privatised 'legislative' texts binding two persons.

However, this theory is plagued with difficulties. For a start, there are many contractual situations that do not involve texts; the everyday transactions made by consumers with suppliers of goods and services do not consist of detailed negotiations to be reduced with great care to paper, although admittedly some of these transactions may involve contractual documents. Rather than legislating, parties are entering into different forms of transaction such as sale, carriage, parking and the like; and these forms can often involve rules laid down by objective law rather than subjective text (see, eg, the Sale of Goods Act 1979). Of course, it is possible to re-conceptualise these objective rules as implied promises flowing between the parties. But a sociologist looking at consumer behaviour is unlikely to theorise it in terms of private legislation.

Another difficulty is that the line between contractual and non-contractual operations is often arbitrary, depending upon the formation rules of the system in question. Thus in France a medical negligence case might well be a contractual problem; while in England, if the defendant is a National Health Trust, it will be tort. Only if the hospital is private will the relationship between hospital and patient be contractual. A similar difficulty can arise in other areas of professional negligence. A bank that gives 'gratuitous' advice is probably not acting within a contractual relationship (*Hedley Byrne v Heller* (1964)); yet the relationship is very close to contract, and in systems where the requirement for consideration is unknown the bank's act might well be contractual. Some employment relationships, which at first sight look contractual, might not be so for reasons of public law; in these situations tort may have to play a 'contractual' role (see, eg, *Lennon v Comr of Police for the Metropolis* (2004)).

The private legislation thesis is at best partial in its portrayal of contract. It undoubtedly reflects certain kinds of contractual behaviour, particularly in the commercial world where the drawing up of contracts requires negotiation and professional skill, and there are similarities on occasions between cases involving the interpretation of contracts and those involving the interpretation of statutes. But the theory breaks down when faced with consumer transactions and with areas of commerce requiring detailed regulation (see in particular the Consumer Protection (Distance Selling) Regulations 2000). Contract is less facultative here and, since at least the middle of the 20th century, much more regulatory. In other words, the idea that commercial and consumer transactions belong exclusively to a world of private law agreements is simply no longer true within the EU.

2.1.3 Contractual obligations and contractual liability

Perhaps another difficulty with the private legislation thesis is that it fails to emphasise what is now seen as an important distinction between the contractual *obligation* and contractual *liability*. In theory the distinction should be meaningless, in that contractual liability is simply the logical outcome of a failure to perform a contractual obligation. Yet in practice the distinction is important, in that many obligation issues become relevant only when the contract has gone wrong and when one party finds itself suffering damage seemingly caused by the other party. Damage and causation thus become the starting point for deciding whether or not the other party ought to compensate. And in deciding this issue of compensation, although the judges might in form refer to contractual promises (terms) contained in the obligation, in reasoning substance they could well base their decision on objective factors like the status of the parties and the allocation of risk (see, eg, *The Moorcock* (1889)). Indeed, liability might well come down to 'reasonableness' rather than rights (see, eg, *Ruxley Electronics Ltd v Forsyth* (1996)).

This distinction between obligation and liability is of even greater importance in English law than in civil law countries where the rules of contract are set out in an abstract code.

In the English system textbooks do, admittedly, try to state the rules in abstract, and a short 'nutshell' may even look like a 'code' of principles if elegantly executed. But it has to be remembered that the rules of contract are for the most part induced out of cases and, as we shall see at **6.3.2.1** below, no *ratio decidendi* of a case can ever be detached from the material facts of the case. There will always be some element of 'contract as remedy' in the common law system (see, eg, *Blackpool & Fylde Aero Club v Blackpool BC* (1990)). This is the reason why one way of understanding contract is to view the subject from a litigation and (or) remedy perspective.

2.1.4 Contract and remedies

When viewed from the position of liability and non-performance, contract can assume, therefore, a rather different shape and form. It can appear much less subjective and can even merge into other areas of the law of obligations, that is to say into tort or restitution (see, eg, Robert Goff LJ in *Whittaker v Campbell* (1984), 327–8). In fact many contract problems are shaped not just by the loss or damage suffered by a party, but also by the actual remedy pursued.

2.1.4.1 Damages

Take, first of all, damages. Where a victim of a breach of contract suffers damage a number of set focal points immediately emerge; the nature of the act complained of is one issue, and the causal link between act and damage is another. Merely because one contracting party is in breach, this does not necessarily mean that the party will be liable for the damage, or all the damage, suffered. Sufficient cause and connection must be shown, and so if, for example, the victim has failed to mitigate a loss, the other contracting party will not be liable for this part of the damage (see **Chapter 10**). Behaviour can become relevant in that causing damage is not always enough; the party causing the damage must be in breach of its promise, and this may in effect mean that it will be liable only if at fault (see Supply of Goods and Services Act 1982, s 13). In this situation a claim for damages in contract looks little different from a claim for damages in the tort of negligence (or, put another way, it might be just as useful to class all the cases under the heading 'fault').

Where the contractual text can become of major importance in a damages claim is when the contract contains an exclusion or limitation clause (see **5.2.4**, below). Such a contractual promise can isolate a party in breach from full or partial liability in damages (see, eg, *Photo Production Ltd v Securicor* (1980)), provided, of course, that it is actually incorporated into the contract (*Thornton v Shoe Lane Parking Ltd* (1971)). Yet even here the approach is not necessarily that far removed from a claim in tort, for consent to the damage (*volenti non fit injuria*) is a defence to most non-contractual claims (although rarely successful).

2.1.4.2 Debt

Yet not all contractual claims are actions for damages. Indeed, most are not. The frequent complaint is that one contractual party has failed to perform his promise to pay a price for a service or for goods supplied. Here the claim is for debt rather than damages. A good example is *Carlill v Carbolic Smoke Ball Co* (see **3.3.2.1**, below) where the plaintiff was not seeking compensation; she was seeking a specific sum of money promised to her on the happening of a certain event (cf PECL, art 9.101(1)). There was no question here of her having to mitigate or prove a causal link between her 'loss' and the defendant's non-performance. The issue was one that focused entirely on the obligation: did the defendant promise to pay and was the promise a contractual one? If so, there is liability for the whole amount; if not, there is no liability whatsoever. In other words debt cases, unlike damages claims (where the claimant might get less than he claimed), are all or nothing (but see, on this point, Swiss Code of Obligations, art 373).

2.1.4.3 Specific performance

In substance, if not in form, debt is a claim for specific performance, in as much as a claimant is asking the court to force a contractor to do what he promised to do, namely, pay a price for goods or services rendered (see, eg, Sale of Goods Act 1979, s 49). Where the promise was one other than to pay a sum of money, the common law courts were helpless when it came to specifically enforcing the primary obligations. There was no form of action available, and all the common law courts could do was to order compensation (damages). The Court of Chancery, however, stepped in to remedy this gap and provided its own action for specific performance. Yet this was only an exceptional remedy; equity would not allow its use where damages would be adequate, and this discretionary aspect to the remedy remains of vital importance in today's commercial world. A claimant might not be able to force a contractor to perform his contractual promise if such performance would, for example, be economically inefficient (*Co-operative Ins Soc v Argyll Stores* (1998)). This remedy, then, should give one an insight into one function of contract, which is economic efficiency, and this function can be perceived in non-specific performance cases as well (see, eg, *Ruxley Electronics Ltd v Forsyth* (1996)).

2.1.4.4 Injunction

Equity can also offer a negative remedy; that is to say, it may issue an injunction to prevent a contractor from breaking his contractual obligation. Thus if an actor, who has contracted to work exclusively for the claimant studio, starts to work for another employer, it may well be that the claimant will be able to obtain an injunction ordering the actor not to work for the other employer (*Warner Brothers v Nelson* (1937)). Injunctions can be used, in other words, to enforce contracts in a negative way, while specific performance (**2.1.4.3** above) is required if the non-performing party is to be forced to do something positive, such as convey property.

2.1.4.5 Rescission

A quite different claim is one where a party wishes simply to escape from the contractual obligation and is asking the court to set aside the contract. In theory there is no question about the actual existence of the contract; what the claimant is arguing is that the other party has spoken, acted or failed to act in such a way that it would be unconscionable for the law to enforce the promises (see **Chapter 4**). The words or act complained of do not, as such, fall within the domain of the contractual obligation; indeed, in the case of misstatements, they often do not form contractual promises (*Hopkins v Tanqueray* (1854)). But in causing the victim to enter into a contract, a situation is arrived at where it would be unjust for the court to insist that the contract be enforced. In other words, a justified form of enrichment is rendered unjust by the pre-contractual behaviour of one of the parties.

Rescission, then, provides yet another perspective from which to view contract. Indeed, this perspective is so important that it acts in itself as one means of understanding an important aspect of contract law. When can a person escape from a contract? The equitable remedy itself will not, it must be said, provide anything like a complete answer to this question. The common law, for example, also allows a contractor to escape from a contract where the other party is in serious breach. Equally statute allows a consumer to escape from a distance selling contract within a statutory period (Consumer Protection (Distance Selling) Regulations 2000, reg 10); this statutory escape is not truly rescission since the contract is deemed never to have existed. In addition a declaration that a contract is non-existent for mistake or frustration often looks similar to the granting of rescission in equity, even if from an internal position the positive rules governing the situation prove very different.

2.1.4.6 Restitution (debt, account or conversion)

Another type of claim, loosely called restitution, is where the claimant is seeking either the return of money or property transferred, or even a service rendered, to another under a purported contractual relationship, or the rendering of a profit made by the other party which the claimant believes should not be retained. There is in truth no such remedy as 'restitution', but the term is valuable in that it acts as a generic category for claims aimed at a specific sum of money or item of property. It includes the remedies of debt, account and damages in the tort of conversion or in the tort of trespass.

Restitution claims may of course follow a claim for rescission of a contract (**2.1.4.5** above): a party seeks the return of money or property transferred under the contract before rescission. Or such claims may arise in situations where the contract turns out not to exist because of a mistake, or because it has been frustrated. For example, in one case the plaintiff had been sold a car that turned out not to be owned by the seller; he successfully sued the seller in debt for the return of the purchase price (*Rowland v Divall* (1923)). In another case, an ex-government employee had secured a nice profit as a result of behaviour that amounted to a breach of contract; the Government could not sue in damages as it had suffered no actual damage from the breach, but it could sue in equity for an account of profits (*Att-Gen v Blake* (2001)). This remedy of account is a kind of equitable debt claim.

2.1.4.7 Self-help

The remedies discussed so far, with the exception of rescission, all involve going to court, and even rescission often requires (or results in) a court decision. However, a contractor may decide to take matters into his own hands and use a self-help remedy. One of the most common in the area of contract is a refusal to perform a contractual obligation because the other party has failed adequately to perform his obligation. In short, this often comes down to a refusal to pay. Thus in one case a householder refused to pay a firm of heating engineers who had contracted to install a central heating system in his house; the firm certainly provided radiators, boiler and pipes, but it could not get the system actually to heat the house. In the end, after the engineers appeared to have given up trying to get the system to function properly, the householder simply withheld payment of the agreed price; the Court of Appeal held that he was entitled to do this (*Bolton v Mahadeva* (1972)).

It needs to be noted, however, that self-help can be a dangerous remedy. If a contractor unilaterally decides to abandon a contract because of the other party's non-performance, this self-help abandonment will be valid only if the non-performance (breach) of contract was serious. If it was not, the self-help behaviour is not only unjustified, it amounts to a breach of contract entitling the other party to damages (see, eg, *Hong Kong Fir Shipping Co Ltd v Kawasaki Kisen Kaisha Ltd* (1962)). Here the situation is analogous to self-help in tort. A victim of some torts, such as trespass (assault, for example), is permitted in certain situations to resort to self-defence. However, if the victim uses more force than was reasonable in the circumstances then the victim himself will become a trespasser, allowing the original attacker to sue the victim for his injuries (this is the reason why some burglars can sue for damages having been assaulted by the house owner).

2.1.4.8 Primary and secondary obligation

One point that emerges from this remedy-orientated view of contract is that some remedies, like debt and specific performance in equity, attach to the primary contractual promise itself. Debt forces a contractor to do what he has promised to do (see, eg, *Carlill v Carbolic Smoke Ball Co* (1893)). Damages, in contrast, arise out of what Lord Diplock has called a secondary obligation. 'Every failure to perform a primary obligation is a breach of contract', said Lord Diplock in *Photo Production v Securicor* (1980); and such a breach gives rise to a 'secondary obligation ... to pay monetary compensation to the other party for the loss sustained by him in consequence of the breach' (at 849). Here, then, is the link between the contractual obligation and contractual liability: contract creates promises (or obligations) at two different levels, the secondary level coming into play when a party fails to perform his obligation under the contract and this failure is not excused (see eg PECL, art 8.101). Of course, if the innocent party suffers no actual loss then damages will not lie (*Lazenby Garages Ltd v Wright* (1976)), but this lack of damage does not necessarily mean that some other remedy might not be available (*Att-Gen v Blake* (2001)).

2.1.4.9 Interests protected

The idea of a secondary obligation is equally useful in understanding that the remedy of damages attracts its own rules (cf **Chapter 10**). The entitlement to damages for breach of contract will not of itself determine what actual interests will be protected. The general rule does try, in the abstract, to protect what is called the 'expectation interest', that is to say to compensate the victim of a breach of contract by reference to the position he would have been in had the contract been performed (PECL, art 9.502). (In tort, in contrast, the general rule is restoration: that is, to be put back into the position the victim was in before the tort: PETL, art 10:101.) However, such an expectation will be the subject of compensation only if it was in the contemplation of the contract-breaker at the time of the making of the contract (*Hadley v Baxendale* (1854); and see PECL, art 9.503). Moreover, the court has some leeway in the determination of what actually counts as damage. It would appear that a product that is defective to the extent that it does not conform to the primary obligation might not be defective from a damage and damages point of view (a swimming pool, for example, that does not strictly conform to the contract measurements but is nevertheless a 'reasonable' pool). In such a situation the interest switches from the thing itself to the mental state of the victim; it becomes a form of mental distress damage (see, eg, *Ruxley Electronics Ltd v Forsyth* (1996)).

2.1.5 Contract and rights

Contract can be approached from yet another perspective, that of rights. This is a perspective that emphasises entitlements, and is perhaps summed up by the judicial observation that a 'person who has a right under a contract ... is entitled to exercise it ... for a good reason or a bad reason or no reason at all' (Pearson LJ in *Chapman v Honig* (1963), 520). Contract, or promise, is from this perspective to be viewed as a form of property. A legally enforceable promise, in other words, is an asset just like an item of property (see Lord Denning MR in *Beswick v Beswick* (1966, CA)).

Now, as we have seen (**Chapter 1**), property, or real, rights are, in strict legal science, to be differentiated from contract, or personal, rights. Yet some contractual rights, in English law at least, are either property rights in themselves – for example a right to a debt – or are capable of creating indirectly rights in an item of property. Thus a contractual right to enter upon land belonging to another can of itself entitle the contractor to a proprietary remedy against a third party who is preventing the contractor from entering (*Manchester Airport Plc v Dutton* (2000)). Normally, however, contract rights are 'weaker' than real property rights in that an owner of land can expel a contractor (for example a decorator) from his property. All that the expelled contractor can do in such circumstances is to rely upon his secondary obligation (or right) to sue for damages for breach of contract; he cannot re-enter the property, complete the contract, and sue for the price of his service (*Hounslow LBC v Twickenham Garden Developments* (1971); cf White & Carter (Councils) Ltd v McGregor (1962)).

Yet not all contract 'rights' have the same status, since some arise directly out of the contractual promise while others are created by ricochet from the existence of a contractual remedy. The householder who refuses to pay for the badly installed central heating system does not have a direct contractual right as such to free services and free heating equipment; it is an indirect right arising out of the failure of the heating engineers to perform their obligations under the contract. Sometimes the right is even more indirect. Thus the family of a contractor who indirectly received compensation for their ruined holiday via payment of damages to the actual contractor were not in theory being compensated for invasion of their contractual rights, for they had no contractual rights (see **3.4.3**, below). All they had was an interest in the performance by the tour operator of its contractual obligations towards the father as contractor. Yet the law of damages, in recognising this interest, in effect bestowed an indirect contractual right on the family members (*Jackson v Horizon Holidays* (1975)).

2.1.6 Structural complexity

Contract as a subject thus turns out to be more complex, structurally speaking, than its definition suggests. Of course it is not untrue to say that it is about enforceable promises or agreements; it is just that the whole of the law of contract often ends up being rooted in more than one conceptual and factual source. Contractual remedies, arising out of loss, damage or disappointment, can shape the contours of the subject as much as contractual rights arising directly out of promise or agreement. Rights, remedies, interests, duties, obligations and reasonableness are also capable of adding structural confusion, since each of these terms varies in the normative (ought) potency. At the level of fact, the sale of an onion and the hire of a ship may both appear to be governed by the same rules, but the factual differences are such that the detailed rules turn out to diverge, often because the *interests* in play are different or what counts as *reasonable* is not the same in the commercial world as in the consumer world. In addition, the comparative lawyer is faced with two rather different contract histories; the civil and common law traditions may both have a law of contract but, from the viewpoint of history at least, the structural foundation of each is not the same.

2.2 Classification of contracts

Accordingly, that there exist different types of contract should be of no surprise, since purchase and sale, employment, the hire of ships, transport, insurance and so on are in the real world all very different transactions. In other words, the facts themselves would appear to determine difference, and in Roman law these empirical distinctions between the various private and commercial operations gave rise to a law of contracts rather than contract (see **3.2.2**, below). Yet with the development of a general theory of contract these differences between empirical transactions became subsumed under the abstract elements of agreement and promise, with the result that contract today is rather 'as if medical students had a first year course entitled "Disease" and consequently came to believe that diseases were all much of a muchness' (Weir, 1992, 1639–40). Classification of contracts ought, therefore, to pay some attention to reality. Yet even if all the different contractual transactions are 'much of a muchness', at the level of form civil lawyers, and to some extent common lawyers, do recognise different kinds of contract.

2.2.1 Civil law model

The French *Code civil* has a list of the different kinds of contract and has whole sections devoted to specific (named) contracts reflecting the different Roman types. Thus the classification operates at two levels. At the level of general theory there are three dichotomies set out in the general introduction to contractual obligations: synallagmatic (or bilateral) and unilateral contracts (arts 1102–1103); *commutatif* and *aléatoire* (uncertain event) contracts (art 1104); and gratuitous (*à titre gratuit*) and advantageous (*à titre onéreux*) contracts (arts 1105–1106). At a substantive level – that is to say at the level of transaction – the codes distinguish between named and unnamed contracts, the former being subject not just to the general rules of contract but also to specific rules devoted to these named contracts (CC, art 1107). These named contracts are based on those to be found in the Roman sources – the main ones being sale, hire, partnership, deposit (D.2.14.7.1) – but the more modern codes often add transactions that appeared only in the modern world. The Quebec Civil Code, for example, has a section on insurance, and this class of contract is in turn subdivided into marine and non-marine (art 2389); and the Swiss Code of

Obligations has articles devoted to publishing contracts (arts 380ff). The Polish Civil Code goes further: there are sections devoted to bank account (arts 725ff) and pension contracts (arts 903ff). The Lando Commission, which drafted the PECL, intends to produce further codes on specific contracts.

2.2.2 Common law model

Some of the civilian distinctions are to be found in the common law. Thus the distinction between unilateral and bilateral contracts is fundamental; and certain specific contracts are governed by their own legislative regimes, of which the most important is perhaps sale of goods (Sale of Goods Act 1979; *Ashington Piggeries Ltd v C Hill Ltd* (1972), 501, *per* Lord Diplock). Even where there is no formal distinction, certain classes of contract do tend to attract their own rules (eg, charterparties and bailment contracts). Moreover, although the civilian distinction between gratuitous and non-gratuitous contracts cannot in theory exist in the common law given the fundamental requirement of consideration (but cf the Law of Property (Miscellaneous Provisions) Act 1989, s 1), the equitable doctrine of estoppel can in practice result, on occasions, in a gratuitous promise being given legal effect (see, eg, *Crabb v Arun DC* (1976)).

2.2.2.1 Unilateral and bilateral contracts

One distinction to be found in French and English law is that between a unilateral contract and a bilateral contract. In the former, only one party makes a promise; while in the latter, promises move from both parties. A unilateral contract is a promise for an act (performance); a bilateral contract is a promise for a promise. Accordingly, in a unilateral contract the promisee can never be in breach (see Diplock LJ in *UDT v Eagle Aircraft Services* (1968)). If, therefore, D declares, in a take-it-or-leave-it fashion, to C that he will pay £100 if C turns up and sings 'My Way' at his birthday party, C will not be in breach if he does not turn up. He will simply not be able to claim the £100. However, if D makes a specific contract with C (or C's agent) for C to come and perform at a certain date, and C agrees to turn up on that date, C could well find himself in breach of a bilateral contract if he fails to perform. Often it is easy to distinguish the unilateral from the bilateral contract – reward cases are usually unilateral – but as the two above examples suggest, there may be situations where it is more difficult (eg, estate agent contracts: *Luxor (Eastbourne) Ltd v Cooper* (1941)).

2.2.2.2 Instantaneous and long-term contracts

Neither the civil law nor the common law makes a formal distinction between instantaneous and long-term contracts (*Total Gas v Arco British* (1998), 218, *per* Lord Steyn). Nevertheless, the distinction is of importance in a number of ways. First, the relationship of the parties is likely to be so different as to generate different expectations. Thus a contractor will not have the same expectations of a shop owner from whom he occasionally buys a newspaper as of his employer for whom he has worked for many years. Secondly, a long-term contract is always subject to the risk of changing circumstances. A contract to supply water at a fixed price in 1929 might appear a most reasonable bargain for both sides at the time of signing the deal; 50 years later, however, the fixed price, thanks to inflation, could prove economically ruinous for one of the parties (*Staffs AHA v South Staffs Waterworks* (1978)). Long-term contracts thus raise a question of whether parties should be under a contractual duty to renegotiate the terms where circumstances have changed to such an extent that it has given rise to hardship (see PECL, art 6.111). Another reason for distinguishing the long-term contract from the instantaneous one is that they may require more long-term planning. This can impact upon formation, upon terms and upon the general structure of the contractual arrangement (see Bell, 1989).

2.2.2.3 Supply of goods and services

Another important distinction to be found in the common law is the distinction between a contract to supply a thing (sale and hire) and a contract to supply a service. This distinction is important when it comes to non- or defective performance: if the quality of goods supplied under a sale or a hire contract turns out to be defective and causes damage (the exploding television that destroys a valuable vase, or food that poisons the purchaser), the supplier of the goods will be strictly liable (*Frost v Aylesbury Dairy* (1905)). However, if the quality of a service proves defective (the electrician who knocks over a valuable vase), the supplier will be liable only if he was negligent (Supply of Goods and Services Act 1982, s 13).

This distinction is to be found in civil law thinking but at a more abstract level. French lawyers distinguish between a contractual obligation to achieve a result (*obligation de résultat*) and an obligation of best efforts (*obligation de moyens*). According to this termi- nology – which has been adopted by UNIDROIT (art 5.4) – a sale of goods contract imposes an obligation of result in respect of the quality of the goods (Sale of Goods Act 1979, s 14) while a contract of service contains an implied term only of best efforts. There are some dif- ficult situations (see Lord Denning MR in *Greaves & Co v Baynham Meikle* (1975); and see *Thake v Maurice* (1986)) and in French law the dichotomy has become increasingly complex with the development of various sub-categories and overlaying obligations (for example, an obligation of safety). But on the whole the distinction is clear enough when applied to the dichotomy between goods and services. One might add, however, that problems can arise over the quality itself. Normally goods must conform not just to the statutory implied terms (eg, s 14 of the 1979 Act) but also to any express term about quality; if there is no such term the PECL stipulate that goods must be of 'average quality' (art 6.108).

2.2.2.4 Contracts to pass title

Another reason why the distinction between supply of goods and supply of service con- tracts is of importance is that the former involve not just obligation rights (*in personam*) but also property rights (*in rem*). In a sale contract the seller promises to pass title (owner- ship) and usually possession in the goods (see Sale of Goods Act 1979, ss 12, 27). However, unlike Roman and German law, England follows the French model, in which it is the contract itself that acts as the conveyance of this title provided the goods are ascer- tained (Sale of Goods Act 1979, s 18), although the seller can always reserve title (s 16). Accordingly, sale of goods contracts are different from service contracts to the extent that they also form part of the law of personal property (see, eg, *Shogun Finance v Hudson* (2003)). One should note here that land is different. Contract does not pass legal title in the property – a separate conveyance is necessary – although it can pass an equitable title, which arises because Equity is prepared to force the seller of land to perform through a claim for specific performance (**2.1.4.3** above).

2.2.2.5 Bailment and contract

Contracts which involve just the transfer of possession in goods also bring the law of personal property into play. This is because the transfer of possession in a chattel from one person (bailor) to another (bailee) gives rise to a legal relationship, independent of contract, called a bailment (cf **1.3.8**, above). Bailment contracts – that is to say contracts for the carriage of goods, contracts of hire, and even some contracts of service (see, eg, *Morris v Martin* (1966)) – need to be distinguished from other contracts because bailment itself creates rights and duties. These obligations may, of course, be modified by the contract itself. However, if a coach company contracts to take C from one town to another and manages to lose C's suitcase on the way, having taken possession of it by putting it into the hold of the coach, C will be able to claim its value from the coach company. This claim will not be based on the contract of carriage to transport C, but on the bailment (property) relationship arising out of the transfer of possession of the suitcase, the remedy itself being, now, the tort of conversion (*Houghland v RR Low (Luxury Coaches) Ltd* (1962)).

2.2.2.6 Administrative and private contracts

The distinction between obligations and property is not the only fundamental distinction to be found in civilian thinking. The dichotomy between public and private law is another important division (cf **1.3.9**, above), and it is reflected in French contract law in the difference of regime between public (administrative) and private contracts. In English law there is no such formal distinction. The ordinary law of contract applies equally to all persons and institutions whether they are in the public or private sectors. However, in substance it may on occasions be important to distinguish between the two sectors, in that public bodies are subject to rules and principles that are not necessarily applicable in the private sector.

In truth the whole public and private question is rather complex in English law for a range of reasons (see generally Rudden, 1989). First, because public bodies themselves differ; the Crown, for example, has a different status in the eyes of the law than local authorities, and an organisation such as the BBC differs from governmental institutions. Secondly, many relations that appear at first sight as contractual may turn out not to be so. Thus the postal services and the supply of gas, electricity and water were not contractual relationships, and privatisation has not necessarily altered this situation. Certain Crown servants may find, also, that their employment is not governed by contract but by a public law relationship. Thirdly, the capacity of local authorities to contract is governed quite rigidly by statute, and if such an authority exceeds its powers any such contract will be void rather than voidable (Turpin, 2002, 627). Fourthly, many government contracts contain adjudication clauses which have the effect of keeping disputes out of the ordinary courts. As Rudden points out, a 'combination of this factor and the use of ... standard terms over a long period means that English courts have been spared the task of fashioning a general law of public contracts' (1989, 103).

Another reason for complexity is that while a private body or an individual is at liberty to refuse to contract with another without giving reasons, or, indeed, because of non-commercial or personal reasons, a public body is not. In fact, were a public body to refuse to contract with a local firm because the authority did not approve of the firm's support of a particular political party or policy, this most probably would be regarded as an abuse of power and subject to judicial review (*R v Lewisham LBC, ex p Shell* (1988)). Indeed, statute specifically restricts the pursuit of collateral policies via certain public works contracts by a local authority (Local Government Act 1988, s 17). In substance, then, the distinction between public and private contracts is not completely devoid of meaning in English law.

2.2.2.7 Commercial and consumer contracts

Abuse of power is not confined to public servants: powerful corporations have on occasions proved quite capable of exploiting those with whom they contract. Such exploitation arose as a result of the principle that parties were deemed by the law always to be equal in terms of their bargaining power. However, abuse of power in the private sector has been remedied to some extent through an increasingly formalised distinction between consumer and non-consumer contracts. The distinction is most evident in respect of two situations. First, unfair or abusive clauses inserted into contracts by commercial suppliers are unenforceable against consumers (see **5.2.4**, below). Secondly, consumers who have entered into a distance selling contract have a right of cancellation within a period of seven working days from the receipt of goods or services (Consumer Protection (Distance Selling) Regulations 2000, regs 10–12). More generally the distinction probably manifests itself with respect to interpretation of contracts: it is unlikely that the courts will approach a written contract between a business and a consumer with the same attitude as they adopt with regard to charterparties.

2.3 Freedom of contract

The distinction between consumer and non-consumer contracts is related to a general principle that has underpinned contract at least since the early 19th century, if not before. This is the principle of freedom of contract affirmed in both the PECL (art 1.102) and UNIDROIT (art 1.1), although perhaps finding its most perfect expression in the French assertion that contracts are a form of private legislation between the parties (CC, art 1134). In its heyday this principle assumed not only that contractual parties were formally and substantially equal, but also that parties were free to make what a third party might consider unreasonable contracts. Contract, in other words, was a matter for the parties and not the courts.

This freedom of contract doctrine is perhaps well encapsulated by an English judge in 1875, who asserted that if:

> there is one thing more than another which public policy requires, it is that men of full age and competent understanding shall have the utmost liberty of contracting and that their contracts, when entered into freely and voluntarily, shall be held sacred and shall be enforced by courts of justice. (*Printing and Numerical Registering Co v Sampson* (1875), 465)

The ideology was to result in a paradox: a party had the freedom to insert in a contract a clause that stipulated that whatever his behaviour, he was in no circumstances to be contractually liable. Such freedom inevitably resulted in abuse where economically powerful parties were able to impose on weaker parties standard form contracts full of exclusion clauses. Courts in the UK and continental Europe developed a number of tactics to deal with this abuse (strict interpretation, *contra proferentem* rule, good faith, abuse of rights, fundamental terms, etc), but it was only with legislative intervention in the 1970s that the problem became fully regulated. This legislation, on the whole, tackled the paradox of freedom and abuse by formally making a distinction between consumer and non-consumer contracts (see EU Directive of 5 April 1993). Freedom of contract was maintained as between commercial parties able to look after their own interests (*Photo Production Ltd v Securicor* (1980)); consumers, on the other hand, were given more or less full protection against abusive terms, although in England much will turn on what 'unfair' means to judges (cf *Director General of Fair Trading v First National Bank plc* (2002)).

In fact the control of unfair clauses is not confined to consumer contracts. Both in English law and at the European level (see PECL, art 4.110) unfair clauses can be struck down in certain types of commercial contracts. Moreover, there is authority to the effect that a small commercial concern might even be treated, in certain circumstances, as a consumer (*R & B Customs Brokers Co Ltd v United Dominions Trust Ltd* (1988)). As is typical with English law, much will depend upon the facts. Further, some cases are controversial in respect of the extent to which they might be said to protect the consumer interest (see, eg, *Director General of Fair Trading v First National Bank plc* (2002); *Shogun Finance v Hudson* (2003)).

2.4 Good faith

One way in which abusive terms could be tackled in civil law systems was through the doctrine of good faith. To contract and not to contract at the same time, or indeed to contract on terms where one party is put under a significant disadvantage, could be seen as evidence of bad faith (cf PECL, art 4.110).

The notion of *bona fides* has its origin in Roman law, where it required equity in contract to the highest degree (D.16.3.31pr). Nevertheless this general statement must be seen in the context that contracting parties were also free to take advantage of each other (D.4.4.16.4; D.19.2.22.3), and thus the exact scope of the duty of good faith in the context of commerce has never been easy to gauge. One Scottish Law Lord has recently pointed out that good faith functioned at the level of the remedy rather than right and was not therefore 'a source of obligation in itself' (Lord Hope in *R (European Roma Rights) v Prague Immigration Officer* (2005), §§ 59–60). Yet in modern civil law the requirement of good faith is to be found in all the codes; thus, for example, art 1134 of the *Code civil* states that agreements 'must be performed in good faith' and it is a general duty to be found in both the PECL (art 1.201) and UNIDROIT (art 1.7) ('good faith and fair dealing'). The rule has been described as a means 'of inserting into positive law moral rules', and as such has 'given rise, because of its imprecision, to many questions' (Terré et al, 2002, § 439).

Certainly the topic has attracted much literature. What makes the duty difficult is whether it is simply a passive duty – that is to say a duty not to act in positive bad faith – or whether it goes further and imposes active duties on contracting parties. Traditionally, in France, good faith has translated itself into two main obligations: the duty of loyalty (*devoir de loyauté*) and a duty of co-operation. Both of these raise interesting questions in themselves. However, more recently French doctrine and jurisprudence seem to have gone further and are imposing a duty to inform and to collaborate, this latter specifically appearing as an independent duty in the PECL (art 1.202). Good faith is, in other words, being used to construct a new philosophy of *solidarisme contractuel*, in which a contracting party has to further not just his own interests but, to an extent, the interests of his co-party (Terré et al, 2002, §§ 41–43, 439–441).

Whether good faith is to be found in English law is a difficult question given that there are judicial dicta pointing in both directions (see generally Bingham LJ in *Interfoto Picture Library Ltd v Stiletto Visual Programmes Ltd* (1989)). One writer has described it as an 'irritant' (Teubner, 1998), while a Victorian Law Lord claimed that it was a term implied in all mercantile contracts (Lord Watson in *Glynn Mills Curie & Co v East & West India Dock Co* (1882), 615). However, what is clear is that English law is very sceptical about any notion of *solidarisme contractuel*, and the case law itself demonstrates that parties are expected to look after their own interests and are not generally under a duty to inform (*University of Nottingham v Eyett* (1999)). The only general duty is not positively to mislead (misrepresentation).

Good faith has in some civilian systems extended itself beyond the contractual obligation and into the pre-contractual domain; this extension is reflected in the PECL, in that negotiations broken off in bad faith may give rise to liability (art 2.301). English law has seemingly rejected such a principle (*Walford v Miles* (1992), *per* Lord Ackner), although not without some dissent in the academic literature. Perhaps the English position has best been summarised by Bingham LJ in the *Interfoto* case, where he said of good faith that (at 439):

> English law has, characteristically, committed itself to no such overriding principle but has developed piecemeal solutions in response to demonstrated problems of unfairness. Many examples could be given. Thus equity has intervened to strike down unconscionable bargains. Parliament has stepped in to regulate the imposition of exemption clauses and the form of certain hire-purchase agreements. The common law also has made its contribution, by holding that certain classes of contract require the utmost good faith, by treating as irrecoverable what purport to be agreed estimates of damage but are in truth a disguised penalty for breach, and in many other ways.

2.5 Domain of contract

The discussion of administrative and ordinary contracts (see **2.2.2.6**, above) raised a question about the scope and extent – or perhaps one should say province – of the law of contract. Some relations that at first sight might appear contractual turn out not to be so, and some rules which appear to be contractual prove on closer examination to fall outside contract. Thus, for example, a claim for damages for misrepresentation belongs to the law of tort and money claims arising after the disappearance of a contract for, say, frustration belong now to the law of restitution (cf **Chapter 11**). Indeed the whole topic of vitiating factors in contract is not really part of contract at all; for the remedy of rescission in equity, which is the vehicle for giving expression to such factors, is in reality founded on the principle of unjust enrichment (*Whittaker v Campbell* (1984), 326–7). The distinction between contract and equity proves important in the area of consideration as well. For example, while it remains perfectly true to say that a promise unsupported by consideration is incapable of forming a contractual obligation, it does not follow that such a promise will be devoid of legal effect (cf **3.4.2.2**, below).

The important point to arise from these domain observations is that knowledge of contract law extends beyond the actual rules of contract law. Knowledge of certain equitable doctrines and remedies, familiarity with aspects of the law of tort, and even an acquaintance with property and administrative law are required if one is to have what might be called a practical and functional view of contract. For example, negligence cases such as *Hedley Byrne v Heller* (1964) (see **8.1.5**) and *White v Jones* (1995) are regarded even by the judges as filling certain gaps in contract law created by the requirement of consideration or the rule of privity (cf **3.4.3**, below). This is, perhaps, the most compelling reason for importing the obligations category from civilian thinking. Obligations as a class provides a perspective which transcends the boundaries between contract, tort, restitution and equity, boundaries that often do more harm than good when it comes to solving litigation problems. Another approach is to switch to the substance of legal reasoning. Here it becomes evident that precise categories and boundaries are not things that necessarily act as reasoning premises for the English judiciary (see generally Waddams, 2003).

3   Enforcing Contracts

Contract is normally approached from an external position. It is generally presented as a closed (or relatively closed) coherent model of interrelated rules waiting to be applied to factual situations as they arise. Both the PECL and UNIDROIT are excellent example of such models. These models broadly fall into two parts: there are rules concerning the formation of the obligation (including obstacles to formation or vitiating factors) and there are rules dealing with the dissolution or non-performance of the obligation, this section often having reference to the contents of the contract. Sometimes, it must be added, the content of a contract is dealt with as a third part falling between the other two parts. Yet there is another view of contract in which cases tell their own story. This is an alternative viewpoint because cases reveal concepts, principles and forms of reasoning that are not always fully exposed by the contract model. They give a view from the bottom-up so to speak. And this is why it is possible to argue that there is another way of understanding contract. This will be the approach of this chapter and the two that follow. They will not cover all the rules in the model – this is something that a standard contract textbook will do – but the bottom-up approach might facilitate understanding from a problem-solving position.

3.1 Contract and methodology

If such a bottom-up approach is to be adopted, something must be said, first of all, about method. Some guidance will already have been provided in the preceding chapter, but a reflection on methods is vital because, when contract cases are viewed from the position of the facts, complexities are revealed that are not always reflected in the standard abstract models.

3.1.1 General rules and problem solving

A general theory of contract impacts upon methodology in two main ways. First, it makes the law of contract, in the common law world, something of an oddity when compared with the law of tort. Tort tends to operate via categories of liability closely linked to different types of factual situation (cf **6.3**, below). Yet, as we have seen, in contract, the hire of a super-tanker, the sale of an onion, the employment of a gardener and the taking out of a loan are all governed by the same legal principle. Secondly, a general theory tends to make problem solving both easy and complex. It is easy in that one can carry a model in one's head to be applied to this vast range of different transactions. Thus formation is a matter of invitation to treat, offer and acceptance, consideration and intention to create legal relations; this structure is then applied to transactions in shops, supermarkets, garages, buses, agencies, offices, factories, constructions sites, ships, and so on and so forth. The general theory is difficult, however, when things go wrong, because it is tempting to think that it always results in the remedy of damages, unless perhaps a defendant is able to offer some convincing defence as to why he should not be liable. This is not helped by the judges. 'Of all the various remedies available at common law,' said Lord Hailsham, 'damages are the remedy of most general application at the present day, and they remain the prime remedy in actions for breach of contract and tort' (*Broome v Cassell* (1972), 1070). This may be true of tort, but it is not actually true of contract since statistically the great majority of claims in contract are in debt (that is to say for money owing and not paid).

This damages and debt point is made in respect of methodology because most contract cases get to court only because something has gone wrong and one party is claiming that the other is in breach of one or more of his contractual promises. Two important methodological questions thus arise when dealing with practical contract problems: What has the non-performing (or defective performing) contractor failed to do? What does the disappointed expectant contractor want in order to remedy the situation?

3.1.2 Deconstructing contract

We have already seen that a general theory of contract tends to mask transactional distinctions that, on occasions, might usefully be revealed. Sometimes these distinctions can be vital, particularly when it comes to non-performance. Take the problem of an exploding bottle of lemonade: if the purchaser is injured after purchase, he or she will be entitled to damages in contract without having to prove fault (*Frost v Aylesbury Dairy Co Ltd* (1905)). However, if after leaving a supermarket, a consumer is injured when the bus in which he or she is travelling crashes, the consumer will be able to get damages from the bus company only if fault is proved (Supply of Goods and Services Act 1982, s 13). Again, if the consumer goes to the cleaners to recover her mink stole, only to be told that it has gone missing, she will be able to recover its value *unless* the firm of cleaners is able to prove that it was not at fault (and that may not always be enough) (*Morris v C W Martin & Sons Ltd* (1966)).

Take another problem: consumer A contracts to hire a standard van from a van hire firm; consumer B contracts to hire a *particular* van from the same hire firm and the firm has only one such van. After the contracts are signed but before either A or B collects the van, there is a fire at the firm and B's particular van is destroyed; however, just two or three of the standard vans are destroyed (and the firm has a dozen of them). Provided the fire is not due to the fault of the firm, it may well be able to say to B that the contract to supply a van no longer exists (*Constantine (Joseph) SS Ltd v Imperial Smelting Corporation* (1942)) while it will not be able to say the same thing to A (*Maritime National Fish Ltd v Ocean Trawlers Ltd* (1935)). We are not talking here of a different type of transaction (hire), yet we can – and must – distinguish between a contract to supply a *specific* thing from one to supply a *generic* thing. Method requires careful consideration of the type of transaction and the nature of the 'thing' promised.

3.1.3 Monetary remedies

Another way of deconstructing contract is from the viewpoint of remedies. When a trans-action goes wrong, or proves unfortunate or defective, what does a disappointed contractor actually want, or what is he entitled to? Take facts similar to those in *Constantine v Imperial Smelting* (1942). H hires a ship from O, and before H can transport his cargo from one destination to another the ship explodes and sinks for some unex-plained reason. H may well want compensation from O for failing to supply a ship, while O may want to know if H remains liable to pay the hire fee. These are two quite different claims: compensation is about *damages*, while claiming hire fees is about *debt*. Mrs Carlill was not, to give another example, claiming compensation for catching influenza; she was asking the court to force the Carbolic Smoke Ball Co to do what it had promised (*Carlill v Carbolic Smoke Ball Co*, **3.3.2.1** below). The £100 promised bore no relation to the harm caused from catching influenza.

The distinction between a claim in debt and one in damages can be vital because normally debt is all-or-nothing: either a contractor is liable to pay the whole sum, or he is not. Damages are not the same. A contractor may well be held liable to pay damages to the other party for a defective or non-performance, but this other party may not get all he asks for. The victim of a breach of contract is not entitled to damages which are too remote or which flow from the victim's own failure to mitigate (ie, cut down his loss) (see **Chapter 10**). These are rules attaching to the *remedy* as much as the contractual right. From a method point of view, damages are an interesting aspect of contract because they seemingly allow the court to apply rules – and economic theories? – that operate inde-pendently from the actual contractual obligation itself. For example, if the victim of a non-performance suffers no recognisable damage, he will be entitled to nominal damages only (*Lazenby Garages v Wright* (1976)).

Thus, to go back to the exploding ship, if O is sued by H for non-performance (ie, not sup-plying a ship as promised), can O say that the non-performance is not due to fault on his part and thus he is no longer under a contractual liability to supply the ship (and ought he to be able to say this)? And if so, who must prove fault or its absence? In French law the burden would be on O to prove that the non-performance is due to an absence of fault (CC, arts 1147–1148; see also PECL, arts 8.101, 8.108). However, English law seemingly puts the burden on H (*Constantine*, above).

3.1.4 Consumer perspective

Yet the *Constantine* rule must be treated with some caution. Imagine that H hires a motor launch for a holiday on the river, but for some unexplained reason the launch catches fire and he has to abandon ship, losing all his possessions. Can it really be said that O could claim he is not liable unless H proves fault? This seems most unlikely (*Reed v Dean* (1949)). All the same, the French make a most useful distinction when it comes to the obligation to supply something under a contract: they distinguish between an obligation to achieve a result and an obligation to do one's best (see **2.2.2.3**, above). Thus the doctor who treats a patient under a contract is not normally promising to cure the patient, only to act with professional care and skill (on which see the Supply of Goods and Services Act 1982, s 13, for English law). The seller in the course of a business promises a result, namely, that the goods will be reasonably fit and of satisfactory quality (Sale of Goods Act 1979, s 14). What does an architect or a builder promise: that he will do his best, or that the building will be reasonably fit for its purpose? (Cf *Greaves & Co v Baynham Meikle & Partners* (1975).) English contract law does not make the distinction at the level of obligation; it makes it at the level of fact, in as much as it distinguishes between supply of goods (strict liability) and supply of services (fault).

3.2 Formation models

If an obligation is a *vinculum iuris* binding two parties, it must, evidently, have a beginning, a content and an end. These three aspects certainly act as focal points for legal rules and analysis, but, depending on the system under examination, they may not always be expressed in quite this way. All systems, however, have rules dealing with the formation of a contractual obligation, and contracts everywhere in Europe are often regarded as agreements, this idea of agreement being a unifying factor. Yet it can hide as much as it can reveal, since behind 'agreement' there are different models of contract. These different models disclose different theories about formation and, thus, enforceability.

3.2.1 Introduction

If one surveys the whole Western legal tradition – Roman law, modern civil law and the common law – three foundational ideas can be identified for the formation of a contractual obligation and thus the possibility of legal enforcement. The first is *causa*, which acted as the basis for contract in Roman law; the second is *conventio* (together with *consensus*), which became the foundation for a general theory of contractual formation in the modern civil law; and the third is *promissio*. This last notion is arguably the basis for contract in the common law.

However, none of this is to say that these three foundational ideas have remained independent one from the other. In French law, for example, *conventio* and *causa* have both become foundational elements (CC, art 1108), and there are those who would argue that contracts in the common law are based upon promise, consent and agreement (*conventio*) (*Shogun Finance Ltd v Hudson* (2003), §§ 123–5). If one had to extract from these notions a single dichotomy it is that between the 'subjective' and the 'objective'. Thus French contract law is, in relation to English law, sometimes said to be more subjective in its approach to formation of contracts and to vitiating factors. Yet even this dichotomy is misleading, in as much as any distinction between subjective legal 'acts' (making wills, entering a contract, etc) and objective legal 'facts' (causing of damage) can break down. How can one judge if a person has consented to something save in respect of his objective behaviour? As will be seen, acts and facts often merge.

3.2.2 Cause (*causa*)

Roman law did not develop a general theory of contract as such. What developed was a law of contracts, each with its own particular *actio* (remedy); and these contracts fell into a number of discrete categories based upon a 'cause', which in turn reflected a range of transactions typical of a commercial society (see Weir, 1992). There were the real contracts (*re*) founded upon the transfer of a thing; consensual contracts based upon the main forms of consensual transactions, namely, sale, hire, mandate and partnership; and verbal contracts arising out of a formal promise. Later Roman law did, it has to be said, develop more informal contracts such as pacts and innominate agreements, but these never really escaped their own particular categories. In a sense, then, it can be said that the obligation arose out of a particular factual transaction and thus *causa* has an objective aspect; it represents particular categories of 'natural' operations (*naturam contractus* said Ulpian: D.2.14.7.5). If there was no cause there could be no contractual *actio* and no contractual obligation, and thus no enforcement (D.2.14.7.4).

This idea of obligations arising from particular categories of transaction is still to be found in contractual thinking and, indeed, in the codes. Thus one can divide up one's daily ('natural') contracts into a limited range of operations such as purchase, carriage, hire and other services (dry cleaning for example, involving the handing over of a thing). Accordingly the codes have not just general rules of contract, but also rules with respect to those specific contracts to be found in the Roman sources (see eg CC, arts 1582ff, 1713ff), with perhaps the addition of post-Roman transactions such as insurance in the more modern codes.

Common lawyers have not made use of *causa* as such, but no contract can be formed without 'consideration', and this does share a common feature with cause. Each promise has to be bargained for, and thus each party must attract an economic detriment and a benefit. Consideration thus provides a kind of objective economic 'clothing' to a 'pact' (Zimmermann, 1996, 554–9). It must be remembered, also, that bailment (see **1.3.8** above), although not as such a contract, does give rise to obligations between bailor (transferor) and bailee (transferee). These bailment obligations are very similar to a Roman real contract, and they arise simply as a result of the transfer of the thing.

3.2.3 Agreement (*conventio*)

Despite the requirement of *causa* (discussed at **3.2.2** above), the Romans observed that all the various contracts shared a common denominator, namely *conventio* (agreement) (D.2.14.1.3). Indeed, agreement was the direct basis of the consensual contracts such as sale, hire and partnership (D.18.1.1.2). Moreover, with respect to *pacta* and the consensual contracts, there was the further idea of *consensus* (D.2.14.1.2; D.44.7.2.1). These two ideas were used by the later civilians to develop a general theory of contract. Domat (17th-century jurist) stated that 'agreements are engagements which are formed by mutual consent', and Pothier (18th century) developed the idea of *consensus* in saying that contract 'contains the coming together of the wills of two persons' (see Zimmermann, 1996, 567).

These two ideas became the foundation of contract in the *Code civil*: a contract is 'an agreement' (*une convention*: art 1101) based upon 'consent' (*le consentement*: art 1108). The German Natural Lawyers equally thought in terms of agreement and consent, but, no doubt stimulated by Roman texts (eg, D.18.1.21), there had to be, in addition to *Vertrag*, a declaration of intentions by the two parties (*Willenserklärungen*). Today, *conventio* has transcended national systems to become the basis of contract in the PECL (art 2.101) and UNIDROIT (art 2.1); a contract is formed if there is 'sufficient agreement' (and note that there is no requirement of either cause or consideration).

3.2.4 Promise (*promissio*)

The Romans might not have developed a general theory of contract, but they did create a general form of contracting, the *stipulatio*, which fell within the class of verbal contracts. The source of the obligation was a promise expressed by set words in the form of a question and answer (D.44.7.1.7): 'Do you promise to do X?'; 'Yes, I promise (*spondeo*).' This, together with the informal *pacta* of later law, became the nearest the Romans got to a general form of contracting; and indeed the *stipulatio* subsequently moved from its oral basis to one where writing was sufficient (D.45.1.134.2).

Now it may seem that this form of contracting would become irrelevant with the development of a general theory based on *conventio* and *consensus*, yet it remains important for several reasons. First, the formality of the operation has left its mark on certain modern contracts which will be valid only if, in addition to agreement, they conform to certain formal requirements such as being in writing (see, eg, the Law Reform (Miscellaneous Provisions) Act 1989, s 2). Secondly, the modern penalty clause, whereby a contracting party promises to pay a specific sum of money if he fails to perform, can be traced back (in civil law) to the *stipulatio* (see **5.2.4**, below).

Thirdly, it is feasible to argue that the formal means of determining agreement and consent, namely the rules of offer and acceptance, owes its form to the *stipulatio* (see, eg, D.45.1.1). It would be quite wrong to say that contract in English law developed out of the *stipulatio*, since the forms of action meant that the building blocks of contract were rather different from those to be found in the Roman sources. The main early actions, and categories of thought, were, as we have seen, trespass and debt (together with covenant) rather than specific types of contracts. However, as the centuries progressed, certain 'contractual' ideas began to emerge, 'with the defendant's 'undertaking' and 'faithful promise' as the central elements of the plaintiff's claim' (Ibbetson, 1999, 135–6). In other words, what emerges is the idea of a liability for breach of promise (*assumpsit*) (Ibbetson, 137–8). Accordingly, in the 19th century, when a general theory of contract was imported and superimposed upon the old common law, the normative basis remained promise rather than *conventio*, with the result that contract is arguably less a meeting of the minds; in terms of form it is a matter of an exchange of promises (see further Samuel, 2001, 285–6).

3.2.5 Promise and agreement

English contract law is, then, built upon the notion of enforceable *promise* rather than agreement, and this distinction is more than academic. In the civil law tradition the emphasis on consent (*consensus*) and agreement (*conventio*) has given rise to an idea of contract that is essentially subjective. The contractual bond is based on the coming together of two wills. In the common law, in contrast, the idea of promise is much more objective; it is a 'thing' that, once launched, assumes a life of its own and upon which others might well rely.

3.2.5.1 *Gibson v Manchester CC* (1978)

There are a number of areas where the objective flavour to English contract law manifests itself. Yet perhaps the most striking decision where the distinction between promise and agreement had a practical effect in terms of enforcement is that of *Gibson v Manchester City Council* (1978, CA; 1979, HL), in which a council house tenant brought an action for specific performance to enforce what he believed was a binding contract of sale to sell him the house in which he was living. The local authority had sent him a number of preliminary letters indicating a willingness to sell the house and stipulating the procedure to be followed. However, half way through this process there was a change of political control, and the incoming Labour group ordered a halt to council house sales except where there was a binding contract.

In the Court of Appeal, Lord Denning MR thought there was a binding contract on the basis of the correspondence between the local authority and tenant. 'If by their correspondence and their conduct you can see an agreement on all material terms, which was intended thenceforward to be binding,' said the Master of the Rolls, 'then there is a binding contract in law even though all the formalities have not been gone through.' However, this decision was overruled in the House of Lords. Lord Diplock asserted that the 'conventional approach' was to examine the actual correspondence itself in order to discover if there was a specific offer made by the council that had been accepted by the tenant. On doing this he found that 'the words ... make it quite impossible to construe this letter as a contractual offer capable of being converted into a legally enforceable open contract'. For the 'words "may be prepared to sell" are fatal to this'.

It is not asserted here that a civil law court would necessarily have arrived at the same decision as Lord Denning. But when one considers that the test of the existence of a contract in Romanist thinking is 'sufficient agreement' (PECL, art 2.101(1)(b)), it is perfectly feasible to argue that Lord Denning's analysis might well be acceptable to a civil lawyer. Lord Diplock, in contrast, is looking for a specific offer (promise) to sell, and for him the word 'may' was objectively fatal, even if at the time the council sent the letter it fully intended to sell the house provided the tenant accepted to pay the asking price (which, after some hesitation, he did).

3.2.5.2 Agreement versus offer

The distinction identified in *Gibson* (at **3.2.5.1** above) between agreement and promise reflects itself in two principal ways with regard to contract formation. First, all Western systems, to a greater or lesser extent, determine contract formation through recourse to a search for an 'offer' and an 'acceptance' (see PECL, arts 2.201 and 2.204; *Shogun Finance Ltd v Hudson* (2003), § 123). However, in civilian thinking a contract can be formed if there is 'sufficient agreement', even (presumably) in the absence of offer and acceptance (PECL, arts 2.101 and 2.211; UNIDROIT, arts 2.1 and 3.2). In English law, on the other hand, there normally has to be offer and acceptance before there can be a binding contract since one has to find a concrete promise. Offer and acceptance (rather than agreement) is, in other words, a matter of English substantive contract law.

The distinction does, of course, have a practical aspect, as *Gibson* indicates. The plaintiff was not seeking damages as such; he was trying specifically to force the owner of the house (the local authority) to do what he considered it had agreed to do, namely, to transfer ownership of the property to him. His whole action, that of specific performance, depended on the existence of a binding contract. *Gibson* is an excellent example of the importance that formation rules can play on occasions.

3.2.5.3 Obstacles to consent

Secondly, in a system based upon *conventio*, the existence of fraud, mistake or duress will logically act as an obstacle to the formation of a contract because they act as obstacles to the coming together of two minds. In a system based on promise, although the law might not be prepared to enforce a contract tainted by a vitiating factor, such a factor does not, as a matter of conceptual logic, prevent the formation of a contract. A promise can still have an objective existence even if it has been induced by fraud, error or duress. This explains why, as Robert Goff LJ once pointed out, fraud in English contract law does not 'vitiate consent' (*Whittaker v Campbell* (1984), 327). Fraud is dealt with by remedies coming from outside contract (damages in tort and rescission in equity). As Lord Nicholls (dissenting) put it, fraud 'can destroy legal rights; it cannot destroy facts' (*Shogun Finance v Hudson* (2003), § 7).

It equally explains why there never really developed, within the common law (as opposed to equity), a general theory of mistake in contract. There is simply no principle at common law similar to the one to be found in the Quebec Civil Code which states that error 'vitiates consent of the parties or one of them where it relates to the nature of the contract, the object of the prestation or anything that was essential in determining that consent' (art 1400). The result is that it is by no means easy for a party to escape from a contract, where the other party is guilty neither of fraud nor of misrepresentation, on the basis that had he known of certain facts he would not have contracted (*Bell v Lever Brothers* (1932)). This is a point to which we shall return in **Chapter 4**.

3.3 Enforceable promises

English contract law is thus based on the promise to do something. In many contract cases this promise is, as one might expect, to pay a specific amount of money. Thus the purchaser or hirer of goods and services normally promises to pay a price in return for receiving some benefit. If such a transaction displays three essential elements or conditions, the promise to pay will be enforceable. These three conditions are:

(a) offer and acceptance;
(b) consideration; and
(c) intention to create legal relations.

3.3.1 General points

With respect to a great many transactions there is little problem with regard to formation since the factual situations are relatively settled. Thus in a supermarket the contract is formed not when the product is taken from the shelf and put into the basket or trolley, but when the price is registered on the till at the cash desk (*Pharmaceutical Soc of GB v*

Boots (1953)). Consequently, if a product explodes and injures a consumer before he or she arrives at the checkout, any claim for injury will have to be brought in tort (Consumer Protection Act 1987, s 2; *Ward v Tesco* (1976)). The idea that it is the customer who makes the offer – products on the shelf being an 'invitation to treat' (an invitation to make an offer) – applies equally to shops, and so goods displayed in a shop window are not offers. Even if they have a price label attached stating, for example, 'special offer', this display will not amount to a contractual offer (*Fisher v Bell* (1961)) and so the customer cannot claim an enforceable contract with the seller.

In the days of bus conductors, the exact time when the contract of carriage formed between a person who jumped on the bus and the bus company could create difficulties in theory. But buses have, on the whole, now changed, with the contract being formed via the driver. Taxis prove interesting from a comparative law viewpoint since some systems treat the 'offer' on the taxi as a legal offer accepted by the customer who hails the vehicle. But, again, in English law it is the client who must make the offer.

Small-scale service transactions are equally well settled in respect of the formation of the contract. Many such transactions are carried out in high-street premises, with the customer making the offer which is accepted by the person behind the counter. The handing over of any item for cleaning or servicing will, of course, create a bailment relationship, but here the customer needs to take some care since the seller of the service may well wish to modify the common law obligations. Such modifications will be incorporated in the contract, and thus be enforceable, only if they are brought to the customer's attention *before* the formation of the contract (*Thornton v Shoe Lane Parking* (1971)). This is normally done by a notice displayed, say, above the counter, or in a ticket or other document supplied to the customer. The latter method is risky, since one could argue that the contract had formed before the customer had had a chance to read the document; but if the client had used the same firm on many occasions, he or she might be bound by reason of a course of dealing. If the clause modifying the contract turns out to be unfair or unreasonable, it may not be enforceable thanks to legislation (Unfair Contract Terms Act 1977; Unfair Terms in Consumer Contracts Regulations 1999).

Service transactions with small builders, plumbers and the like are usually negotiated through an estimate and, in the case of a builder, a written contractual document. The estimate possibly amounts to an offer accepted by the customer when he or she asks the builder or plumber to proceed. One might note here that it might be particularly important to determine if a written estimate amounts to an offer if the customer's acceptance is made by post; for if it does, the offer will, in English law, be accepted the moment the client posts the letter of acceptance. This is the so-called posting rule, specifically rejected by the PECL (art 2.205(1); but cf Consumer Protection (Distance Selling) Regulations 2000, reg 10(4)(b)).

Window cleaners are more interesting from a contract point of view since nothing may be in writing, the window cleaner arriving every month or so and cleaning the windows without gaining the actual assent of the house owner. Usually the owner has specifically agreed with a particular window cleaner that the latter will maintain the windows, and thus each time he arrives to do the cleaning it is implied that he is doing the work expecting to be paid. A similar situation will apply with respect to the family solicitor. Each time a client needs a service, he will no doubt telephone the solicitor with the request and this will be carried out, the solicitor then sending his bill. Given that the solicitor will have provided the service expecting to be paid, there is no question of 'past consideration', that is to say the rendering of consideration (the service) that does not connect with any actual promise to pay moving from the other party. The offer, acceptance and consideration are part of the ongoing relationship (family solicitor).

3.3.2 Difficult cases

There are, however, a number of difficult situations which could easily result in litigation if sufficient amounts of money are at stake, or if a person faced with a bill decides not to pay. These difficult cases can arise out of a number of typical situations.

3.3.2.1 Non-serious promise: *Carlill v Carbolic Smoke Ball Co* (1893)

Imagine the following situation. A potential restaurant customer sees a notice outside a pub stating that any person ordering a meal who has to wait more than 45 minutes for the food to arrive will be entitled to eat free of charge. The customer orders a meal, waits more than 45 minutes for the food to arrive, eats it, and then, when faced with the bill, refuses to pay. The contract question is, of course, this: can the customer refuse to pay the bill, or can the pub owner claim that the promise is not to be taken seriously since it is simply an advertising gimmick? The foundational case is *Carlill v Carbolic Smoke Ball Co* (1893), in which the defendants, manufacturers of a medical product, placed an advert for the product in a popular magazine. The advert stated that the defendants would pay a £100 reward to any person who purchased the medical product and used it according to the directions, and who nevertheless caught influenza. In addition, there was a statement in the publicity that £1,000 had been deposited with a bank in Regent Street 'showing our sincerity in the matter'. The plaintiff purchased and used the product, and on contracting influenza demanded her reward money. When the company refused to pay, she brought an action in debt for the £100. The Court of Appeal upheld the decision of the trial judge that the defendants were to be liable for the sum.

The case raised several fundamental points about contract formation. The Court of Appeal confirmed that offers could be made to the world at large (as opposed to individuals), and that individuals accepting such an offer need not communicate an acceptance since the advertisement contained an implied waiver. However, it is with respect to consideration that the case is of particular importance. AL Smith LJ noted in his judgment that the defendants had argued that there was no consideration. He replied that there were two considerations: '[one] is the consideration of the inconvenience of having to use this carbolic smoke ball for two weeks three times a day; and the other more important consideration is the money gain likely to accrue to the defendants by the enhanced sale of the smoke balls, by reason of the plaintiff's user of them' (275).

Smith LJ's approach is indicative of the methodology. One takes each party and asks if there is a benefit and if there is a detriment. From the position of Mrs Carlill, there is the detriment of having to use the product, but the benefit of the possibility of a reward. From the position of the Carbolic Smoke Ball Co, there is the detriment of putting oneself under an obligation to pay a reward if the flu condition materialises; on the benefit side, however, there is the extra profit generated by the advertisement with its reward offer. Smith LJ was thus able to conclude that there was 'ample consideration to support this promise'.

What is important about this precedent is that it can apply to so many contemporary situations. A pub or restaurant that states on a board outside its premises that customers who are kept waiting for more than a certain period of time before their food arrives will not have to pay for their meals, may well find that it has made a contractual offer which legally it will have to respect. The same is true for a manufacturer of a consumer product who promises free air tickets to the USA to any consumer who purchases one of its products. *Carlill* makes it very clear that such specific promises are not always mere advertising 'puffs', and this is one of the reasons why the case remains an important precedent.

Another form of offer to the public is an auction sale without reserve. In this situation the auctioneer offers to sell the auction item to the highest bidder, this offer being accepted when the bid is made (*Barry v Davies* (2000)). This contract is of course one that is collateral to the actual contract of sale between the seller of the auctioned item and the highest bidder (buyer).

3.3.2.2 Battle of forms: *Butler Machine Tool Co v Ex-Cell-O-Corp* (1979)

Difficult formation problems can also arise where two contractors send out contradictory documentation to each other. This is not necessarily untypical in the commercial world, where parties often contract using their own printed conditions of contract. B orders material from S using its standard contract form full of conditions; S does not read the conditions but delivers the requested material along with his own printed contractual document equally full of contractual conditions; a dispute subsequently arises, say, about the amount to be paid, after B has consumed the ordered material, and lawyers have to decide which set of conditions forms the contract. Now strictly speaking it could be said that there is no contract between B and S because there was no actual offer and acceptance of each other's terms (*Trollope & Colls v Atomic Power Constructions* (1962), 1040). But this would be commercially inconvenient since S has delivered and B has consumed the requested material. There must, in other words, be some sort of contract. Indeed both the PECL (art 2.209) and UNIDROIT (art 2.22) lay down that there is in principle a contract, founded upon the agreed and any standard terms, even if there is a conflict with regard to the exchange of contractual forms; a party unhappy with this situation must without delay inform the other party that he will not be bound.

English law seems not so generous. The Court of Appeal in *Butler Machine Tool Co v Ex-Cell-O-Corp* (1979) approached this kind of problem from the position of the contractual documents themselves and reduced it to a 'battle of forms'. The battle is won by the last form which is sent and which is received without objection, for these are seen as the conditions and terms 'offered', and if the other party then performs the contract without raising an objection to these latest terms he is deemed to have 'accepted' them. Yet, as Lord Denning MR observed, there are other cases where 'the battle is won by the man who gets the blow in first', or 'where the battle depends on the shots fired on both sides' (at 405).

These battle of form situations are complex, because if an 'acceptance' does not accord with the offer it can amount to what is called a counter-offer. This has the effect of depriving the original offer of its legal force, and so if the 'acceptance' (ie, counter-offer) is not accepted by the original offeror, the counter-offeror cannot then purport to accept the original offer. For example, if S offers his car to B for £2,000 and B purports to 'accept' for £1,500, this latter 'acceptance' is no acceptance but a counter-offer, which S can either accept or reject. If S rejects the counter-offer, B cannot then claim to accept the original offer to sell for £2,000. What if B purports to accept S's offer to sell the car for £2,000 by replying that he accepts for £1,995 since that is all the cash he has and he knows that S would like to be paid in cash? According to English law, where the foundation of contract is promise, the reply is no less a counter-offer than the £1,500 reply. But civil law, based on agreement, can be different since there may be a sufficient accord between the two parties (PECL, art 2.208(2)).

3.3.2.3 Lack of clarity

Offer, acceptance and consideration will not be sufficient to create a contract if the subject matter itself is too uncertain to uphold such an obligation. Vague transactions will not, in other words, be treated as contracts; a contract 'must contain mutual obligations and a commitment by each party' (Peter Gibson LJ in *Firstpost Homes v Johnson* (1995), 1573). Thus it could be argued that in a contract of sale there must be a commitment to pay a specific price for a specific object. For example, if B merely promises to buy S's car without anything being agreed as to price, it is doubtful if a contract would form. Indeed in Roman law there could be no contract if there was no price (D.18.1.2.1). Yet English law is prepared to be much more subtle, in that it accepts that there can in certain circumstances be a binding contract even if no price is agreed. In such a situation the buyer is under an obligation to pay a reasonable price (Sale of Goods Act 1979, s 8). Accordingly, in a commercial setting, where S periodically delivers raw material to B's factory and B consumes the material, there will, if only for practical reasons, be a contract. Should a dispute arise, the law will be that B must pay a reasonable price for any material delivered (although, as we have seen at **3.3.2.2** above, there might in such a situation be a battle of forms problem). The same is true for a contract for the supply of a service (Supply of Goods and Services Act 1982, s 15). A contract can equally form in situations where it is agreed that a price will be determined in the future; what the law looks for is a means by which the uncertain can be rendered certain. *Certum est quod certum reddi potest* (what can be rendered certain is certain), a maxim that is probably valid equally in Roman and in English law. Perhaps one should add here that there is a general principle (*favor contractus*) to be found in the civil law systems that contracts should, if at all possible, be upheld rather than declared inexistent (Crépeau, 1998, 13–37).

The certainty rule has been held to apply to a contract to contract, that is to say a contract to negotiate (*Courtney & Fairbairn v Tolani Brothers* (1975)). Such a contract is too vague and, anyway, there is a further general principle that a duty to negotiate in good faith is repugnant to the adversarial position of contractual parties (*Walford v Miles* (1992)). There are, however, exceptions. Potential purchasers and sellers of real property can bind themselves in a lock-out agreement (not to sell to anyone else) and an invitation to tender has been held in one rather exceptional case to be an offer capable of being accepted, to form a collateral contract, merely by the submission of a tender (*Blackpool & Fylde Aero Club v Blackpool BC* (1990)).

3.3.2.4 Lack of consensus or intention

The distinction between promise and agreement is also reflected in the role that subjective intention plays in the formation of a contract. Here it has to be said that it is not true that *consensus* has no role in the common law, because offer and acceptance does have a subjective dimension. If by chance two offers, for example one to sell an item and one to buy this precise item, were to cross in the post, and the cross-offers were identical in terms of price and the like, there would not be a contract. There has to be *consensus ad idem* between the parties (*Shogun Finance Ltd v Hudson* (2003), § 123).

This *consensus* principle has two aspects. The subjective aspect is that of intention and the meeting of the minds. In the cross-offers example there is certainly an intention to sell and an intention to buy on identical terms, yet the minds themselves have not been brought into contact. On the other hand there is an objective dimension. An acceptance can be sufficient to create a contract even if the acceptor had no subjective intention to accept on the terms offered. As Lord Diplock has stated, 'what is necessary is that the intention of each *as it has been communicated to and understood by the other* (even though that which has been communicated does not represent the actual state of mind of the communicator) should coincide.' And he went on to say that this 'is what English lawyers mean when they resort to the Latin phrase *consensus ad idem* and the words ... italicised are essential to the concept of *consensus ad idem*, the lack of which prevents the formation of a binding contract in English law' (*The Hannar Blumenthal* (1983), 915).

Lord Diplock also added this. He said that the

> rule that neither party can rely upon his own failure to communicate accurately to the other party his own real intention by what he wrote or said or did, as negativing the *consensus ad idem*, is an example of a general principle of English law that injurious reliance on what another person did may be a source of legal rights against him.

Here Lord Diplock is perhaps going further than the rules of contract and, possibly, into the realm of equity, which has a general doctrine that one can be estopped from denying the legal force of a statement (representation) where another has relied upon it to his detriment. It would appear, therefore, that the equitable principle of estoppel can produce a binding contract even although there is no *consensus* (on the notion of estoppel see Hudson, 2001, 105–15; and see also Lord Phillips in *Shogun Finance v Hudson* (2003), § 123). However, care must be taken here because estoppel does not in fact create a 'contract'. What it does is to create a situation at the level of procedure and (or) remedies, where a party who has led another by his acts or words to rely upon him is prevented from raising in court his own lack of intention. This may have the effect, objectively, of creating a contract, but it might be more helpful, as indeed Lord Diplock himself went on to suggest, to see it as creating an equitable 'obligation' (cf *Shogun*, § 123).

3.3.2.5 Consensus and pre-contractual obligation

The *consensus* rule might also have the effect on occasions of putting onto one contractual party a special obligation to bring to the attention of the other party any onerous terms (promises) that he is deemed to have accepted (or made) (UNIDROIT, art 2.20). Thus in one case a contractor hired some photographic transparencies from an agency and, by an oversight, failed to return them on time. The agency then claimed an exorbitant sum of money as a debt from the hirer, pointing to a clause in the delivery note allowing them to charge such a sum. The Court of Appeal rejected the plaintiffs' debt claim on the basis that the hirer never agreed to the charge. To be enforceable the plaintiffs would have had to bring to the hirer's attention the specific clause; merely inserting it into the written delivery note alongside other clauses was not enough (*Interfoto Picture Library v Stiletto Visual Programmes* (1989)).

3.3.2.6 Intention to create legal relations

Some promises may be treated as outside the law of contract on the basis that there is a lack of intention to create a legally binding contract. The courts take the view that any commercial agreement in which there is offer, acceptance and consideration is prima facie a legal contract. There is, in other words, a presumption of an intention to create legal relations if the agreement is a commercial one. This presumption can be displaced; and so, for example, a negotiation letter may specify that it will not be capable of giving rise to a contractual obligation. Or if a 'contract' contains a clause stating that it will not be enforceable at law, the agreement will lack an intention to create legal relations and be unenforceable (*Jones v Vernon's Pools Ltd* (1938)). If the agreement is a non-commercial one – that is to say within the family or between friends – there is a presumption that it will not be legally binding (*Balfour v Balfour* (1919)). Again, however, this presumption can be displaced by the evidence, and there are therefore cases where family separation arrangements and agreements between friends have been held to be contracts. An informal agreement among friends to share a prize will probably be a contract if each member has contributed entrance money to the competition (*Simpkins v Pays* (1955)).

One might add here that the essential condition of an intention to create legal relations can appear superfluous given the requirement of consideration, certainty and *consensus*. But it does have a practical role in as much as it can be used to remove from the law of contract a number of agreements that the courts consider, for policy reasons, to be unsuitable for contractual regulation. For example, the courts have been most reluctant to see the supply of energy as contractual arrangements; gas, water and electricity are supplied pursuant to a statutory rather than a contractual duty, and the difference between the two relationships was explained in terms of a lack of intention to create legal relations (*Willmore v SE Electricity Board* (1957)). One way of viewing these statutory duty cases was in terms of the public and public divide; but the privatisation of energy would suggest that this explanation is no longer valid, although the courts continue to insist that even after privatisation the legal status of the supply relationship has not changed (*Norweb v Dixon* (1995)).

3.3.2.7 Abusive revocation of an offer

In the case of a unilateral contract acceptance is complete only when the offeree has performed what is required of him, and this rule implies that in principle the offeror could withdraw his offer even after the offeree has entered upon performance. The classic example is the offer to pay £100 to anyone who walks between London and York. The offeror can in theory revoke his offer even when the walker has reached the outskirts of York, since acceptance would not at that point be complete. In fact English law would not allow the offeror to revoke until the offeree had been given a reasonable opportunity to complete, and the conceptual basis of this rule is probably to be found in equity. At common law the offeror would have the right to revoke, but equity would regard this as an abuse of a 'right' and would hold that the offeror would be estopped from revoking until the offeree had had a reasonable opportunity to complete. This example possibly has a practical commercial application in the area of house sales. It may well be that the contract between the vendor of a house and an estate agent is unilateral (an interesting question), the latter being able to claim its fee only if it introduces a buyer (*Luxor (Eastbourne) Ltd v Cooper* (1941)). If a potential vendor agrees that a particular estate agent should handle the sale, it may well be, especially if the agent has invested time and money in advertising the property, that the owner will have to give the agent a reasonable opportunity to sell before the house can be withdrawn (unless perhaps there is a good reason for the withdrawal).

An offeror will no doubt be equally estopped from revoking an offer when he indicates that an offer is irrevocable, or states a fixed time for its acceptance (PECL, art 2.202(3)). Yet these rules can be ambiguous, in that if a revocation reaches an offeree before he has actually accepted the offer, it is prima facie a valid revocation (UNIDROIT, art 2.3(2); and see in particular *Financings Ltd v Stimson* (1962)). The equitable rule will come into play if the offeree has relied to his detriment upon the offeror's statement that the offer will not be withdrawn.

3.4 Enforceability and consideration

One of the main differences between civil and common law contracts is that consideration is a vital requirement for an enforceable promise. A promise to pay a sum of money as a gift is enforceable only under 'property' legislation if the promise conforms to certain requirements (Law of Property (Miscellaneous Provisions) Act 1989, s 1). It is not enforceable as an ordinary contractual 'obligation'. 'A valuable consideration,' said Lush J, 'in the sense of the law, may consist either in some right, interest, profit, or benefit accruing to one party, or some forbearance, detriment, loss, or responsibility, given, suffered, or undertaken by the other' (*Currie v Misa* (1875), 162). In short, a benefit and a detriment must attach to each contracting party in order for the contract to be enforceable (see **3.3.2.1**, above).

3.4.1 Enforceability and performance

It is necessary to be clear as to what actually amounts to consideration in contract, and here two distinctions need to be made. The first is between the formation of a contract and its performance (or execution). The second is between bilateral and unilateral contracts (cf **2.2.2.1**, above).

In a bilateral contract, where both contracting parties make promises, what amounts to consideration is not actually the physical object that makes up the economic value, it is the promises themselves. Thus if S offers to sell his car to B for £2,000 and B accepts the offer, the consideration is not actually the car and the money. The contract is formed before delivery (and indeed B may well become owner of the car) and payment, and what amounts to consideration are the promises moving from each party (promise for a prom-ise). It is thus a mistake to think that when one goes into a shop to buy a newspaper the consideration consists of the handing over of the money and the paper. This handing over is the *performance* of the contract. In theory the contract is formed beforehand, and the consideration consists of the promise to pay and the promise to convey title in the paper. Of course reality may telescope the two aspects of contract, but that does not mean that they should be telescoped at the level of contract theory.

Unilateral contracts are different, for here only one party makes a promise (eg, the Carbolic Smoke Ball Co) while the other party (eg, Mrs Carlill) promises nothing. Consequently the consideration moving from the promisee can only be the performance. This can be problematic though. What if a person does an act, such as returning a lost wallet to its owner, ignorant of the fact that the owner had advertised a reward? The *con-sensus ad idem* rule would seemingly declare that there can be no contract, and so the person returning the wallet could not claim the sum as a contract debt.

3.4.2 Variation of existing contracts

Most consumer and commercial contracts do not give rise to consideration problems since goods and services are rarely supplied free (but cf *Esso Petroleum v Commissioners of Custom and Excise* (1976)). Promises within the family can of course be problematic, but this is partly because the courts do not always wish to turn family arrangements into bind-ing contracts. Where problems can arise in the commercial world is in two situations, the first being the variation or modification of an existing set of promises. This can be difficult because one party may agree to a modification, and the only way the English courts seemed to have been able to handle this was by treating the variation or modification as a new promise. Accordingly, it must in theory be supported by consideration

3.4.2.1 *Williams v Roffey Brothers* (1991)

In *Ward v Byham* (1956), Denning LJ thought that a promise to perform an existing duty ought to be regarded as good consideration because it is a benefit, and this view seems now to have been accepted by the Court of Appeal. Or, at least, it seems to have been accepted in certain commercial circumstances. In *Williams v Roffey Brothers* (1991), a car-penter brought an action for an extra sum of money promised to him by a building contractor. The sum had been promised in return for the carpenter completing within a particular time limit the refurbishment of 27 flats, a job that the carpenter had already been contracted to do, by the contractor, for an agreed price of £20,000, and on which he had completed about third of the total job. After the completion of some more flats, the carpenter claimed the extra sum promised, but the defendant building contractor argued that the extra sum promised was not supported by consideration. The Court of Appeal allowed the carpenter's claim for the extra money to succeed on the basis that 'there was clearly a commercial advantage to both sides from a pragmatic point of view' (Purchas LJ, at 22). And, with respect to the rule of consideration, 'the courts nowadays should be more ready to find its existence so as to reflect the intention of the parties to the contract where the bargaining powers are not unequal and where the finding of consideration reflect the true intention of the parties' (Russell LJ, at 18).

This case may be exceptional. For a start, the Court of Appeal did not discard either the necessity of consideration, or the original case (*Stilk v Myrick* (1809)) that established the existing duty rule. It made a decision within a particular commercial context. Furthermore, the facts disclosed no improper pressure on the part of the carpenter; he had genuinely under-priced the job and was not trying to blackmail the contractor into paying more (cf *D & C Builders v Rees* (1966)). In addition, *Roffey* is not authority for the proposition that a promise by a creditor to accept a sum less than the debt is enforceable as a contractual promise (*Re Selectmove Ltd* (1995); and see **3.4.2.2**, below). Nevertheless, despite these reservations, *Roffey* remains to date a leading consideration case and is a clear example of a commercial promise being held enforceable on the basis of the facts before the court.

3.4.2.2 Unenforceable debts

Even if consideration is insufficient to support a contractual promise, this does not necessarily mean that the promise is without legal effect. A promise is a specific form of representation (statement), and certain representations made by one party to another can have legal effects in equity if they have been relied upon to that person's detriment. Equity, using its doctrine of estoppel, will prevent a person going back on his promise in such circumstances (see generally Hudson, 2001, 105–106, 113).

This doctrine of estoppel was extended to situations where one contractor promises not to enforce his full contractual rights and the other contractor relies upon this statement (Hudson, 2001, 113). For example, where a landlord, in order to encourage a tenant to remain in one of his flats, informs the tenant that he need pay only half the rent stipulated in the lease, this promise, although not supported by consideration (see *Foakes v Beer* (1894)), will be effective in equity. The landlord will be estopped from enforcing his right to the full debt during the period he has indicated to the tenant that he need pay only the reduced amount (*Central London Property Trust Ltd v High Trees House* (1947)).

This principle can be seen as an equitable intervention to prevent a contractor from abusing his common law (contract) right. However, if the person seeking equity's aid is himself guilty of abusive behaviour, the aid will be withheld under the principle that he who comes to equity must come with clean hands. This will allow the other contractor to enforce his full contractual right to the original debt (*D & C Builders v Rees* (1966)). What if a contractor subsequently promises more than the original sum? The Court of Appeal has left open the question as to whether estoppel might apply (*Williams v Roffey Bros*). But it is generally considered that estoppel is a shield and not a sword, and this presents a difficulty; estoppel is not a cause of action and functions only at the level of remedies. All the same, it could be used to prevent a defendant from raising in court the inexistence of a contract.

3.4.3 Privity of contract

The second situation where consideration, or the lack of it, can cause problems is where it has not moved from the actual claimant or victim of the breach of promise. This rule is closely associated with another principle known as privity of contract, and basically declares that only the actual parties to a contract can be bound within the contractual nexus (see Law Commission Report No 242, Cm 3329; *Darlington BC v Wiltshier Northern Ltd* (1995)). Thus, at common law, if A promises B, in return for consideration supplied by

B, that he will pay C a sum of money, C cannot, in principle, according to the case law, sue to enforce the promise. This rule – or at least the rule of privity of contract – was confirmed by the House of Lords in *Beswick v Beswick* (1968). Equally, if A makes a contract with B containing a clause that neither B nor C will be able to sue A for damages should A be in breach, C will not in principle be bound by the clause (see, eg, *Morris v CW Martin & Sons* (1966)). The principle of privity arises out of the nature of an obligation itself: it is strictly *in personam* and thus cannot bind third parties (otherwise it would be effectively creating rights *in rem*). In civil law this rule is known as the relative effect of contract.

3.4.3.1 Avoidance and exceptions

The principle of privity is, then, clear enough, and it would be misleading to suggest that the rule has not created difficulties for third parties harmed by another's breach of contract. Equally it has created problems for contracting parties hoping to limit their liabilities arising out of poor or non-performance of contracts. It would, however, be just as misleading to overstate the effects of the privity rule since the courts have developed a range of important exceptions. Moreover, statute has now intervened in order to give a third party beneficiary a general right to sue, in certain circumstances, for a breach of a contractual promise.

3.4.3.2 Contract (Rights of Third Parties) Act 1999

The Contracts (Rights of Third Parties) Act 1999 permits a third party who is not a party to a contract to enforce in his own right a term of the contract in two situations:

(a) if the contract expressly provides that he may (s 1(1)(a)); and
(b) where a contract term purports to confer a benefit on him (s 1(1)(b)).

The third party must be expressly identified in the contract by name, as a member of a class or as answering a particular description, although he need not be in existence at the time of the contract (s 1(3)). In the leading English privity case of *Beswick v Beswick* (1968), the wife of a dead contractor was not allowed to enforce the contract in her own name despite being specifically named as a promisee. Today she would probably be able to sue thanks to s 1 of the 1999 Act.

The most troublesome cases have been in the area of carriage of goods by sea where contracts have purported to confer benefits on, for example, stevedores (*Scruttons Ltd v Midland Silicones Ltd* (1962)). Although the 1999 Act excludes carriage of goods contracts covered by their own international conventions, it expressly allows third parties in such contracts to take the benefit of exclusion or limitation clauses (s 6(5)). More generally it has to be said that the 1999 Act stands in stark contrast to the short provision in the PECL, since there are many restrictions and defences that make the 1999 statute rather long and complex. Moreover, it is by no means clear, despite its length and complexity, that the 1999 Act has resolved all of the traditional problem areas in this part of the law of obligations. A father contracts with a tour operator for a holiday for himself and his family; the holiday, in breach of contract, proves a most unpleasant experience (*Jackson v Horizon Holidays* (1975)). Does the 1999 Act allow the mother and children each to sue the tour operator for breach of its contractual promise to provide a reasonable holiday? Perhaps a more fundamental example is *Donoghue v Stevenson* (see **8.1.4**, below). Would Mrs

Donoghue now have a claim against the seller of the contaminated ginger-beer for breach of s 14 of the Sale of Goods Act (assuming the facts arose in England)? Care must be taken, therefore, before asserting that the privity rule has been abolished in English law; it has not. What the Act does is to recognise the civilian notion that a contractor can stipulate for a third party; and it does this not by abolishing the privity rule, but by granting a remedy, in certain circumstances, to the third party.

3.4.4 Deed of covenant

Form can equally be important in ensuring that a promise is enforceable even in the absence of consideration. English law has for most of its history recognised that a promise made under seal is enforceable as a deed, and what gives the promise its legal force is the form in which it is made (document plus seal). The theory in some ways echoes the one behind the Roman *stipulatio*, but the history of the deed is very different. It arises out of the tradition that the courts would never look behind the sealed document (Ibbetson, 1999, 241). In 1989 the requirement of an actual seal was abolished and, in its place, Parliament has declared that a deed need only be described as such and should carry an attested signature (Law of Property (Miscellaneous Provisions) Act 1989, s 1). The potential of this statutory form of contracting is rather interesting; it is rather like the *stipulatio* in as much as it is a method of pure form for creating a binding promissory obligation free of all the substantive necessities associated with the parole contract. But it seems that only those with a sense of history appreciate this potential (see Ibbetson, 241).

4 Escaping from Contracts

If one examines the contract cases to be found in a contract casebook, they can be reclassified in ways that are different from the scheme probably used by the author of the book. As we have already suggested, one such reclassification could be along the lines of the transaction in issue: cases could be grouped under headings such as carriage of goods, sale of land, sale of goods, charterparties, insurance, carriage of persons and so on. Indeed some specific types of contract – notably contracts of employment, insurance and sale of goods – form the subject matter of courses and books independent of general contract law. Another group of headings might be remedies: cases could be grouped under debt, specific performance, rescission, self-help, damages, and one or two other remedies. **Chapter 3** went some way in grouping cases under debt and specific performance (enforcing contracts), and **Chapter 5** will focus primarily (if not exclusively) on compensation (damages) for failure to perform. This chapter will, in part, examine rescission; that is to say, on escaping from the contractual bond.

4.1 Defective contracts

The distinction between promise and agreement underpins a section of contract formation law known to a civil lawyer as defects or obstacles to consent. In English law these issues are treated under the heading of vitiating factors. If contract is founded upon agreement and *consensus ad idem*, any obstacle that impedes the meeting of the two *volontés* (wills) must by definition threaten the coming into existence of the *vinculum iuris*, and this is why French lawyers talk of *vices du consentement*. English law, in contrast, is based on promise, and it does not necessarily follow that because a promise was given under conditions that might be seen as an 'obstacle' or *vice*, such an obstacle threatens the very existence of the promise.

4.1.1 Effects of a vitiating factor

Article 1109 of the *Code civil* declares that: 'There is no valid consent if the consent was given only by error, or was extorted by violence or obtained by fraud'. This provision is, of course, perfectly logical given the *conventio* basis of contract. Thus a person who consents, labouring under a mistake, is said not to consent at all (*non videntur qui errant consentire*: Pothier). Yet even where the foundation of the contract is promise, duress and fraud must equally impact upon the normative force of the promise that results.

Consequently, the idea of *vices* or defects in formation is to be found, to a greater or lesser extent, in all Western contract systems (although the idea itself is quite recent: Lévy and Castaldo, 2002, § 556).

However, as between the civilian and the common law traditions, there is an important difference of emphasis that in turn can be related to the subjective and objective approaches. Generally speaking, although this is not fully and reliably reflected in the whole of the case law, promise, being more formal than agreement, is less sensitive from an internal position to problems of *vices du consentement*. Now this not to say that such *vices* will not impact upon the enforceability of the promise. The point to be made – particularly given the dichotomy in England between law and equity – is that *vices* are approached more from an external position. In other words, the law of equity and of tort impact upon the law of contract.

4.1.2 Defective offer and acceptance: void contracts

As we have seen, offer and acceptance plays a role in most Western systems, including French law, despite the fact that the *Code civil* says nothing about it. Now, given this general mechanism, the possibility clearly exists that a contract may be fundamentally defective simply because there is no matching offer and acceptance (*Shogun Finance Ltd v Hudson* (2003), §§ 123–5, 183). One leading case here is that of *Raffles v Wichelhaus* (1864), which concerned a contract for a cargo on board a ship called the *Peerless*. In fact there were two ships of the same name, and one of the parties was thinking of one while the other was thinking of the other ship. It was held that there was no binding contract. How is this case to be analysed given the ambiguity of the law report (Zimmermann, 1996, 583)? One answer is to say that it is not a matter of 'mistake' as such; there is no contract simply because there is no offer and acceptance in respect of the same object (or person), and thus *no enforceable agreement or set of promises*. A similar analysis might be made in situations where there is extreme duress ('an offer he cannot refuse'); an acceptance in such circumstances is simply not an 'acceptance'. In such a situation a common lawyer would talk here of a *void* contract, that is to say a contract that never existed. And it never existed because there was a lack of proper offer and acceptance.

4.1.3 Voidable and unenforceable contracts

The expression 'void' contract needs to be distinguished from 'voidable' contract. The former expression, as several judges have pointed out, is actually a contradiction in terms since there never was a contract. A voidable contract is quite different. Here the contract exists but is subject to one party's right to set the contract aside, normally for misrepresentation, duress or undue influence. If the party decides to exercise this right, the contract will come to an end. However, this termination will not act retrospectively, unless it is rescission *ab initio*; it will not result in a situation where the contract never existed.

The right to rescind does not, as a matter of history, arise from internal contractual rules; it was granted by the Court of Chancery through the equitable remedy of rescission. One distinction, then, between void and voidable contracts is that the former usually involves rules of common law while the latter is a matter of equity. One interesting question that arises out of this dichotomy between law and equity is this. If a party does have a right to rescind the contract, does this mean that the other party is guilty of a breach of duty capable of giving rise not just to rescission in equity, but also to a claim for damages? A clear answer to this problem has been given by Lord Millett in *Agnew v Länsförsäkringsbolagens AB* (2001): it gives no such right to damages. Nevertheless, what is intriguing about Lord Millett's analysis is that he recognised that what counsel was trying to do was to turn the equitable 'duty' (giving rise to rescission) into a common law duty via the medium of an obligation of good faith. In rejecting this analysis, the Law Lord was, of course, reaffirming not just the distinction between common law and equity, but also the absence of an independent doctrine of good faith (see **2.4**, above).

Void and voidable contracts need to be distinguished from an unenforceable one. This idea of an unenforceable contract arises as a result of English law traditionally distinguishing between rights and remedies: a contract might exist at the level of legal rights but the courts, perhaps because of the illegality of one or more of the promises, refuse to grant any remedy. The contract thus becomes unenforceable. This situation may give the impression that the contract is in reality void (or has been rescinded), yet an unenforceable contract is different because it can, unlike a void contract, have some effects. It can, for example, act as a means of passing title in property (cf *Shogun Finance Ltd v Hudson* (2003)).

4.1.4 Remedies

This distinction between right and remedy illustrates another external approach to the problem of error, duress or fraud: the law can provide remedies independent of contract for the innocent contracting party. This is the approach to be found in Roman law in respect of fraud and duress, for these were wrongs giving rise to delictual actions and thus were designed to protect victims against loss by allowing them to sue for damages. Another possibility was for the law to grant an action in restitution, which indeed, if available, would take precedence over an action for *dolus malus* (D.4.2.14.1).

This remedies approach is an important characteristic of the common law as well. It was the Court of Chancery that provided the remedy of equitable rescission to relieve a party who had been induced to enter a contract as a result of a false statement (misrepresentation) or duress (which includes undue influence). A misrepresentation is traditionally defined as an untrue statement of existing fact which induces the representee to enter into a contract with the representor. The word 'statement' is not confined literally to speech; various other kinds of acts and omissions can be construed on occasions as representations. And the word 'fact' now includes, as a result of a major House of Lords decision in the law of restitution, an untrue statement of law (*Kleinwort Benson Ltd v Lincoln CC* (1999)). If the misrepresentation was made fraudulently this also gave rise to a damages action in tort for deceit, and today this tort is available to a contracting party even in the absence of fraud (Misrepresentation Act 1967, s 2(1)). One might note here how the emphasis is not on error or fraud as such, but on the words uttered by a party to induce a contract. This is why an English judge has observed that 'there is … no general principle of law that fraud vitiates consent'. The 'effect of fraud is simply to give the innocent party the right, subject to certain limits, to rescind the contract' (Goff LJ in *Whittaker v Campbell* (1984), 326–7; confirmed *Shogun Finance Ltd v Hudson* (2003), § 7).

4.1.5 *Bell v Lever Brothers* (1932)

What if there is an error but no misrepresentation? The leading authority on mistake is the House of Lords decision in *Bell v Lever Brothers* (1932). A company, which had made termination contracts with two of its directors, brought an action to have the contracts set aside after subsequently discovering that the directors had committed breaches of their contracts of employment while working for the company. The company equally sought return of the compensation payments it had made in performance of the termination contracts. The jury returned a verdict that the two directors had not fraudulently concealed their breaches. The trial judge, the Court of Appeal and two Law Lords thought that the termination contracts were void for mistake, but the majority of the House of Lords thought that the contracts were valid. Lord Atkin stressed two fundamental points:

(a) that it was vital to keep in mind the jury verdict acquitting the directors of fraudulent misrepresentation or concealment; and

(b) that the company got exactly what it bargained for, namely, the retirement of the directors. 'It seems', said the Law Lord, 'immaterial that [the company] could have got the same result in another way' (at 224).

Lord Atkin went on to give a number of analogous examples. Most of these involve buying something that either the buyer or both parties believed to be much better quality than it turned out to be; provided that the seller has made no representation or warranty the contract is not void. This may be unjust on the buyer, but, said the Law Lord, the example

> can be supported on the ground that it is of paramount importance that contracts should be observed, and that if parties honestly comply with the essentials of the formation of contracts – ie, agree in the same terms on the same subject-matter – they are bound, and must rely on the stipulations of the contract for protection from the effect of facts unknown to them. (at 224)

This mention of stipulations does, however, provide an insight into how the courts can declare a contract void for mistake even if there is no misrepresentation. If a fact is so fundamental to the whole transaction, it is possible for a court to imply a condition into the contract to this effect.

4.1.6 Role of equity

The rigour of this common law position was, until recently, partly mitigated by the equitable remedy of rescission. According to a decision given in 1950, equity could set aside a contract for mistake (*Solle v Butcher* (1950)), but the Court of Appeal has more recently ruled that this decision is wrong and that there is no such equitable jurisdiction (*The Great Peace* (2002)). It may well be, therefore, that the remedy of rescission in equity is no longer available for mistake. However, equity is still not excluded entirely. Another important remedy for mistake is rectification, and this is available to correct a written contractual document that wrongly records what was clearly agreed between the parties, for example a £200,000 price stated as £20,000. What the court does here is to order that the document itself be corrected. Such a remedy is not one that strictly allows a party to escape from the contract, but it does allow him to escape from the contract as recorded in a contractual document.

4.1.7 Implied term

Another approach to mistake is to imply a condition (promise) into the contract that if the object of the contract turns out to be quite different from the object promised then the contract is annulled. For example, if S promises to sell to P a sterile cow but, before delivery, the cow proves to be fertile (and thus of much higher value), the contract could be said to be void on the basis that there was an implied condition precedent that the cow be sterile. It has to be said that the courts are very reluctant to do this since they tend to put the emphasis on the form rather than the substance, treating the latter as a question of risk (*William Sindall Plc v Cambridgeshire CC* (1994)). And this reluctance might even have been strengthened by the knowledge that equity could always intervene (although even here the courts were not prepared to interfere with normal commercial risks: see *William Sindall*). However, it may be that the whole conceptual basis of mistake in English law has changed as a result of a Court of Appeal decision. For the Court has stated that it does 'not consider that the doctrine of common mistake can be satisfactorily explained by an implied term' even if 'an allegation that a contract is void for common mistake will often raise important issues of construction' (*The Great Peace* (2002), § 82).

One might note here that the topic of implied terms in the common law covers what in civil law is often described as simply 'interpretation of contracts'. Accordingly, mistake in English law might now be summed up as follows:

> Where it is possible to perform the letter of the contract, but it is alleged that there was a common mistake in relation to a fundamental assumption which renders performance of the essence of the obligation impossible, it will be necessary, by *construing* the contract in the light of all the material circumstances, to decide whether this is indeed the case. (*The Great Peace* (2002), § 82, emphasis added)

4.1.8 Europeanisation and globalisation: validity and good faith

The PECL and UNIDROIT have on the whole amalgamated the two approaches to *vices du consentement*. That is to say, they have internalised the approach so that fraud, mistake and duress are now matters of validity (see PECL, Ch 4; UNIDROIT, Ch 3). Nevertheless, a trace of the English law of misrepresentation seems to have found its way into the PECL (art 6.101) and UNIDROIT (art 3.8); and the concept of an implied term is specifically retained both in the PECL (art 6.102) and in UNIDROIT (art 5.2). There remain, also, traces of a remedies approach, in as much as damages and avoidance of contract are retained as separate entitlements (PECL, art 4.117; UNIDROIT, art 3.18); and, under UNIDROIT, a party cannot avoid the contract for mistake if he has an alternative remedy for non-performance (art 3.7; but cf PECL, art 4.119).

One important development in the PECL is that mistake has now been made the subject of good faith (PECL, art 4.103(1)(a)(ii)), although in UNIDROIT there is the (lesser?) obligation of 'reasonable commercial standards of fair dealing' (art 3.5(1)(a)). Subjecting mistake to an obligation of good faith could have far-reaching consequences for the traditional English approach, since it might put a contracting party under a positive obligation to inform. Thus two of the most fundamental English mistake cases, *Smith v Hughes* (1871) and *Bell v Lever Brothers* (1932), might have been decided quite differently if the PECL had applied to their facts. It is, of course, unlikely that the PECL will replace English contract law in the foreseeable future, but one might still reflect upon whether the interpretation (construction) approach asserted in *The Great Peace* allows for the presumption of reasonableness or good faith.

4.1.9 Error and property

The distinction between void and voidable contracts (see **4.1.3**, above) becomes vital in situations where a contractor is mistaken as to the identity of his co-contractor (*error in persona*). Most of these cases follow a common pattern and give rise to a similar property problem: a rogue (R) assumes the identity of a famous celebrity in order to induce the seller (S) to hand over an item that he is offering for sale in return for a cheque, which subsequently turns out to be worthless, R having in the meantime sold the item on to an innocent third party purchaser (D). The problem arrives in court when S sues D for the return of 'his' item, and the question thus to be decided is whether S or D is the owner (*Shogun Finance Ltd v Hudson* (2003), § 56). Now it is clear that such a contract is *voidable* for misrepresentation, but this is often of little help to S because a voidable contract will nevertheless pass title from S to R and, provided that the contract has not been unilaterally rescinded by S, R then has a title he can pass on to D (Sale of Goods Act 1979, s 23). However, if the contract between S and R is *void* at common law because S's offer was aimed only and exclusively at the celebrity, title in the item cannot pass to R and S will thus succeed in his claim against D in the tort of conversion. The question, therefore, in these cases is whether the seller intended to contract with the celebrity, or with the person actually standing before him (*Shogun*).

In some legal systems this problem cannot arise because a possessor of a chattel vis-à-vis an innocent third party buyer is deemed to be owner (see CC, art 2279). However, English law has never adopted this rule in its entirety and, moreover, has held on occasions that contracts can be void for mistake of identity (*Ingram v Little* (1961)). In 1972, the Court of Appeal appeared to come down, definitively, on the side of D (*Lewis v Averay* (1972)) – for if anyone is in a position to prevent this kind of fraud it is S rather than D – but the definitiveness of this approach has more recently been reversed by the House of Lords in yet another case involving a car (*Shogun Finance v Hudson* (2003)). As one dissenting Law Lord observed, '[g]enerations of law students have struggled with this problem' and they 'may be forgiven for thinking that it is contrived by their tutors to test their mettle' (Lord Millett in *Shogun*, § 56). He went on to observe that German law favours protection of the innocent third party buyer and that English law, having adopted a different approach (Lord Millett dissented), has now put itself in a position that 'would make the contemplated harmonisation of the general principles of European contract law very difficult to achieve' (*Shogun*, § 86).

A similar property problem can arise out of an error in respect to the nature of the transaction itself (*error in negotio*). Again these errors usually arise out of fraud, when one party misrepresents to the other the nature of the contract or the document to be signed; the object of the misrepresentation is for the representor to get possession of or title to property, which is then transferred for money to an innocent third party. The point to note here is that the equitable remedy of rescission is not really helpful since it makes the contract only *voidable*; what the claimant wants is an order or declaration that the contract is *void* in order to prevent the third party obtaining a property right. In this situation the common law does not approach the problem as one of formation but as one where the victim raises a defence of *non est factum* (this is not my deed). This plea was originally designed to apply to forgery cases where the victim had not signed at all, but it was extended to cover certain cases where the victim had signed.

However, for this defence to succeed and the victim to escape from the contract, the facts must be exceptional, because there is a presumption that a contractor will read any contractual document presented to him or her. The plea will be effective (and the contract declared void) if, first, the representee signed without any negligence on his or her part and, secondly, the contract is radically different from the one the signer believed it to be (*Saunders v Anglia Building Society* (1971)). The object of this rule is to effect a compromise as between victim and innocent third party. However, if the third party is less than innocent, it may find itself unable to enforce, for example, any contract it has as a result of the fraud with the victim (*Avon Finance v Bridger* (1985)).

4.2 Duress

The French *Code civil* talks not just of error, but also of fraud and duress as obstacles to consent (art 1109). Where they exist they create difficulties at the level of formation. In English law, fraud and duress do not function at the level of formation even if they are seen as impacting on consent; a contract can certainly exist at common law despite the presence of these two factors. However, they both have the capacity to make a contract voidable. As we have seen at **4.1.4** above, there is no general rule that fraud vitiates consent. What fraud does is to give the victim a right to rescind the contract and (or) to sue for damages in the tort of deceit. Many fraud cases involve a fraudulent statement by one party to the other, and this means that most of the fraud cases end up under the heading of misrepresentation.

Duress, like fraud, gives rise to a right to rescind the contract, but, as with fraud, it seems that the rules relating to duress are not strictly internal to the law of contract. No doubt it could be argued that certain kinds of menaces are so intense that they impact directly upon the very existence of consent, thus making the contract void rather than voidable. But this is not the approach of English law. Most fraud and duress cases were the concern of equity, and the modern law probably reflects principles developed in Chancery (Ibbetson, 1999, 235). Thus duress to the person or to goods will generally give rise to a right on the part of the victim to rescind, provided that the duress has been a (not necessarily *the*) cause for entering the contract (*Barton v Armstrong* (1976)). Lesser forms of duress are more problematic.

4.2.1 Economic duress

One lesser form of duress that has given rise to a body of case law is where the threat is economic. Equity has been prepared to aid a victim of this form of behaviour in an indirect way (see *D & C Builders v Rees* (1966)), but as a direct basis for obtaining rescission the development is relatively recent and belongs more to the law of restitution (unjust enrichment) than to contract (see **Chapter 11**). English law now accepts that the equitable remedy of rescission will be available for certain kinds of economic duress (*Pau On v Lau Yiu Long* (1980)).

The starting point is probably clear enough: a contractor who threatens to do a legally wrongful act (a crime, tort or breach of contract) will prima facie be guilty of economic duress rendering any contract resulting from the exercise of the threat voidable. This rescission rule is also to be found in the PECL (art 4.108(a)), but the provision in UNIDROIT is in many ways more interesting. 'A party may avoid the contract', states art 3.9, 'when he has been led to conclude the contract by the other party's unjustified threat which, having regard to the circumstances, is so imminent and serious as to leave the first party no reasonable alternative'. This provision is more restrictive than the one in the PECL in that it specifically incorporates the 'no reasonable alternative' test. As a result it may be closer to English law. Yet what both the PECL and UNIDROIT accept is that certain threats, even if not unlawful, may be sufficient to amount to economic duress ('lawful act duress'). There is some authority that this may be true of English law as well (*The Evia Luck* (1992)), but a decision of the Court of Appeal suggests otherwise (*CTN Cash & Carry v Gallaher* (1994)). This is an area of law that depends very much on the facts and the context within which the alleged economic duress is exercised.

4.2.2 Undue influence

Equity has made a further fundamental contribution to this area in recognising an equitable form of duress, namely undue influence (*Royal Bank of Scotland plc v Etridge (No 2)* (2002), §§ 6–7). This form of duress grew out of the idea that certain relations of themselves gave rise to a situation where one party could exercise domination over the other (Ibbetson, 1999, 209). In the 19th century undue influence remained largely confined to particular categories of relations such as parent and child, doctor and patient, and the like, but in the latter half of the following century it saw an expansion into a fully developed principle applicable to commercial and consumer transactions.

Thus in *Lloyds Bank v Bundy* (1975), the Court of Appeal set aside a contract between a bank and a farmer, in which the farmer had charged his farm in support of his son's business debts. The Court was of the view that the bank had abused its long-term relationship in failing to urge the elderly farmer to seek independent advice before signing the forms. In *Barclay's Bank v O'Brien* (1994), the House of Lords went further and confirmed that a bank may be under an equitable duty to warn a client with whom it is negotiating a mortgage contract to seek independent advice, even in cases where it is not the bank, but a third party, exercising the undue influence. If the bank has constructive knowledge of the undue influence, and fails to warn the client to seek independent advice, it will find that its contract might be subject to rescission. The case law is now complex, but if the undue influence is clear and obvious the bank will be under a high duty specifically to warn the client of his or her potential liabilities (*Credit Lyonnais Bank Nederland v Burch* (1997); *Royal Bank of Scotland plc v Etridge (No 2)* (2002)).

4.2.3 Duress and remedies

The principal remedy for duress is rescission in equity. However, economic duress could be said indirectly to have facilitated the victim's debt claim in *D & C Builders v Rees* (1966) in that the court refused to allow the perpetrator to take advantage of promissory estoppel. And in *Williams v Roffey Brothers* (see **3.4.2.1**, above), had the carpenter threatened not to continue with his existing contract, he would not have been able to claim the extra money. One who obtains a profit through duress might be liable to account to any victim through an action of account of profits (*Att-Gen v Blake* (2001)). The interesting question is whether a victim can sue in damages. To be able to do this, the victim would have to prove damage and a cause of action in contract or tort. It is not easy to see how duress could amount to a breach of the actual contract that it induces, but causing damage through unlawful threats may give rise to a claim in the tort of intimidation (see **7.3.3.8**, below). However, the 'use of economic duress to induce another person to part with property or money is not a tort per se' (*Universe Tankships v ITW* (1983), at 385, *per* Lord Diplock). But it will give rise to a claim in restitution (debt) for the return of any money paid, together with, of course, the rescission of any contract (*per* Lord Diplock).

4.3 Capacity and illegality

Capacity and illegality have little in common, save that they both can result in defective contracts the restitutionary effects of which are quite complex. In fact, like fraud and duress, they are topics that in English law technically fall outside contract and, for the most part, now fall within the law of restitution. Nevertheless, they are both capable of acting as vitiating factors.

4.3.1 Capacity

In French contract law capacity is an essential condition for the formation of a contract (CC, art 1108). In English law it is not, except perhaps in one or two situations. Thus a contract tainted by incapacity – usually one where one party is a minor (below the age of 18), or perhaps a contract with a mental incompetent – is prima facie valid and not void. It is only voidable or unenforceable, and rescission or enforceability will depend upon the nature of the transaction and upon whether or not enforceability is unconscionable (*Hart v O'Connor* (1985)). The exception is a public or a private corporation that has no power to contract; here the contract will be void on the basis that the corporation was acting *ultra vires*. In the case of commercial companies, thanks to statutory intervention, *ultra vires* contracts are no longer of great practical concern; the same could not be said for public authorities (see *Hazell v Hammersmith and Fulham LBC* (1992); *Westdeutsche Landesbank Girozentrale v Islington LBC* (1996); *Kleinwort Benson Ltd v Glasgow CC* (1996); *Kleinwort Benson Ltd v Birmingham CC* (1997); *Kleinwort Benson Ltd v Lincoln CC* (1999)), although statute has intervened in respect of local authorities (Turpin, 2002, 627).

4.3.1.1 Restitution

One of the most serious problems that arises out of contracts made with a minor is in respect of money or property transferred to a minor under an unenforceable or voidable contract. Can the minor keep either the money, or the property without having to pay? A minor or other human incompetent must pay for necessary goods supplied to him (Sale of Goods Act 1979, s 3), and now a court has been given power to order the return of 'property' acquired by a minor 'if it is just and equitable to do so' (Minors' Contracts Act 1987, s 3). The Act does not define 'property', and so it is not clear from the text itself whether it covers money conveyed to a minor.

4.3.2 Illegality

Illegality is even more complex because, unlike French law which focuses on illegal cause (CC, arts 1131, 1133) and object (art 1128), there is no single starting point, and it is not even clear whether an illegal contract is void or unenforceable. Moreover, the topic also embraces certain contracts that are not illegal in any moral sense but which are void or unenforceable for reasons of public policy. The line between illegal and public policy contracts is not always easy to discern.

4.3.2.1 Scope of illegality

The first difficulty is to pin down exactly what is meant by 'illegality', since it encompasses, at one extreme, serious criminal behaviour (*mala in se*) and, at the other extreme, breach of a technical statutory provision (*mala prohibita*). Historically no distinction, it seems, was made, but one key concept did emerge, that of public policy, and this proved useful because of its flexibility (Ibbetson, 1999, 212–3). Flexibility is needed in this area because contracts can be tainted by illegality in a number of ways. There are contracts which in their very substance are illegal because the transaction itself is criminal (a contract to sell drugs, or to have someone killed); there are other contracts which are illegal because of general social policy and (or) morality. There is a further class of contracts which are not illegal per se but become illegal because of motive and performance (a contract to hire a carriage for prostitution: *Pearce v Brooks* (1866)). In this latter situation the question then arises as to whether both parties were aware of the illegal motive, or whether one party was innocent.

4.3.2.2 *Ex turpi causa* rule

The primary practical question comes down to one of enforceability. Here two principles are said to govern. The first is the rule *ex turpi causa non oritur actio* (no action arises out of an illegal cause), which gives expression to the idea of unenforceability. Where both parties collude in the illegality, it may well be that neither party will be allowed to sue if there is a breach of the contract (*Ashmore, Benson, Pease & Co v AV Dawson Ltd* (1973)). Equally a contractor guilty of illegal behaviour will not be allowed to sue on any contract connected with this behaviour if it would result in an unjustified enrichment (*Geismar v Sun Alliance Insurance* (1978)). Yet the rule is not rigidly applied; much will depend upon the circumstances and the relative guilt of each party.

4.3.2.3 *In pari delicto* rule

The second principle used by the courts looks to the position of the parties: *in pari delicto potior est conditio defendentis (possidentis)* (where both parties are equally in the wrong, the position of the defendant (or possessor) is stronger). This rule evidently overlaps with the *ex turpi causa* maxim, but it is wider in that it would prima facie seem to prohibit any action – even one that is not contractual – from coming to the aid of a party who has transferred money or property pursuant to an illegal contract (see, eg, *Parkinson v College of Ambulance* (1925)). One point to note is that both parties must be *in pari delicto* (equally guilty). Yet, more generally, it can be said that the rule is not rigidly applied, and if a claimant is able to found his claim on a cause of action independent of the tainted contract – for example, if he can sue in tort, quasi-contract, or even on a collateral contract –

he may succeed. Thus the owner of some machinery delivered under an illegal hire-purchase contract was able to sue for damages in the tort of conversion when the other party converted the property (*Bowmakers v Barnet Instruments* (1945)).

4.3.2.4 *Tinsley v Milligan* (1994)

There has been a further development in recent years with respect to the *in pari delicto* rule. In *Tinsley v Milligan* (1994), a majority of the House of Lords decided that a woman who had transferred her share in a jointly purchased house to her partner, in order that the two of them could facilitate a social security fraud, could reclaim her equitable interest in the property despite the illegality. Several points emerge from the decision. First, that a person can at law enforce property rights against the possessor provided that one does not have to rely upon the illegal contract. Secondly, the court will no longer distinguish between common law and equitable property rights, thus allowing the claimant to avoid (perhaps) the maxim that he who comes to equity must come with clean hands (cf Lord Goff's dissenting judgment; and see *D & C Builders v Rees* (1966)). Thirdly, the courts are taking a measured approach towards restitution and illegal contracts; much will depend upon the facts, including the nature and seriousness of the illegality, knowledge of the parties and so on. Two focal points perhaps emerge from this more flexible and discretionary approach: the courts will weigh deterrence (public interest) on the one hand against proportionality (private interests and unjustified enrichment) on the other. If the judges had refused to aid the claimant in *Tinsley*, the private interest and enrichment of one of the fraudsters would have been much enhanced, thus affirming that, for her, crime pays. In other words, if the court had allowed the party effectively to escape from the contract, it would have resulted in an unjustified benefit for the fraudster. The majority decision meant only that the status quo was restored.

4.3.3 Void contracts

In addition to contracts that are unenforceable because of illegality, common law and statute also treat certain other contracts as being 'void' for reasons of public policy. These contracts are not illegal as such since they often lack the moral dimension associated with illegality (although there is overlap). They are simply unenforceable for social or economic reasons. Thus gambling contracts are 'null and void' (Gaming Act 1845, s 18), although insurance and investment transactions are outside of this provision; and contracts in restraint of trade and certain anti-competitive agreements are void for economic policy reasons. Certain other contracts also fall into this public policy voidness class. Whether 'void' really means void or whether such contracts are just unenforceable is a debateable issue (cf *Shell UK v Lostock Garages* (1976), *per* Lord Denning, at 1198), for parties to a gambling contract are not liable to make restitution (but cf *Lipkin Gorman v Karpnale* (1991)) and restraint of trade provisions can be severed from unobjectionable parts of a contract. Yet, whatever the situation, restraint of trade and competition agreements are now specialist areas of commercial law and European economic law, and the statute book itself is littered with sections declaring void or unenforceable either various types of agreements or particular provisions inserted into what are otherwise valid contracts.

4.3.4 Cancelled contracts

A contract may also be in effect 'void' if it is of a type in which one of the parties – normally a consumer – has a statutory right to cancel. Such a right is a real means of escape and, indeed, brings the whole idea of a binding contract concluded through offer and acceptance into question. Thus, with respect to a distance selling contract, a consumer has a right to cancel within seven working days of the receipt of the goods or services. If the consumer does cancel, 'the contract shall be treated as if it had not been made' (Consumer Protection (Distance Selling) Regulations 2000, reg 10(2)). In other words, the contract is void. This right of cancellation is rather similar to the right of rescission accorded to a minor, since they both could be said to depend upon the status of the contracting party. One might be tempted to say, therefore, that consumers are now a class of persons who should be considered from the angle of contractual capacity. Suppliers may well find that certain kinds of commercial contracts are not as binding as the traditional textbooks might lead them to believe.

4.4 Non-performance of a contract

So far the primary, although not exclusive, means of escape from a contract has been via the equitable remedy of rescission. However, the common law allows a contractor, both directly and indirectly, to escape from the contract in a number of situations where performance of the contract has failed or is defective. In particular, a contractual party faced with a serious breach of a fundamental contractual promise (called a condition) has the remedy at common law of escaping from the contract and, if he has suffered damage, suing in damages. Put another way, one contractor is obliged to perform his promise only if the other contractor performs his basic promises (*Bolton v Mahaveda* (1972)). This is a real escape hatch, so to speak, and a well-drafted commercial contract could be phrased in such a way as to allow a contractor to repudiate the whole contract even if, say, a payment is five minutes late.

A contractor may find himself freed from a contract as a result of an intervening event, arising through the fault of neither party, which destroys the commercial basis of the contract. Thus a contractor who undertook to pay a high rental sum for use of rooms to view the King's coronation was freed from the contractual debt when the coronation was cancelled (*Krell v Henry* (1903)). Another means of escape is for a party to renegotiate the whole contract with the other party. If successful, the first contract will be replaced by a second contract. Perhaps the most obvious way of 'escaping' from a contract is to perform one's promises. However, all of these performance issues will be discussed in more depth in the next chapter, since many such situations involve claims not just for freeing oneself from the obligation but, more importantly, for compensatory damages.

5 Unperformed Contracts and Monetary Remedies

English works on the law of contract do not on the whole have sections or chapters devoted to non-performance of contracts. Indeed to subdivide contract into just two parts – formation and non-performance – is very civilian. Moreover, to try to approach English law from this general viewpoint has been described as 'somewhat alarming' because 'it is so general, too general for … intellectual comfort' (Weir, 1999, 71). Interestingly, Tony Weir gives as one of the reasons for discomfort the distinction between promise and contract, pointing out that non-performance in English law tends to centre on the unperformed promise rather than the unperformed contract (cf **3.2.5**, above). Nevertheless, in a general work on the law of obligations the idea of non-performance as a viewpoint can be helpful in the understanding of the structure of English contract law. It can also contribute to contract method, since failure to perform is what usually gives rise to practical problems (see **3.1**, above). Working back from these practical problems, one often has to examine and to interpret the contract itself.

5.1 Defining performance: interpretation

The contractual obligation having been formed, the next rational step is to examine its content. Where the contract has been reduced to writing this formal content will be evident from the written document. However, because natural language can be ambiguous, and because the parties cannot always foresee and provide for future events, certain clauses in the contract may well give rise to disputed interpretations. In substance, then, the content of the contract may be uncertain. Where a contract is silent about a particular event or factual circumstance a further interpretation problem arises. Can the court read into the contract certain obligations? Nevertheless, all this can be unrealistically abstract in as much as interpretation and content issues usually arise only when something has gone wrong and one of the parties is threatening to have recourse to a legal or self-help remedy. This is why content and interpretation should be seen as part of the more general topic of liability.

5.1.1 Structure and contents of a contract

In civilian thinking a contract is more than the sum of its parts; it is an obligation – a *vinculum iuris* – binding two parties and having an existence, so to speak, of its own. English law, in contrast, enforces promises, and thus a contract is simply a bundle of promises. As we shall see, these promises may vary in importance and status. Yet when things go wrong the reaction of contract lawyers is to locate the precise promise, or promises, that remain unfulfilled or broken.

Now this promise approach has the merit of focusing attention on very precise areas of the contract, and in commercial contracts, which are normally reduced to writing, this means that the text becomes the object of attention. Contractual interpretation might easily, then, have developed rules analogous to interpretation of statutes. Yet this did not happen – or at least the rules of interpretation did not become fixed and assessable in quite the same way as for statutes – and one reason for this is that the structure and status of promises became so dominant that they focused attention on a number of terms of art. Remedies came to be dependent upon whether a promise (term) was a 'condition' or a 'warranty'. In addition, another dichotomy – that between express and implied terms – had the effect of fragmenting interpretation behind tests that looked to structure and content rather than linguistic analysis. And perhaps the same can be said of the distinction between 'terms' and 'representations' (see *Hopkins v Tanqueray* (1854)). Interpretation and content have tended, therefore, to merge in English contract law.

5.1.2 Interpretation of written contracts

In the civil law, interpretation of contracts is recognised as a specific aspect of contract knowledge. This is largely because the *Code civil* and other codes have a section specifically devoted to this issue (see PECL, Ch 5). Yet there is also a general tendency in the civilian world to treat interpretation of contracts within the topic of interpretation of texts in general, and thus contracts are subjected to the same methods as statutory texts. In the common law world, in contrast, interpretation of contracts is not traditionally to be found as a free-standing topic in the textbooks (but cf Lewison, 2003). In addition, it is very rare for statutory interpretation methods to be cited as the means to be adopted with respect to contracts, although there are exceptions (see Lord Denning in *Staffs Area Health Authority v South Staffs Waterworks Co* (1978)). In fact, while there are specific textual interpretation cases in the common law contract books (see, eg, *Genossenschaftsbank v Burnhope* (1995); *Mannai Investment Co v Eagle Star Life Assurance* (1997)), many problems are to be found in chapters on express terms, implied terms and exclusion clauses; and these problems often take as their starting point the issue of liability.

5.1.2.1 Difference of approach

Common law and civil law appear to take diametrically opposed approaches in respect of the interpretation of contracts. The PECL declare that a 'contract is to be interpreted according to the common intention of the parties even if this differs from the literal meaning of the words' (art 5.101(1)). And this provision in turn has doubtless been influenced by a provision in the French *Code civil* (art 1156). In the common law, in contrast, intention 'is determined by reference to expressed rather than actual intention' (Lord Steyn in *Genossenschaftsbank v Burnhope* (1995), 1587). The policy behind this approach has been explained by Lord Bridge in *The Chikuma* (1981):

> The ideal at which the courts should aim, in construing such clauses, is to produce a result, such that in any given situation both parties seeking legal advice as to their

rights and obligations can expect the same clear and confident answer from their advisers and neither will be tempted to embark on long and expensive litigation in the belief that victory depends on winning the sympathy of the court.

As he admitted, this 'ideal may never be fully attainable, but we shall certainly never even approximate to it unless we strive to follow clear and consistent principles and steadfastly refuse to be blown off course by the supposed merits of individual cases' (at 322). A similar view has been expressed by Lord Goff. An 'objective interpretation is of paramount importance in commercial affairs' since not only is it important that they can rely on courts and arbitrators but 'in the commercial world contracting parties have to look after their own interests' (*The General Capinpin* (1991), 9).

5.1.2.2 Contractual background

The comments quoted in **5.1.2.1** above have, of course, to be understood in the context of the actual contracts in issue, namely, charterparties. And these contracts are notorious not just because they often raise interpretation issues, but also because they function within a 'hard nose' business world. It may well be that other contracts, even commercial ones, attract a more flexible approach. In *Mannai Investment Co v Eagle Star Life Assurance* (1997), Lord Hoffmann said that 'the restriction on the use of background has been quietly dropped' (at 779); and in the same case Lord Steyn was of the view that one looked for 'the intention of the parties', which often meant that 'the reasonable commercial person is hostile to technical interpretations and undue emphasis on niceties of language' (at 771). Indeed, Lord Hoffmann has subsequently gone on to reinforce what he calls the 'common sense' approach to interpretation and so, in short, a strictly literal approach to the interpretation of a contractual text has now been definitively abandoned with respect to many commercial contracts (see *Investors Compensation Scheme v West Bromwich Building Society* (1998); see also *Sirius Insurance Co v FAI General Insurance* (2004), § 19). The approach is probably much closer to the one to be found in the PECL (art 5.102), although it is unlikely that English law would fully subscribe to the good faith provision.

5.1.2.3 *Contra proferentem*

One principle that English law does share – or at least partly share – with civil law is the *contra proferentem* rule, which states that where 'there is doubt about the meaning of a contract term not individually negotiated, an interpretation of the term against the party who supplied it is to be preferred' (PECL, art 5.103). In English law this rule applies to any clause that attempts to take away or cut down the customer's common law rights (*Adams v Richardson & Starling* (1969)), and thus it is usually encountered in the area of exclusion and limitation clauses. However, it may equally have a role in the interpretation of insurance contracts (*Houghton v Trafalgar Insurance Co* (1954)).

5.2 Determining performance: terms

The dichotomy between agreement and promise, and the importance of promise with respect to the contents of an English contract, have already been mentioned. Promise explains the English approach to the structure of a contract. A contract is not a *vinculum iuris* founded on a single obligation; it consists of a bundle of promises, called 'terms', of differing intensity and status. These different classes of terms have attracted their own labels, and these labels in turn have determined the contents and structure. Two classification dichotomies are particularly important:

(a) the distinction between 'conditions' and 'warranties'; and
(b) the distinction between express and implied terms.

5.2.1 Total failure of consideration

Before examining these dichotomies, something must again be said about the starting point of an English contract. It is in structure nothing more than the sum of its parts, that is to say a bundle of promises. Nevertheless, the courts have recognised that a contract usually has some fundamental, or basic, promise upon which the whole contract rests. Thus, in a contract for the sale of a car, the fundamental promise made by the seller is that he will pass ownership in the vehicle to the buyer; and if he fails to do this (passing only possession) there will be a 'total failure of consideration', allowing the buyer to reclaim the whole of the price of the vehicle even if he has had use of the car for six months (*Rowland v Divall* (1923)). This kind of thinking has given rise to the idea that there are certain 'fundamental' terms in every contract. In principle there is nothing wrong with this idea, but in the context of English law the idea of fundamental terms proved unfortunate because the expression was used to mean different things. In particular, the fundamental term was seized upon as a weapon in the war against exclusion clauses and this, in the end, resulted in its demise as a term of art. One is left, all the same, with the notion of a 'total failure of consideration' and, by ricochet, with the idea that some promises are fundamental to the whole contract.

5.2.2 Conditions and warranties

The idea of a fundamental term proved difficult for another reason: it seemed to share much the same status as a 'condition'. 'In civilian legal systems', observed Lord Steyn, 'a condition is sharply distinguished from the actual terms of a contract' in as much as it 'is reserved for an external fact upon which the existence of the contract depends'. In English law, in contrast, 'a condition frequently means an actual term of the agreement', and thus it is 'necessary to distinguish between promissory and contingent conditions' (*Total Gas v Arco British* (1998), 220).

5.2.2.1 Ambiguity of 'condition'

A contingent condition is one where the contract is dependent upon the happening of an event (see now PECL, art 16.101). Thus Mrs Carlill was entitled to claim her reward of £100 only on the happening of a condition, namely, that she caught influenza (see **3.3.2.1**, above; and see PECL, art 16.103(1)). But, as Lord Reid pointed out in *Schuler AG v Wickman Machine Tools* (1974) (250–51), in 'the ordinary use of the English language "condition" has many meanings, some of which have nothing to do with agreements'. Thus 'it may mean a pre-condition: something which must happen or be done before the agreement can take effect', or 'it may mean some state of affairs which must continue to exist if the agreement is to remain in force' (on which see CC, art 1168 and PECL, art 16.103(2)).

5.2.2.2 Condition and repudiation

Lord Reid added a third meaning: it 'is a term the breach of which by one party gives to the other an option either to terminate the contract or to let the contract proceed and, if he so desires, sue for damages for the breach' (*Schuler AG v Wickman Machine Tools* (1974), 251). According to this third meaning, a condition is a promise that is fundamental to the contract, and this is why, if it is broken, the other party has the right to refuse to go on with the contract. One contractor's performance is conditionally dependent on the other party's performance, performance here signifying the 'fundamental' substance of the contract itself reflected in the idea of a fundamental promise or term.

5.2.2.3 Warranty

If the term broken is only a 'warranty', the other party will not have a right to terminate; he will have a right only to damages (Sale of Goods Act 1979, s 11(3)). Like 'condition', the word 'warranty' has several different meanings and this, equally, can cause confusion. For example, the expression 'warranty' is sometimes used to describe a pre-contractual statement that is more than a mere 'representation'. It is a term of the contract itself, or, if not part of the main contract, a promise capable of being a contractual promise collateral to the main contract (*Dick Bentley Productions v Harold Smith (Motors)* (1965)). Again, in insurance contracts, the expression 'warranty' has a meaning of its own (see, eg, Marine Insurance Act 1906, ss 33–41).

5.2.2.4 Condition and performance

The main purpose of the dichotomy between conditions and warranties is to distinguish between what a civil lawyer would call fundamental and non-fundamental failures to perform. Only if the other party's non-performance is fundamental may a contractor terminate the contract (PECL, art 9.301(1)). In focusing on the term, English law is achieving the same objective; but in placing the emphasis on the status of the promise it has created a structure whose logic could on occasions lead to difficulty. What if the harm arising from a breach of a promise labelled a condition turned out only to be slight? According to the logic of the dichotomy, if the promise broken is a 'condition' then the victim can terminate the contract irrespective of the extent or seriousness of the harm. The logic can seemingly apply in reverse: if a contracting party suffers very serious damage, yet the term broken is only a minor one, it could be argued that he has no right to repudiate (but see *Aerial Advertising Co v Batchelor's Peas Ltd* (1938)).

5.2.2.5 Innominate term

In the PECL, where the focus is on the non-performance, the position is more flexible, in that the effects of the non-performance are taken into account in assessing whether or not the non-performance is fundamental (cf *Aerial Advertising*, at **5.2.2.4** above). The non-performance must substantially deprive the other party 'of what it was entitled to expect under the contract' (art 8.103(b)). The logical difficulty created by the English approach was appreciated by the Court of Appeal in 1962, with the result that the Court attempted to introduce into English law an approach not dissimilar to that in the PECL. Before a contractor could be allowed to terminate the contract for breach of a term, it should be asked if the innocent party had been substantially deprived of the whole benefit of the contract (*Hong Kong Fir Shipping v Kawasaki Kisen Kaisha* (1962)). The conditions and warranties dichotomy might work well enough in the area of sale of goods, but this was not necessarily true of undertakings in general in the common law (Diplock LJ).

The effect of the *Hong Kong* case proved ambiguous. Was it abandoning the condition and warranties dichotomy as a model generally applicable in contract, or was it introducing a third class of term or promise that fell mid-way between these two? Many commentators took the latter view, and thus was created the 'innominate' term. Such a term has been accepted by the case law, but it was re-asserted in 1981 that freedom of contract and contractual certainty dictated that parties ought to be allowed to continue to use 'condition' as a term of art (that is to say, if broken, the remedy of termination will be available). And so if the parties clearly label a term as a condition, the court should give effect to their intentions (*Bunge Corp v Tradax SA* (1981)). Indeed, this point is possibly recognised by the PECL (art 8.103(a)).

5.2.3 Implied terms

The idea of promise equally explains one of the most important conceptual devices of English contract law, the implied term. To paraphrase Lord Wright, the expression is used in different senses; sometimes it denotes a term which is not dependent on the actual intention of the parties but on a rule of law, such as the terms, warranties or conditions which, if not expressly excluded, the law imports, as for instance under the Sale of Goods Act and the Marine Insurance Act. Sometimes the law, in certain circumstances, holds that a contract is dissolved if there is a vital change of conditions (as we have seen with mistake). Sometimes what it is sought to be implied in a contract is based on an intention imputed to the parties from their actual circumstances (*Luxor (Eastbourne) Ltd v Cooper* (1941), 137).

5.2.3.1 Term implied in fact

Implied terms are central to the whole question of contractual liability in the common law, and although they are said to be based on the presumed intention of the parties, questions of risk and status may have their role as well. This is particularly so in cases where a party seeks to imply a term on the actual facts of a case. Here the test is one of giving 'efficacy to the transaction' (Bowen LJ), which in commercial contracts is shortened to the business efficacy test (*The Moorcock* (1889)). The court will imply a term on its facts if the contract would otherwise fail. However, a number of requirements or reference points will guide the court, and some of these are helpfully set out in UNIDROIT. They are:

(a) the nature and purpose of the contract;
(b) the practices established between the parties and usages;
(c) good faith and fair dealing; and
(d) reasonableness (art 5.2).

All of these reference points, except perhaps good faith (see *Reid v Rush & Tompkins* (1990)), are to be found in English law and so, for example, the term to be implied must be reasonable. Lord Denning once tried to raise reasonableness to the test itself of when to imply, but this was subsequently rejected by the House of Lords (*Liverpool CC v Irwin* (1977)).

5.2.3.2 Term implied by law

Terms can also be implied by law. Here what the court or the legislator does is to stipulate that in certain classes of contract particular promises will be implied as rules of law. For example, before 1982, case law laid down that in commercial or consumer contracts to supply a service a term would be implied to the effect that the provider of the service would use skill and care; after 1982 this term is now implied by statute (Supply of Goods and Services Act 1982, s 13). Thus an employer and employee both owe mutual duties of care, not just in tort, but as implied terms of the contract (*Lister v Romford Ice & Cold Storage Co* (1957); but cf *Reid v Rush & Tompkins* (1990)). In contracts for the supply of goods, there is an implied term that the goods will be of satisfactory quality and reasonably fit for their purpose (see, eg, Sale of Goods Act 1979, s 14).

5.2.3.3 Level of duty

This distinction between contracts for the supply of a service and one for the supply of goods raises an important question about the link between liability and content of the implied term duty or obligation. In French law this is to be found in the famous distinction between *obligation de résultat* and *obligation de moyens*, a distinction that has been specifically adopted by UNIDROIT (art 5.4). Does a contractor promise or agree to achieve a specific result, or just to use his best efforts? This question is clearly of importance in English law as well, but it has become hidden behind a distinction between a contract to supply goods and a contract to supply a service, as we have seen (see **2.2.2.3**, above).

5.2.4 Unfair terms

Express terms, unlike implied terms, tend to give rise to textual interpretation problems as one might expect. Yet there is one area that has proved particularly difficult, and indeed is an area where express terms, interpretation and liability intersect with contract theory and ideology. This is the area of exclusion, limitation, indemnity and penal clauses. The area was once very difficult because the fundamental principle of freedom of contract clashed with the problem of abuse of economic power. In all of the EU countries it is generally true to say that, today, the consumer is largely protected (see EU Directive of 5 April 1993) and standard form contract terms, even in commercial contracts, might be avoided if very unreasonable (UNIDROIT, art 7.1.6; PECL, art 4.110; Unfair Contract Terms Act 1977, s 3). However, contract law tries to avoid declaring that parties should be under a duty to make reasonable contracts (PECL, art 4.110(2); Unfair Terms in Consumer Contracts Regulations 1999, reg 6(2)); the emphasis, instead, is on open dealing and, in civil law thinking, on good faith (PECL, art 4.110, but cf art 8:109; Unfair Terms in Consumer Contracts Regulations 1999, reg 5(1)). The distinction between commercial and consumer contracts is thus vital (Unfair Contract Terms Act 1977, s 12; Unfair Terms in Consumer Contracts Regulations 1999, reg 3). In consumer contracts unfair terms are void (1999 Regulations), while in commercial standard form contracts clauses are subject to a reasonableness test (1977 Act, s 3). Clauses that attempt to exclude personal injury liability for negligence are void in business situations and must be reasonable in relation to other forms of damage (1977 Act, s 2).

Penal clauses have raised their own special problems. These are clauses whereby a contractor agrees to pay a fixed sum of money on failure to perform his contractual obligations, and they can be unfair in that the sum stipulated could far exceed any damage suffered by the victim of the non-performance. Indeed, English law takes the view that if the sum stipulated is a fair estimation of the damage likely to be suffered the term will not be a penalty clause; it will be a liquidated damages clause and fully enforceable virtually as a debt (Ibbetson, 1999, 150–151). However, if it exceeds any likely estimation – that is to say, if it was intended to operate *in terrorem* – it will become penal and, thanks to equity, will not be enforceable (*Jobson v Johnson* (1989)).

5.3 Performance and non-performance of the contract

Many cases concerning terms of the contract arise because one of the parties either has failed to perform his contractual promise or promises, or has rendered defective performance. Interpretation of terms is necessary in order to discover what remedies are available to the innocent party. Of course it must not be forgotten that the great majority of contracts are formed and performed without giving rise to problems. And even in those statistically rare cases when things do go wrong, the victim may decide that the defective performance is not worth pursuing in or outside the courts; other problems are solved mutually between the parties. Yet when a party to a contract does feel aggrieved the first question that needs to be asked is whether or not there has been performance. This may well involve looking back at the promises, but equally, as the *Hong Kong Fir Shipping* case illustrates (see **5.2.2.5**, above), it will require examination of the quality of the performance itself.

5.3.1 Performance and non-performance

Non-performance is not an expression that is often used in English contract law, and this is why it is necessary to look at the civil law and transnational contract codes in order to understand its significance. Non-performance of a contract 'is failure by a party to perform any of its obligations under the contract, including defective performance or late performance' (UNIDROIT, art 7.1.1). Two general questions arise from this definition:

(a) What amounts to performance (or alternatively non- or defective performance)?
(b) What can the victim (aggrieved party) do when faced with such a non-performance?

Now civil law systems start off from this idea of non-performance, and thus it is possible to approach these two questions from the top-down so to speak (see PECL, art 8.101). But common lawyers do not. They have tackled non-performance from the bottom up through a number of specific categories forming part of a general topic called discharge of contract. There is an equal logic or symmetry to this approach, in that discharge or dissolution of contract is the mirror image of formation. Nevertheless, when it comes to reconciling the two approaches – that is to say, if one looks at the consequences of non-performance in English law – it is necessary to bring together a range of disparate areas (Weir, 1999).

5.3.2 Non-performance and remedies

The question of what amounts to performance is vital both for the alleged non-performing party and for the aggrieved party. The alleged non-performer will no doubt be seeking performance from the other party (for example, payment), while the aggrieved party will want to know what he can do about the non-performance. With regard to the question of what amounts to performance, the PECL state that 'a party must tender performance of at least average quality' (art 6:108) and UNIDROIT says it must be 'reasonable' (art 5.6). Common lawyers certainly talk from time to time about performance, but the emphasis on promise has resulted in many performance problems being dealt with under the heading of 'breach' of promise and the remedies available to the aggrieved party. Thus, prima facie, a failure to perform, including defective performance, amounts to a breach of contract. The question then becomes one of liability and remedies, in turn relating back to the type of promise (term) breached. Was the promise one to pay a sum of money, to transfer a thing (of perhaps a particular quality) or to render a service? Was it a fundamental term (condition) (cf PECL, art 8.103; UNIDROIT, art 7.3.1) or a non-fundamental term (warranty)?

These questions are vital with regard to remedies, but performance questions can arise when one party renders defective performance and the other party, as a result, refuses to perform his promise (usually an obligation to pay). If the defective performance is so defective that it amounts to no performance at all, the aggrieved party can refuse to pay (*Vigers v Cook* (1919); *Bolton v Mahadeva* (1972)). If, however, it amounts to defective but substantial performance, the aggrieved party cannot refuse payment; he is liable for the price less an amount to remedy the defects (*Hoenig v Isaacs* (1952)) or which represents the damage (*Ruxley Electronics Ltd v Forsyth* (1996)).

5.3.3 Excused non-performance

According to the French model, a non-performing contractor will be liable in damages to the other contracting party (CC, art 1147). However, the non-performing party will have a defence to any such damages claim if he can show that the non-performance is due either to a *force majeure*, or to a *cas fortuit* (CC, art 1148). This is the model that has been adopted by the PECL (arts 8.101, 8.108) and by UNIDROIT (arts 7.1.7, 7.4.1); in these codes *force majeure* is defined as an impediment beyond the control of the non-performing party and one which could not have been foreseen at the time of the conclusion of the contract (UNIDROIT, art 7.1.7(1); PECL, art 8.108(1)).

5.3.3.1 Frustration of contract

English law, as we have seen at **5.3.1** above, does not operate in this top-down way. Instead it deals with the problem of *force majeure* as an event that frustrates the contractual venture and discharges the whole contract. The effect is often the same, in as much as the discharge of the contract will prevent the non-performing party from being liable in damages. Yet the concept of frustration was developed on the basis of the implied term (implied condition precedent) and as a result shared a conceptual similarity with mistake at common law (see *The Great Peace* (2002), §§ 61–75). This conceptual similarity disappeared in 1956 when the implied term theory for frustration was abandoned on the basis that it was self-contradictory (how could the parties theoretically foresee something which was theoretically unforeseeable?) (*Davis Contractors Ltd v Fareham UDC* (1956)). But it may be that the relation has been re-established now that the Court of Appeal has seemingly abandoned the implied term theory for mistake at common law (*The Great Peace*). At all events, the court now has a power to set aside a contract for frustration.

73

5.3.4 Onerous performance

According to Lord Simon:

> Frustration of a contract takes place when there supervenes an event (without default of either party and for which the contract makes no sufficient provision) which so significantly changes the nature (not merely the expense or onerousness) of the outstanding contractual rights and/or obligations from what the parties could reasonably have contemplated at the time of its execution that it would be unjust to hold them to the literal sense of its stipulations in the new circumstances; in such case the law declares both parties to be discharged from further performance. (*National Carriers Ltd v Panalpina (Northern) Ltd* (1981), 700)

As Lord Simon makes clear, an increase in expense or onerousness does not amount to a frustrating event, and a similar conclusion has been reached in French private law. Contracts, like statutes, are binding (CC, art 1134) and severe inflation does not amount to a *force majeure* (*Canal de Craponne* (1876)).

However, in administrative law the theory of unforeseen change of circumstances (*la théorie de l'imprévision*) was adopted in the famous *Gaz de Bordeaux* case (1916) on the basis that the public interest takes precedence over the binding nature of contract (it was not in the public interest that the lighting company should go bankrupt). Interestingly, English law has reached a similar result as the *Gas de Bordeaux* case in *Staffs Area Health Authority v South Staffs Waterworks Co* (1978); but for the majority of the Court of Appeal this result was simply a matter of interpretation of the contractual document (see **5.1**, above). Lord Denning, however, went beyond the interpretative approach and based his decision both on frustration and on a *rebus sic stantibus* (things remain the same) implied clause giving rise to a right to have the contract re-negotiated. In fact Denning's approach, although rejected by the other judges, now finds expression in both the PECL (art 6.111) and UNIDROIT (arts 6.2.1–6.2.3).

5.3.5 Protected non-performance

A non-performing party may also be protected from the effects of non-performance by an express clause in the contract. Such clauses, as we have seen (**5.2.4** above), can take many forms and in principle, even if they exclude liability, are effective unless they fall within the Unfair Contract Terms Act 1977. However, if the aggrieved party is a consumer, any such clause will, thanks to the Unfair Terms in Consumer Contracts Regulations 1999, be void if it amounts to unfair term. Just what amounts to good faith and unfairness in this context may well vary as between civil and common law systems (see, eg, *DGFT v First National Bank* (2002)).

5.3.6 Performance and third parties

A contract might stipulate that a benefit or burden be placed on a third party, or that the contract will be performed by someone other than the contracting party (which is always the case with corporations). Can the third party demand performance? Can a contracting party disown performance if the third party performs defectively? Originally a person who was not a party to the contract could not sue, but this has now largely been modified in most systems (see **3.4.3**, above; and see also PECL, art 6.110). Where performance is carried out by a third party, the contractor will remain responsible for non- or defective performance (PECL, art 8.107), unless, perhaps, the third party acted outside the scope of his employment (see, eg, *Photo Production Ltd v Securicor* (1980); *Wong Mee Wan v Kwan Kin Travel Services Ltd* (1996)) or is clearly independent of the contractor and whose performance is not warranted (through an implied term) by the contractor (*Wilson v Best Travel* (1993)).

The great danger for this area of contract law is that it becomes infected with what might be called tort thinking. In tort an employer is liable for the tortious acts of its employees only if the latter were acting in the course of their employment (see **9.4**, below). Ought a similar rule to apply in contract? That is to say, should a contractor be able to escape liability for breach of contract where the damage is caused by his employee or independent contractor? It is tempting to say that a contractor ought not to be liable if the damage is caused by a third party ('it is not my fault but his'); but difficulties arise when that third party is the very person charged with carrying out the contract. In *Photo Production Ltd v Securicor* (1980), where a contractor's factory was destroyed thanks to the act of the other contractor's employee (in a contract to provide a security service to the factory premises), the House of Lords ended up by rendering an ambiguous decision. The House certainly refused to allow the security company to argue that its employee was acting outside the scope of his employment when he started a fire at the plaintiff's factory. But the House did allow the security company to rely upon an exclusion clause limiting its liability for acts committed by its own employee. From an insurance position – and it must be remembered that in truth this was an action between the subrogated insurance companies of the two contractors – it seems reasonable enough that the judges should see the whole case in terms of risk. Which insurance undertook the risk of this kind of fire? The problem is that it in putting the emphasis on the fire and building insurance risk, the House of Lords has suggested that a corporate contractor might be able to escape liability for non-performance simply by pointing to a causal link between 'another person' and the innocent contractor's damage (see *Tesco Supermarkets v Nattrass* (1972)).

5.3.7 Inexcused non-performance

Non- or defective performance, unless excused by agreement or frustration, will prima facie amount to a breach of contract. Now, breach of a contractual promise cannot of itself result in termination of the contract (although Lord Denning MR once tried to argue that it could: *Harbutts Plasticine v Wayne Tank & Pump Co* (1970), now overruled); what is required are two conditions:

(a) that the breach is serious enough to justify termination; and
(b) that the victim actually elects to terminate. An innocent party can thus elect to keep the contract alive and, in certain (limited) circumstances, render performance and then sue for the contract price in debt (*White & Carter (Councils) Ltd v McGregor* (1962)).

The central question is the seriousness of the breach. It must go to the root of the contract before a party is entitled to discharge the contract for breach (*Decro-Wall International v Practitioners in Marketing* (1971)). However, we have seen that the traditional approach of English law was not to look at the breach itself but at the status of the term broken; only if the promise or term broken was a 'condition' did the innocent party have the right to terminate (see **5.2.2**, above). All the same, if the effect of the breach is not serious it may well be that a court would treat the term broken as an innominate one, thus allowing them to switch the emphasis to the seriousness of the breach itself.

5.3.7.1 Anticipatory breach

A victim who wishes to terminate a contract for serious breach does not actually have to wait for the breach itself to occur. If the other party declares that he is not going to per-form – or if he acts in a way that will prevent performance (for example, going on an extended holiday in a far-off land a day or so before he is to perform) – the victim can treat this declaration or act as an anticipatory breach and make his election from that moment. He may decide to keep the contract alive, or he may terminate and sue immediately for damages (*White & Carter (Councils) Ltd v McGregor* (1962)).

5.3.8 Non-performance excused by agreement

A contract can of course be discharged before performance by agreement between the parties. However, this is yet another area where the promise basis of English contract law manifests itself with something of a vengeance. The agreement to vary a contract or to discharge it completely is valid at common law only if it amounts to what is in effect a new contract; in other words, the contract is discharged as a result of new promises moving from each party. If the contract has not been performed (executed) by either party there is no problem, since each promise will act as consideration for the other. But if one party has performed his obligations under the contract to be discharged or varied, the new contract will fail because there can be no benefit for the new agreement and thus no enforceable promise. A contractor who agrees to pay a premium to his co-contractor over the agreed contract price might be seen to be providing only a gratuitous promise, although when this was tested the Court of Appeal did find consideration (see **3.4.2.1**, above). Equally, the creditor who agrees to accept a lower sum than the one stipulated in the original contract is, at common law, not bound by this promise (*D & C Builders v Rees* (1966)). Equity will no doubt step in with its remedy of estoppel, provided that the promisee comes with 'clean hands'; and a party who agrees not to enforce some term or other in the contract will be bound by such a variation under the doctrine of waiver (*Hartley v Hymans* (1920); *Charles Rickards Ltd v Oppenheim* (1950)).

5.3.8.1 Variation promise and contractual obligation

The rules on variation and discharge by agreement confirm that an English contract amounts to nothing more than its promissory parts. There is no obligation that transcends these promises. If there were, the problem of variation and discharge would not need to be based on consideration. The contractual obligation having been formed, consideration, it could be said, ought no longer be relevant, since the sheer obligatory force of the contract now in existence could act as the means for variation or discharge. In other words, any sub-sequent contractual promises would gain their contractual obligatory force from the existing contractual relation. The doctrine of waiver might appear to go some way in accepting this analysis, but *Williams v Roffey Brothers* (see **3.4.2.1**) shows that this is wishful thinking. Every contractual promise, at common law, must be the product of a bargain.

6 Tortious Obligations: General Provisions

When one moves from contractual to non-contractual obligations, the idea of an abstract *vinculum iuris* which exists independently of the law of actions becomes more difficult to envisage. The distinction between the formation of an obligation and the performance of it has a practical dimension in a contractual obligation; a party may wish to know independently of any liability whether or not he is under an obligation to do or to convey in some specific manner. With respect to non-contractual obligations it is often the causing of harm or the acquiring of a dubious enrichment that first gives rise to a legal question. And this question is as much concerned with the availability of any remedy as with any idea of a pre-existing obligation. In other words, the remedy question in practice often precedes, or at least becomes combined with, the obligation question.

6.1 Historical and definitional considerations

In spite of what has just been said, claiming a remedy was – and is – never enough to establish liability. A claimant must also establish a cause of action upon which the remedy is based, since claims and obligations are intimately bound together; 'obligations are the mother of actions' said the later Roman lawyers (cf D.3.3.42.2; D.44.7.53pr).

6.1.1 Causes of action in the common law

In order to succeed in a damages claim in English law, a claimant must establish a cause of action in contract, tort or under statute (*Banque Keyser Ullmann v Skandia Insurance* (1990)). Equally, to obtain an injunction in equity a claimant must in principle show the invasion, or threatened invasion, of some substantive legal or equitable right which is normally linked to a cause of action (*Kingdom of Spain v Christie Ltd* (1986); but cf *Burris v Azadani* (1995)). Debt claims are mainly associated with contractual obligations, in that such claims are the means of specifically enforcing a contractual promise to pay a price for goods or services (**Chapter 3**; and see Sale of Goods Act 1979, s 49). However, with respect to a non-contractual debt claim, that is to say a claim in restitution, the link between (implied) contract and debt has now been severed. A quasi-contractual debt claim is based on unjust enrichment, and this is a category of obligation completely separate from either contract or tort (see **Chapter 11**). Civil liability thus requires a knowledge both of *remedies* and of *rights*, and these latter are a matter of *causes of action* to be found in the substantive categories of contract, tort and restitution. If these categories fall within the generic category of the law of obligations, as seems the case according to Lord Goff (*Henderson v Merrett Syndicates Ltd* (1995), 184), it would logically follow that such obligations have a process of formation. But the idea of formation proves elusive, since on the whole it is only when damage is incurred (or threatened) that the law comes into play.

6.1.2 Tort(s)

The term 'tort' is an Anglo-Norman word that simply means 'wrong', and thus tort can be seen as the law of wrongs. In the common law, the law of tort, like the law of contract, is historically founded on the forms of action, the most important of which was trespass, which in the 18th century came to be seen as being concerned with damage *directly* caused. *Indirect* harm was covered either by other writs such as nuisance, or by a development from trespass called the action on the case (the boundary between trespass and case had earlier been much more fluid) (*Wainwright v Home Office* (2003), § 8). When the procedural forms of action were abolished in 1852, the category of 'tort' was used to house those claims for compensatory damages that could not be accommodated under contract. However, the names of the old forms of action were retained and they acted as the basis for a cause of action in tort. Thus trespass, nuisance, conversion (trover), detinue and the like became specific 'torts'.

In 1932 the law of tort took an important step towards a general principle of liability when the House of Lords in *Donoghue v Stevenson* established the tort of negligence, based upon the idea of a general duty of care owed by one person to his 'neighbour' (see **8.1.4**, below). Nevertheless, the older causes of action did not disappear. Accordingly, even today there is no general theory of liability in tort; in order to succeed in a tort claim, a claimant must establish the constituents of a specific tort (see, eg, *Gibbs v Rea* (1998)).

6.1.3 Duty

Nevertheless, if one is going to talk in terms of a law of obligations, it would seem logically to follow that tort is about non-contractual rights and duties. Yet the difficulty in trying to analyse English tort law in terms of a pre-existing obligation is that the analysis works, if at all, only at a very high level of abstraction. One can talk of an obligation not to harm others. In terms of actual vocabulary English law tends to use 'duty', and thus one can talk of 'duty of care' and 'breach of statutory duty'. But the language of duty does not easily work for torts like trespass (*Stubbings v Webb* (1993), 508) and, in addition, it often attaches to the nature of the harm and (or) the status of the defendant. Restitution is less problematic in that one can talk of a duty arising out of unjustified enrichment (cf **Chapter 11**). But a duty to repay can be based on an *in rem* right, which undermines the obligation aspect of the 'duty' to make restitution (Hudson, 2001, 150–59). In other words, restitution is as much about *owning* as *owing*. Attempts have been made to analyse contract, tort and restitution in terms of primary and secondary obligations or duties; but this again is awkward given the forms of action legacy. The idea of a formation of a pre-existing abstract *vinculum iuris* can, then, be unrealistic. Instead one must often think, at best, in terms of a mixture of duties (eg, negligence), rights (eg, defamation), interests and causes of action arising out of factual situations. Only with regard to certain activities (eg, driving, manufacturing) can one think in terms of a pre-existing undertaking or obligation: might one talk here of a kind of 'contract' with those others undertaking the same activity (cf *Clarke v Dunraven* (1897))?

6.1.4 Definition of tortious obligation

Examining tort from an historical perspective is also one way of defining it. Tort claims are those causes of action (formerly forms of action) that cannot be classified under contract or, now, restitution. Such an historical approach partly informs those writers who are sceptical of normative definitions. For example, Tony Weir writes in the preface to his introductory work on the subject that tort law 'is what is in the tort books, and the only thing holding it together is the binding'. He adds that the courts in tort cases 'function as a complaints department – though the claimant, unlike the customer, is not always right'. These 'complaints are of such different kinds that very different reactions may be appropriate, and though there are horses for courses, the tort course sports quite a lot of horses, and they are of very different breeds and speeds'. One cannot, according to Weir, produce a definitional theory, or even discuss the purpose of tort, without first becoming 'familiar with what that ragbag actually contains: otherwise we shall be like adolescents spending all night discussing the meaning of life before, perhaps instead of, experiencing it' (Weir, 2002, ix).

There is, of course, much truth in these observations. Nevertheless, this has not stopped many authors in the common law world from producing definitions, and these definitions can broadly be classed into two groups characterised in turn by two questions: What *is* tort? And what does tort *do*? The first group of definitions can be labelled *formalist*, and they in turn fall into two sub-categories. There are formalist definitions based on inference from a pre-established model of rights, remedies, legal categories, legal rules or whatever; and there are formalist definitions based upon an axiological (science of morals) model. An example of the first kind of formalist approach is the definition fashioned by Winfield. He said that tortious 'liability arises from the breach of a duty primarily fixed by the law: such duty is towards persons generally and its breach is redressible by an action for unliquidated damages' (Winfield, 1931, 32). Winfield goes on to explain how the terms 'fixed by the law', 'towards persons generally' and 'unliquidated damages' mark off tort from other areas of the law such as contract, property and crime. Tort, in other words, is inferred from a classification model of legal rules.

A definition of tort based on principles of justice or upon the moral behaviour of individuals can be regarded as *axiological* in its approach, and any resulting definition can be labelled as formalist. Perhaps one recent example of an axiological approach is to be found in Peter Cane's definition. He says 'that the law of tort can be viewed as a system of ethical rules and principles of personal responsibility for conduct'. Cane contrasts this approach 'to the traditional one of seeing tort law as made up of a number of discrete "torts", that is, legal formulae which can be used to obtain remedies from courts or as bargaining counters in out-of-court negotiations' (Cane, 1997, 1).

6.2 Purpose and policy of tort

Another, and more common, approach is to fashion a definition in terms of the ends that tort is intended to achieve. This group of definitions can be called *functionalist*. What is the function of the law of tort? For example, John Fleming began his introductory work to tort by noting that the

> toll on life, limb, and property exacted by today's industrial operations, methods of transport, and many another activity benignly associated with the 'modern way of life' has reached proportions so staggering that the economic cost of accidents represents a constant and mounting drain on the community's human and material resources. (Fleming, 1985, 1)

He thus went on to assert that the 'task of the law of torts is to play an important regulatory role in the adjustment of these losses and the eventual allocation of their cost'. Other writers have talked in a similar vein. Tort is about spreading the cost of accidents. In fact, as we shall see, although personal injury litigation statistically makes up the bulk of tort law, loss-spreading is not the only aim of this area of law.

6.2.1 Functional definitions

Defining tort from the position of its purpose and function is by no means easy. The subject's fragmentary basis in a wide range of old forms (now causes) of action is at the heart of the problem, since this fragmentation is equally reflected in its functions. One should note, also, that the absence of any formal distinction between administrative liability and civil liability means that tort ends up playing an important administrative and constitutional law role (see, eg, *Keegan v Chief Constable of Merseyside* (2003)). This constitutional role has become more acute, and in some ways more complex, with the incorporation of the European Convention for the Protection of Human Rights and Fundamental Freedoms into English law (Human Rights Act 1998). Moreover, the further absence of any strict divisions, at the level of remedies at any rate, between property and obligations, and between personal and patrimonial rights, results in yet further roles for tort: it ends up as the category providing remedies for the 'vindication' of property rights (see, eg, Torts (Interference with Goods) Act 1977) and of personal rights such as harassment, if not privacy (cf *Wainwright v Home Office* (2003)). This said, it must be remembered that statistically the great majority of tort claims are for personal injury arising out of accidents on the road or in the factory. Personal injury thus dominates the purpose and policy dimension.

6.2.2 Claims for damages

One broad way of defining tort in terms of its purpose and policies is through the remedies associated with this category. By far the most important of these is damages; only the equitable remedy of injunction has any other real claim, and this remedy is more or less limited to certain specific torts. Viewed from the position of damages, one can talk of the law of tort as being concerned with compensation. However, several qualifications must be made here.

First, a claim for damages is an important remedy in contract, and so tortious liability must be distinguished from contractual liability. To an extent this can be done by reference to aims

– contract tends on the whole to protect economic interests as opposed to personal injury interests – but the overlap between the two areas is considerable (see, eg, *Henderson v Merrett Syndicates Ltd* (1995); *Lennon v Comr of Police of the Metropolis* (2004)).

Secondly, to talk in terms of compensation is to view tort from the position of the claimant; tort can, and must, equally be viewed from the position of the defendant (see, eg, *Elguzouli-Daf v Comr of Police for the Metropolis* (1995)). One might add that the subject can also be viewed from the perspective of society (see, eg, *Tomlinson v Congleton BC* (2004)). Can society afford to compensate all accident victims?

Thirdly, *damages* and *damage* are not the same; not all damage will attract compensation (damages), and thus a second descriptive concept, that of an *interest*, needs to be brought into the model. Tort can thus be seen as a matter of protected and unprotected interests, with perhaps varying degrees of protection between these two poles (see eg PETL, art 2:102). However, attempting to define tort in terms of protected interests will again prove extremely difficult not just because of overlap with other subjects (contract, public law, property, etc), but also because some interests are protected at different levels in the law of tort. One cannot say that 'mental distress' is not a recognised interest, yet it is not always well protected (cf PETL, art 2:102(5)).

Fourthly, an award of damages in tort is not the only means of securing help and compensation for harm; private insurance, social security, criminal injuries compensation (see Criminal Injuries Compensation Act 1995), family support, charity and, of course, the National Health Service (NHS) are other support systems. Tort needs to be considered in relation to these other systems, and not just because this contextual perspective is an accepted part of any tort course. These other systems are also of importance because they can influence, directly or indirectly, the actual reasoning and decisions of the judges.

Fifthly, damages as a remedy has a variety of aims and functions not all of which are compensatory. These differing functions are directly reflected back into the causes of action that give rise to the remedy, and thus compensation has to be distinguished, for example, from restitution and from deterrence.

Lastly, damages as a common law monetary remedy needs to be distinguished from other monetary claims such as an action for debt, an action for account, or a claim for damages in equity. Indeed, some claims for 'damages' are in substance really 'debt' (see, eg, *The Stonedale (No 1)* (1956); *Yorkshire Electricity Board v British Telecom* (1986)) or account actions (see, eg, *Att-Gen v Blake* (2001)), and as a result they belong in substantive categories different from tort.

6.2.3 Aims of the law of tort

In a famous article published more than half a century ago, Professor Glanville Williams identified a number of differing aims of the law of tort (Williams, 1951); and see also Williams and Hepple, 1984, 27–30). Moreover, these aims were given a measure of judicial approval in a speech by Lord Steyn in *Smith New Court Securities v Vickers Ltd* (1997), where he recalled Glanville Williams's conclusion that where 'possible the law seems to like to ride two or three horses at once; but occasionally a situation occurs where one must be selected'.

The first of these aims (as set out in William and Hepple, above) is the protection of an *expectation interest*. Now this is normally an aim of the law of contract, but it needs to be added to the law of tort since it has been judicially recognised on occasions that tort fills the gaps of the law of contract, and while an expectation interest is not normally the subject of a duty of care there are exceptions (see, eg, *White v Jones* (1995)). Moreover, one might refer to the more general question of whether a breach of contract is itself a 'tort'. Secondly, there is *compensation for harm*. This is regarded as tort's most important aim, and it is sometimes described as the protection of a person's reliance interest. However, it might be better described as the protection of a restoration interest, since in personal injury and physical damage (and indeed in many economic loss) claims the claimant is demanding to be put back into the position before the tort occurred. Thirdly, there is the *rectification of unjust enrichments*. This aim is less central to tort than it once was now that the law of restitution has become an independent category in English law (**Chapter 11**). Nevertheless, conversion, trespass and exemplary damages can have an important restitutionary function, and these claims remain formally within the category of tort.

Another important aim is *punishment and deterrence*. In Roman law these were central aspects of liability *ex delicto*, but the punishment objective was in later Europe taken over by criminal law. A similar development can be traced in the common law. Nevertheless, the punishment and deterrence aim still has a place in tort law; it directly motivates exemplary damages, which are non-compensatory damages awarded to punish the defendant (on which see *Kuddus v Chief Constable of Leicestershire* (2001)), and has been used to justify more stringent damages in the tort of deceit than in negligence (*Smith New Court Securities Ltd v Vickers Ltd* (1997), *per* Lord Steyn). In other words, by making such a person pay, the law is attempting to deter certain kinds of behaviour that it considers wrongful. One might add here that while this deterrence aim would appear to be totally undermined by the existence of insurance, the idea of punishment and deterrence might still be reflected indirectly via the contract of insurance. Lost no-claims bonuses and higher premiums could be seen as adjustment mechanisms that attempt to continue the deterrence aim.

A further aim of the law of tort is the protection of *rights*. At one level all legal categories could be said to be about rights. But the term 'right' has many meanings, and in this tort context it means rights in the strong sense of the word (infringement rather than behaviour gives rise to a claim). Thus causes of action such as conversion and trespass to goods protect property rights, while malicious prosecution and false imprisonment (trespass to the person) protect constitutional rights. Trespass to land and private nuisance protect rights in land, while some other rights are protected by statutory torts (see, eg, Protection from Harassment Act 1997). The incorporation of the European Convention of Human Rights into English law is clearly of major importance in respect of right protection. The Human Rights Act 1998 itself gives rise to a statutory claim for damages against a public authority that infringes a human right, although it would seem that such a claim is not to be regarded as an action in tort (*R (Greenfield) v Home Secretary* (2005), § 19).

Lastly, although this is not to suggest that the list of aims is closed, Williams and Hepple mention status as an indirect aim and cite how the tort of defamation might be used indirectly to declare a claimant's marital *status*. One might add to this example the protection offered to a private purchaser of a motor vehicle which turns out not to have been owned by the seller but is the subject of a hire-purchase agreement with a finance company. This is a tort problem in as much as, at common law, the purchaser might well be liable in conversion (on which see **7.3.3.3**, below). However, statute offers protection to private purchasers of such motor vehicles, and the question of who is a 'trade and finance' buyer, who will not get protection, is, according to the Court of Appeal, one of status (*Stevenson v Beverley Bentinck Ltd* (1976)). Nevertheless, perhaps this status aim is now too limited. Given that status forms part of the law of persons, it might be now possible, especially since the Protection from Harassment Act 1997 and the Human Rights Act 1998, to think in terms of personality rights. That is to say, tort will protect certain rights which are not patrimonial but attach directly to the person as a human. Such a category would include defamation, which protects the reputation interest, and certain other torts protecting, or coming close to protecting, privacy.

6.2.4 Philosophy of the law of tort

In addition to the doctrinal work on the purpose, policy and aims of the law of tort, there is a huge body of literature, especially North American, devoted to the theory and philosophy behind tort liability. Indeed, there is enough to fill a whole course on the subject. Some theories are based directly on particular notions of justice; thus an emphasis on individual *corrective justice* usually focuses on the balance between individuals in society and the moral imperative behind the obligation to pay damages. Theories of *distributive justice* often emphasise the statistical cost (human and economic) of certain activities, and the unrealistic nature of moral imperatives in a legal structure where most defendants are insured and accidents statistics are predictable. These theories motivate the debate between fault and no-fault liability (see brief extracts in Samuel, 2000, 67–9). In the USA, the law and economics school has been particularly active in the area of tort law, but old ideas about individual responsibility and freedom to act are by no means dead.

6.2.5 Confusion of aims, theories and schemes

Given the discursive nature of common law judgments, these policy, aims and philosophy questions remain important to the understanding of the case law itself. Different judgments can reveal differing theoretical perspectives. Nevertheless, the judges themselves do tend to agree on one thing – that English tort law has committed itself to no single theory (*Broome v Cassell & Co Ltd* (1972), 1114). The effect of such judicial statements is not, of course, to render aims, policy and philosophy irrelevant, for, as the Privy Council has put it, '[o]il and vinegar may not mix in solution but they combine to make an acceptable salad dressing' (*The Gleaner Co Ltd v Abrahams* (2003), § 54). What the judicial scepticism indicates is a point made by Stephen Waddams in his analysis of common law reasoning and categorisation. Discussing the difficulty of trying accurately to 'map' English law, he points out that a 'related problem is the absence of uniformity in the reasoning and conclusions of judges, both within particular jurisdictions and from one jurisdiction to another'. Professor Waddams uses *White v Jones* (1995) as an example. He notes that 'the three majority judges and the two dissenting judges all took different approaches' and that a 'differently constituted panel of English judges could very well have reached the opposite conclusion, as has indeed occurred on this question in other common law jurisdictions' (Waddams, 2003, 13). It needs hardly to be stated that, if this is an accurate picture of

English methodology (which arguably it is, see **6.3** below), then each judgment is likely to reflect a particular philosophical and policy bias. It is the very nature of the judicial system that prevents the adoption of a single theory.

6.3 Tort and methodology

The observations by Professor Waddams noted at **6.2.5** above are fundamental to an understanding of the law of tort in general: for anyone who wishes to understand this (or in truth any) area of the common law must have an appreciation of much more than just the cases (precedents) and legislative texts that form the rule-basis of this subject area. Tort, in particular, requires a sophisticated appreciation of the common law method, which in turn requires a sound grasp of both the history and the methods of common lawyers. An understanding of the law of tort requires, in short, a thorough understanding of its methodology.

6.3.1 Absence of codes

It is of course trite knowledge that the English common law is uncodified and that the two main sources of law are case law and statute. It would, however, be dangerous if cases were approached as if they acted as the source of 'unwritten' rules and principles which can be abstracted from their factual foundations. Statutes, also, are in style often rather different from the continental codes. Moreover, these sources of law can be properly understood only in the context of the methods of reasoning which are brought to bear on them, and these methods are in many ways more open-ended than those formally used by, for example, French lawyers (but cf Lasser, 1995). In addition, there is a political and social mentality behind this reasoning that in some important ways is rather different from the political and social mentality to be found in other European countries which, at first sight, might appear to have similar principles in the area of non-contractual obligations.

6.3.2 Case law

The law of tort is one area of English law (and there are not so many these days) whose foundation is largely in precedent. The main concepts have been formed by the common lawyers over the centuries; and even where the legislature has intervened to reform or alter the law, it often uses, without definition, these concepts. The precedents can be analysed in terms of rules, but such an approach is largely misleading for several reasons.

6.3.2.1 Precedent and material facts

For a start, what binds is not actually a rule but the *ratio decidendi* of a precedent, and this is a notion that by definition includes the 'material facts' of the precedent itself. This means that an important part of any judgment in a tort case will be devoted not just to the facts of the case in hand, but equally to the facts of any relevant precedents. The problem here is that the relationship between facts and law is extremely complex. As Stephen Waddams explains, the facts 'may be stated at countless levels of particularity, and legal issues and legal rules may be formulated at countless levels of generality'. Thus no 'map or scheme could possibly classify all imaginable facts, for there is no limit whatever to the number of facts that may be postulated of a sequence of human events'. Moreover, facts do not exist independently of their perception. A small ship sinks leaving no survivors: could it be said, as a question of fact, that all aboard the vessel died *simultaneously*, or must one conclude that their deaths occurred at different times? How one processes this factual situation can of itself determine how a case will be decided (see *Re Rowland* (1963)).

6.3.2.2 Inference and logic

Yet the traditional ideal is that legal solutions in any litigation problem flow from a pre-defined set of rules through the application of a syllogism. Lord Simon explained the method in *Lupton v FA & AB Ltd* (1972, 658–9):

> A judicial decision will often be reached by a process of reasoning which can be reduced into a sort of complex syllogism, with the major premise consisting of a pre-existing rule of law (either statutory or judge-made) and with the minor premise consisting of the material facts of the case under immediate consideration. The conclusion is the decision of the case, which may or may not establish new law – in the vast majority of cases it will be merely the application of existing law to the facts judicially ascertained.

Lord Simon took as an example the case of *National Telephone Co v Baker* (1893). He said the major premise was the rule in *Rylands v Fletcher* (1866–68) and the minor premise was that the defendant brought and stored electricity on his land for his own purpose; it escaped from the land, and in so doing it injured the plaintiff's property. The conclusion was that the defendant was liable in damages to the plaintiff (or would have been but for statutory protection). The importance of this syllogistic approach is that the liability is seemingly not the result of the personal prejudices of the judges, but a matter of mechanical logic. It flows automatically from the rule in *Rylands v Fletcher* (on which see **9.3.5**, below).

6.3.2.3 Reasoning by analogy

On closer inspection, however, Lord Simon's description of the reasoning process turns out to be more ambiguous. 'Analysis shows', he said, 'that the conclusion establishes a rule of law, which may be stated as "for the purpose of the rule in *Rylands v Fletcher* electricity is *analogous* to water" or "electricity is within the rule in *Rylands v Fletcher*".' And that 'conclusion is now available as the major premise in the next case, in which some substance may be in question which in this context is not perhaps clearly analogous to water but is clearly analogous to electricity' (*Lupton*, **6.3.2.2** above, emphasis added). The point has already been made that the *ratio decidendi* of a precedent includes its material facts, and this means that when a new set of litigation facts arrives before a court, the barristers and judges need to compare two sets of facts in order to see if the new facts are governed by the *ratio* of the precedent. Lord Simon indicates that this is not actually a matter of logic but of *analogy*. This reasoning by analogy is of particular importance when it comes to extending the tort of negligence (duty of care) to new factual situations; the approach is not one of applying an abstract principle like art 1382 of the *Code civil* to a set of facts. The new situation needs to be analogous to the facts of an existing duty of care case (*Caparo Industries plc v Dickman* (1990), 635). Thus one reason why the plaintiff's action for damages was dismissed in *Goodwill v British Pregnancy Advisory Service* (1996) was because the facts of her case were not *analogous* to those of the precedent established by *White v Jones* (1995).

6.3.2.4 *Esso v Southport Corporation* (1952–56)

Reasoning by analogy does not, of course, of itself undermine the idea that legal reasoning in tort is a matter of applying rules. One is simply using analogy as a means of *applying* a legal rule. Nevertheless, it does offer a certain latitude to judges. Thus in *Esso Petroleum v Southport* (1952–56), an action for damages was brought by a local authority against the owners of a ship for damage arising out of the pollution of beaches by crude oil, when the tanker captain deliberately discharged the oil into the sea to protect the ship and its crew. Devlin J (High Court) reached his decision that the defendant was not liable because he drew an analogy between ships on the sea and motor vehicles on the highway, thus allowing the authority of *Holmes v Mather* (1875), which insisted that the victim of a highway accident must prove fault, to govern the case. Denning LJ (Court of Appeal), in contrast, used a different analogy. The causing of damage by pollution was, for him, more like the image of a horse polluting the highway, thus giving rise to a public nuisance and a line of authorities which included *Benjamin v Storr* (1874). This nuisance case, and others, have been interpreted as laying down that such a liability could be avoided only by the defendant disproving fault. The defendants had failed to prove that their ship was seaworthy when it put to sea and thus, for the Court of Appeal, the company would be liable to the local authority. In the House of Lords, the vision of Devlin J was re-adopted, and judgment was finally given for the defendants.

The fundamental reasoning point that flows from *Esso* is, accordingly, that the difference of result between the High Court and House of Lords on the one hand, and the Court of Appeal on the other, was not a matter of reasoning by logic. It was a question of different analogies. And this reasoning by analogy aspect to tort is inherent in the very concept of the *ratio decidendi*, the basis of which is as much the material facts of a precedent as any identifiable rule.

6.3.2.5 Policy and functionalism

The complexity of reasoning in tort does not end with analogy. In *Home Office v Dorset Yacht Co* (1970), Lord Diplock gave his own description of the reasoning methods used in negligence (duty of care) cases. At a formal level it was a matter of the *induction* out of all the duty of care precedents of a proposition about situations in which the courts have recognised a duty of care to exist. This induction stage was followed by a second, *deductive* stage, whereby the facts of the case before the court were examined in the light of the induced proposition. If the facts display all the characteristics to be found in the induced proposition, 'the conclusion follows that a duty of care does arise in the case for decision'. However, Lord Diplock did not stop there. He went on to admit that there was an element of choice in reaching the conclusion, since the facts of the case before the court will by definition *not* contain all the characteristics to be found in the induced proposition (and that is why the case has gone to court). This choice, said Lord Diplock, 'is exercised by making a *policy* decision' (at 1059, emphasis added). This notion of policy has become a major reasoning focal point in the contemporary law of tort (see, eg, *Hill v Chief Constable of West Yorks* (1989)).

Yet what does it mean? In terms of methodology, policy reasoning can be contrasted with syllogistic or logical reasoning in that solutions are not determined by way of *inference* from a model of rules. It is not like saying if A=B and B=C therefore A *must* equal C. Instead it represents a different kind of method called *functional* reasoning. A solution is fashioned in terms of the intended social *purpose* of the rule in question. In other words, one asks: what is the function of this rule?

6.3.2.6 *Spartan Steel v Martin* (1973)

A good example of this approach is to be found in the important tort precedent of *Spartan Steel & Alloys v Martin & Co* (1973), where an action for damages was brought in negligence by the owner of an alloys factory against contractors working in the street outside the plaintiffs' premises. The contractors had carelessly cut through an electricity cable and this deprived the owners of the factory of electricity for 15 hours or more, with the result that the valuable metal in their furnaces hardened and caused damage. In addition to claiming compensation for the physical damage to the furnaces and the metal, the factory owners also demanded damages for the economic loss caused by their inability to use the furnaces during the power cut. Now there is, or at least was, a well-established rule that no duty of care in negligence exists in respect of pure economic loss. If one focused simply on the claim for lost profit, it would appear as a matter of logical inference that the factory owners were not entitled to damages for this head of damage. Yet not only was the rule ambiguous in this situation – there exist cases that have permitted a claimant who has suffered some physical damage to recover for any economic loss 'parasitic' to it – but some lawyers were beginning to question whether the rule itself was justified. Edmund Davies LJ, who dissented in *Spartan*, thought that the fine line between economic loss associated with physical damage and pure financial loss had nothing to do with legal principle.

Lord Denning MR, as one of the majority, took a different view. He certainly discussed the precedents but asserted that at 'bottom ... the question of recovering economic loss is one of policy' (at 36). He later explained that the cutting off of the supply of electricity is 'a hazard which we all run'; that in general 'most people are content to take the risk on themselves'; that 'they do not go running round to their solicitor'; and that this 'is a healthy attitude which the law should encourage' (at 38). The policy, in other words, is to spread the loss arising from hazards. Physical damage caused through the fault of another can be transferred onto the shoulders of the person at fault; but the *function* of the economic loss rule in negligence is to limit the amount that the defendant has to bear. These economic losses are spread more widely and between perpetrators and victims.

6.3.2.7 Interests and rights

One might note here how this economic loss rule can be translated into yet another concept that often has an important *functional* role to play in tort reasoning. This is the notion of an *interest* (see PETL, art 2:102). The tort of negligence will protect some interests like personal injury and physical damage to property, but will often exclude the pure economic interest (see, eg, Consumer Protection Act 1987, s 5(1)). In this context the notion of an interest is basically descriptive; it cannot in itself provide the *normative* force that will determine whether or not the interest is one that can attract compensation. This force has to come from a concept that does have normative force, such as a 'right' or a 'duty' (determined in turn by the existence of a cause of action such as trespass or negligence; and see PETL, art 1:101). Consequently, the law expresses the economic loss rule in terms of the defendant's 'duty' (no duty of care) or the claimant's 'right' (no right to economic loss).

Nevertheless, there are occasions in tort when 'interest' can be used in a normative way. In *Burris v Azadani* (1995), the Court of Appeal had to decide if a woman being harassed by a particular man was entitled to the injunction that had been granted at first instance to prevent him from coming within 250 yards of her address. The man claimed that the injunction went too far and prevented him from exercising his lawful 'right' to use the public highway that passed by her house. However, Sir Thomas Bingham MR analysed the situation in terms of two *interests* that needed to be reconciled. The defendant's liberty must be respected; but, equally, 'the plaintiff has an interest which the court must be astute to protect'. Normally the court would grant an injunction only to restrain an actual tort, such as trespass or interference with goods. However, 'the court may properly judge that in the plaintiff's *interest* – and also, but indirectly, the defendant's – a wider measure of restraint is called for' (at 1380–81, emphasis added). The Court of Appeal accordingly upheld the injunction on the functional basis of an interest.

6.3.2.8 Axiological (moral) reasoning

In addition to logical, analogical and functional (policy) reasoning, the judges will often in tort cases employ moral (axiological) reasons. In *Smith New Court Securities Ltd v Scrimgeour Vickers* (1997), the House of Lords had to decide whether a more generous measure of damages could be awarded in the tort of deceit than would have been the case if the claim had been one in, say, negligence. Lord Steyn stated that 'as between the fraudster and the innocent party, moral considerations militate in favour of requiring the fraudster to bear the risk of misfortunes directly caused by his fraud.' Moreover, he made 'no apology for referring to moral considerations' since the 'law and morality are inextricably interwoven.' Indeed, to 'a large extent the law is simply formulated and declared morality' (at 280). A couple of years later, Lord Steyn made very similar comments in *McFarlane v Tayside Health Board* (2000). Here he accepted that the role of the court is to apply the law; but the 'judges' sense of the moral answer to a question, or the justice of the case, has been one of the great shaping forces of the common law' (at 82). Other judges have exhibited similar views. In *Fairchild v Glenhaven Funeral Services Ltd* (2002), Lord Hoffmann stated that

> as between the employer in breach of duty and the employee who has lost his life in consequence of a period of exposure to risk to which that employer has contributed, I think it would be both inconsistent with the policy of the law imposing the duty and morally wrong for your Lordships to impose causal requirements which exclude liability. (at 75)

6.3.2.9 Argumentation

Several other methodological points need to be stressed. The first is that it is not just the judges who are the sources of law; they make their decisions on the basis of arguments presented to them by the parties' barristers (see Weir, 2005, 890). Indeed, the judges rely on the barristers to research the law (*Copeland v Smith* (2000)). The presentation of these arguments is itself dialectical (for and against) because of the nature of the legal process;

thus nearly all English judgments consider in turn the arguments presented first by the claimant's counsel and then by the defendant's counsel. The judge then decides between them, sometimes after a lengthy analysis of the precedents (and/or the statutory provisions) and sometimes after a detailed consideration of the factual context. This decision is often supported by a series of justifications that may, as we have seen, use reasoning internal to the law (eg, the interpretation and application of a precedent or text) or external to strict positive law (eg, arguments of policy or morality).

Recourse to metaphor is not unusual. For example, in *Spartan Steel* (**6.3.2.6**, above), another form of reasoning employed by Lord Denning to reject the claim for 'parasitic' damages was to say that he did not like the very word 'parasite'. 'A "parasite",' he said, 'is one who is a useless hanger-on sucking the substance out of others' and the 'phrase "parasitic damages" conveys to my mind the idea of damages which ought not in justice to be awarded, but which somehow or other have been allowed to get through by hanging on to others.' And if 'such be the concept underlying the doctrine, then the sooner it is got rid of the better' (at 35). In contrast to this reasoning, one might note that in *White v Jones* (1995) the decision of the majority allowing the plaintiff to succeed for what was in effect a pure economic loss claim was based on 'practical justice', a form of argumentation blending the *functional* with the *axiological*. A similar intermixing of the functional with the moral is often to be found in Lord Steyn's, and sometimes Lord Hoffmann's, judgments. Indeed Lord Hoffmann often brings in arguments from economics (see *Transco plc v Stockport MBC* (2004), § 29; but cf Lord Hobhouse, at §§ 55–60)

Finally one should, perhaps, bear in mind Tony Weir's observation that until recently all senior judges were, before their elevation, practitioners who had largely specialised in a particular area of law. On the bench they immediately become generalists with the result that they 'are often not at all familiar with the area of law being discussed before them by the barristers' and thus 'are sometimes less dismissive of feeble arguments than they might be, perhaps out of deference to their future colleagues'. And even when they do reach 'the correct result, [they] may not be able to give the best reasons for it' (Weir, 2005, 890). Of course what judges declare has legal authority, but that does not mean that their reasoning is not open to critical appraisal.

6.3.3 Statutory interpretation

The foundational source of the law of torts is the common law (precedent). However, legislative intervention and the methods that attach to the interpretation of statutes cannot now be ignored in tort, even if the intervention is relatively modest. In the remedial field of damages the intervention is such that the texts have an important role in personal injury claims (see Fatal Accidents Act 1976, Damages Act 1996, Social Security (Recovery of Benefits) Act 1997, etc). And in the area of liability for defective premises (occupiers' liability) the foundation is almost entirely statutory, as will be seen in **Chapter 9**.

The methods applied to the interpretation and application of statutory texts are traditionally seen as being rather different from the application of precedents since the starting point is not analogy with pre-existing factual situations. The method is *hermeneutical* in the more traditional sense of working directly on the words of a text (signifier) to discover what Parliament 'intended' (signified). It is a matter of focusing on the text and *interpreting* the words in a way that will give expression to the author's intention. But this 'intention' is normally to be gauged only from the words of the text, with the result that, in order to avoid circularity, other reasoning methods find themselves creeping into the justifications. These other methods are, as one might expect, those used in case law analysis and so, for example, one can apply a statutory text in a *literal* (see, eg, *Fisher v Bell* (1961)) or a *functional* manner (what is the purpose of the statute?). The courts seem to oscillate between the two methods, or indeed sometimes to combine them (see, eg, *Birmingham CC v Oakley* (2001)).

Reasoning by *analogy* does not usually have a direct role, in as much as one cannot normally use a statutory provision such as the Animals Act 1971, s 2(1) as the basis of creating by analogy a strict liability for, say, dangerous objects other than dangerous animals. But recourse to images by way of analogy is often used to test whether or not a word or phrase covers a particular fact ('an elephant is difficult to define but easy to recognise': *Young v Sun Alliance Insurance* (1977), *per* Lawton LJ, at 107). One might add that traditional distinctions, such as those between physical and mental injury (*Morris v KLM Royal Dutch Airlines* (2001)) and physical and pure economic damage (*Merlin v British Nuclear Fuels plc* (1990)) can still influence the way texts are interpreted.

In the past the approach was often quite literal, the judges stopping at the text itself and not considering the contextual situation (see, eg, *Haigh v Charles W Ireland* (1973)). It is not what the legislature aims at but what it hits that counts (*St Aubyn v Att-Gen* (1952), 32). But some judges now approach statutory interpretation in a more flexible way. Thus, where the statute is ambiguous the judges have abandoned their rule that they could not look at Parliamentary debates; and where human rights are involved, the courts are under a statutory duty to interpret in such a way that, if at all possible, the Act in question is compatible with European Convention rights (Human Rights Act 1998, s 3(1)). However, artificial distinctions are still to be found, especially in cases where, for example, the judges feel they are being forced to make policy decisions which would be better made by Parliament, especially if there are huge financial implications (see, eg, *Birmingham CC v Oakley* (2001)).

The methodology associated with literal interpretation might also be termed a 'shallow' hermeneutical approach in that it takes as its point of focus only the text. This, of course, restricts the type of reasoning and research that can be applied, for the emphasis is on the dictionary and on technical legal concepts rather than on the function of the rule. One searches, for example, for a definition of a 'road' and, logically applying it to the facts in issue, arrives at the conclusion that it does not include a 'car park' (*Clarke v Kato* (1998)). Had one looked at the function of the actual statute, and asked whether it had as its *policy* the exclusion of the claimant from receiving compensation, a wider definition of a 'road' might have resulted. One might add that this lack of partnership between judge and legislator has, in turn, resulted in textual characteristics that can only be described as detailed if not opaque (see, eg, *Mirvahedy v Henley* (2003)).

6.3.4 Concluding remarks

It is by no means easy to offer any general summary of the reasoning methods used in tort. One can say that judges by tradition focus on the case in hand and their primary aim, even in the House of Lords, is only to settle a dispute between two parties (*Read v J Lyons & Co* (1947), 175). It is not the judges' job to rationalise the law. Yet this does not always mean they are backward-looking and irrational; what it does mean that they take at best 'one step at a time' (Lord Simon in *Miliangos v George Frank (Textiles) Ltd* (1976), 481–2), working from factual situation to factual situation, often by way of analogy. Thus English judges, on the whole, do not see the common law as a system of formal positive rules and concepts waiting to be applied in a logical manner. They tend to see problems in terms of their substantive social, moral and economic context, these contexts often being encapsulated in concepts such as 'practical' or even 'distributive justice' (Lord Steyn in *McFarlane v Tayside Health Board*, at 82).

This is not to suggest that they have abandoned 'applying the law'; but in the application judges are quite prepared to have recourse to open-ended reasoning tools such as 'policy', 'reasonableness' and 'justice'. Of course, different judges can take different approaches. Indeed, sometimes the same judge can adopt differing approaches in different cases. One might compare, for example, the judgment of Devlin J in *Esso v Southport* with that of Denning LJ in the same case (see **6.3.2.4**, above). One adopted a reasoning approach to liability founded on general principle; the other started out from liability and duty attaching to particular tort categories. In other cases Lord Denning seemingly abandoned the category approach in favour of broad-based principle (see, eg, *Letang v Cooper* (1965)). Perhaps Stephen Waddams best sums up legal reasoning in private law cases. 'It is not so much that various *alternative* approaches are *permissible*', he says, 'as that various *complementary* approaches are *necessary* (to the understanding of a complex phenomenon)' (Waddams, 2003, 232).

7 Liability and Intentional Harm

The frontiers between tort and other areas of the law of obligations suggest that tort obligations have a substantive existence of their own. Yet, as we have already seen with regard to contract, the notion of liability acts as a meeting point between the *vinculum iuris* (legal bond) and the *actio* (remedy). In the civilian world the distinction between obligation and liability is once again attracting attention, even if in the common law the distinction is often masked by the emphasis on causes of action and on remedies. Accordingly, liability, as a focal point in itself, has attracted its own theorising in that it raises a general question about accident liability and the factual sources of such accidents.

7.1 Liability and fault

In the civil law systems non-contractual compensation claims have traditionally been closely interrelated with fault (PETL, art 1:101(2)(a)). Indeed, until relatively recently, it could generally be said that loss and damage accidentally caused would lie where it fell, and could be transferred onto the shoulders of another only if that other was to blame for the harm. Roman law was particularly influential here given the central importance of *injuria* (wrongfulness) and *culpa* (blame) in both contractual (see D.13.6.5) and non-contractual damage claims (D.47.10.1pr). However, this Roman foundation was given added support by Christian notions of individual responsibility in the later civil law, with the result that fault became an 'axiomatic truth' (see Zimmermann, 1996, 1033–35).

With the rise of industry, technology and, later, widespread insurance this individualistic attitude to liability began to change and a second principle developed to challenge fault. This is the principle of risk (PETL, art 1:101(2)(b)). The problem with fault is that, when viewed from the position of the victim, it is an arbitrary way of determining who should receive compensation, especially when statistics indicate that the accident rate is relatively constant from one year to the next. Moreover, the statistics suggest that making wrongdoers pay was not a deterrent; indeed, the existence of (often compulsory) insurance could, anyway, be said to negative such deterrence. Nevertheless, despite the growth of risk liability in France and in some other systems, the fault principle is proving harder to abandon than one might think. Its moral force seems irrepressible and it does have the economic advantage of limiting liability, thus providing scope for liberty of action for those engaged in activities that ultimately benefit the public (cf *Tomlinson v Congleton BC* (2004)).

In English law the fault principle remains central to tort liability in a number of ways. First, despite the existence of several strict liability torts, the House of Lords went far in indicating that, in an action for personal injuries (by far the most important type of tort claim), fault normally had to be proved (*Read v J Lyons & Co* (1947); confirmed *Transco v Stockport MBC* (2004)). Secondly, the 'pull of the negligence principle – pay for the foreseeable harm you are at fault in causing – is immensely strong' (Weir, 1998, 137); so strong, indeed, that it has tended to subvert other ideas. Thirdly, as we have seen, English law has committed itself to no single theory or aim when it comes to tort liability. 'It cannot lightly be taken for granted, even as a matter of theory, that the purpose of the law of tort is compensation' said Lord Wilberforce; as 'a matter of practice English law has not committed itself to any of these theories, it may have been wiser than it knew' (*Cassell & Co Ltd v Broome* (1972), 1114). English doctrine can sometimes be similarly sceptical, although academics on the whole like to propound theories, even if far removed from judicial reality.

In fact, Lord Wilberforce's statement hides a continuing commitment to an 'individualistic philosophy' (Lord Hoffmann in *Reeves v Comr of Police for the Metropolis* (2000), 368) and to the requirement of fault. At a formal level liability is dependent upon the existence or non-existence of a cause of action, and a 'cause of action is simply a factual situation the existence of which entitles one person to obtain from the court a remedy against another person' (Diplock LJ in *Letang v Cooper* (1965), 242). And in tort these causes of action are traditionally presented in list form, seemingly bound together only by the alphabet, with the result that, at first sight, it might appear that fault is a requirement of some but not all torts. However, when tort is viewed from the perspective of damage, the picture changes, in that personal injury damage and, to some extent, physical damage to property usually require fault before liability is established (strict liability cases becoming the exception). Fault for this purpose does include illegal acts (breach of a statute), and in the area of industrial injuries this gave rise to the tort of breach of statutory duty, which in turn resulted in a marked shift towards risk (*Groves v Wimborne* (1898)). However, such a regime was rejected in respect of traffic accidents (*Phillips v Britannia Hygienic Laundry Co* (1923)).

The position in France seems quite different in that the French *Cour de cassation*, during the 20th century, created a whole area of risk liability on the basis of art 1384 of the *Code civil*. As the advocate general stated, in one of the principal decisions holding the family liable for a traffic accident caused by a young person: 'In civil liability law the notion of fault is becoming more and more restricted and the need to compensate victims for their harm is leading to the search for objective situations where a right to compensation will flow automatically.' And he continued, the 'liability for harm done by things under one's control, that of employers for their employees, the law of 5 July 1985 on traffic accident victims are examples of this' (Cass.civ. 19.2.1997). One should add that the French public law courts have been equally adventurous in developing no fault liability. This does not mean that liability for fault under art 1382 of the *Code civil* is redundant. Indeed this is not so. What it means is that liability can now be presented under a number of broad general headings, and these headings can perhaps be used to map out a general pattern of liability (and see also PETL, art 1:101). These patterns of liability will be the focus of this chapter and the next.

7.2 Liability for individual acts (1): general elements

The first head of liability is the one that normally attaches to fault, and it is expressed in its most concise and abstract form by art 1382 of the *Code civil*. According to this article, three conditions must be proved before liability is established:

(a) damage;
(b) fault; and
(c) causation.

Each condition has given rise to a mass of case law and doctrine in Western legal systems, and it would be idle even to try to summarise this material, or to try to draw out of it any normative propositions that can be succinctly stated. Several points ought nevertheless be made about each of these conditions of liability.

7.2.1 Damage

Physical damage to person or property is normally easy enough to identify. One can point to the broken limbs, or to the wrecked car. However, psychological damage can be much more difficult and has given rise to problems in various legal systems. Pure economic loss is equally problematic in some systems (and see PETL, art 2:102(4)). Put another way, harm which constitutes a wrong ought no doubt to be remedied, but 'the world is full of harm for which the law furnishes no remedy'. And thus, for example, 'a trader owes no duty of care to avoid injuring his rivals by destroying their long-established businesses' (Lord Rodger in *D v East Berks Community Health NHS Trust* (2005), § 100). In fact the more intangible the damage – for example, loss of a chance – the more likely it is that the case law in Western systems will be complex. In common law systems damage problems arising out of accidents are normally dealt with under the duty of care question (cf **8.1.3**, below). However, negligence is not the only tort. In private nuisance, for example, an important distinction is made between tangible and intangible damage (in respect of the defence of locality); and, more generally, the relationship between damage and the remedy of damages has created a whole sub-section of case law precedents (since damage is defined in relation to 'a legally protected interest': PETL, art 2:101).

A further problem that arises in the common law is the possibility of liability in situations where no damage is proved. Some torts, such as trespass and defamation, are said to be actionable *per se* (see now *Jameel (Yousef) v Dow Jones & Co* (2005)); and, with respect to the latter, large sums of money have been awarded in situations where the relationship between compensation and discernible damage can appear tenuous. In fact several unfortunate defendants have been forced to pay damages for failing to prove true in court things that subsequently turned out to be perfectly true. Trespass is a little different in that this tort has a range of aims and objectives. In situations where it is protecting constitutional rights (eg, false imprisonment) the awarding of damages is made to fulfil aims other than direct compensation (and this is true of abuse of public office as well: *Watkins v Home Secretary* (2005)). There are intangible aspects. In other trespass situations the award of damages might be made to fulfil restitutionary aims (cf **Chapter 11**). This restitutionary aim lies behind some of the exemplary damages cases, that is to say situations where damages are awarded not to compensate but to punish.

7.2.2 Fault

The second requirement for liability is normally fault (PETL, art 4:101). In civil law systems fault is a broad category encompassing deliberate harm at one extreme and the slightest degree of negligence at the other (D.9.2.44pr). These two poles turn out, however, to be more complex than mere points at either end of a spectrum. In the case of deliberate harm, liability is based on what might be called a subjective state of mind; carelessly caused harm, in contrast, is different in that one cannot talk of a particular state of mind. Thus in Roman law the existence and non-existence of fault was determined objectively: 'to do a certain act at a certain time and place was *culpa*, but at another time or place was not' (Lawson, 1950, 38). The result was that even a learner (mule) driver could be held liable for damage caused by his inexperience since, objectively, he should have known that he presented a danger to others (D.9.2.8.1). English law has arrived at a similar conclusion (*Nettleship v Weston* (1971)). One effect of this approach is that fault comes to embrace not just behaviour as such but also risk, which in turn can act as a means of moving liability beyond fault.

The idea of minimal fault as sufficient to trigger liability is usually to be found in most systems, although different degrees of fault can result in different measures of damages if not different forms of liability (*Smith New Court Securities v Vickers Ltd* (1997)). But of course proof can be a problem (as the victims of the Potters Bar rail crash have discovered: letter, *The Guardian*, 18 September 2003). Ideas of risk can again come into play here in that the law might deem some forms of damage arising from some forms of activity as raising a presumption of fault (PETL, art 4:201); the onus will then be on the defendant to disprove fault if he wishes to escape liability. Equally, other activities might be treated more favourably by the courts, especially if they are perceived to have a high social and moral value (for example, cricket: *Bolton v Stone* (1951); *Miller v Jackson* (1977)).

In the common law fault is not employed as a generic category since liability did not develop through abstract principle but through a system of individualised forms of action. The result is that different types of fault give rise to different torts. Fraudulent behaviour that causes damage will give rise to deceit, while negligent damage must be remedied through the tort of negligence. Deliberate physical harm to another will normally be a trespass and certain kinds of abuse of power by public officials may result in other specific torts (see, eg, *Gibbs v Rea* (1998)). Economic loss deliberately caused attracts yet other torts. One point that must be made at the outset is this. In several famous late 19th-century decisions the House of Lords confirmed that the intention and damage are not sufficient in themselves to generate liability in tort; there must be something more (see, eg, *Bradford Corporation v Pickles* (1895)). Nevertheless, this categorisation of fault into specific kinds associated with specific torts has been breaking down to some extent with respect to negligent behaviour. For the 'pull of the negligence principle ... is immensely strong' (Weir, 1998, 137).

7.2.2.1 No fault liability (strict liability)

Yet the expansion of negligence as a general basis of liability in the common law world implies that there is a field of liability where fault does not have to be proved. In French law such strict liability is associated with art 1384 of the *Code civil*, which imposes liability upon a defendant in respect of persons and things under his control and which cause damage. The PETL base such liability on abnormally dangerous activities (art 5:101) and on liability for 'auxiliaries' (arts 1:101(2)(c), 6:102(1)). In English law, as one might expect, there is no equivalent general provision; instead there is a number of specific 'strict liability' torts, such as trespass, public and private nuisance, breach of statutory duty, the rule in *Rylands v Fletcher* and defamation. There is also a more general rule that an employer will automatically be liable for a tort committed by an employee acting in the course of his employment (vicarious liability).

7.2.3 Causation

The third condition for liability is that there must be a causal link between the blameworthy act (or even non-blameworthy act in the case of liability without fault) and the damage (see **Chapter 10**). This is generally regarded as the most difficult, yet philosophically intriguing, part of obligations liability, and the conundrums start in Roman law itself (cf D.9.2.11pr) to end up as competing theories in modern legal thinking (PETL, arts 3:101–3:106). As a result the topic has two distinctive dimensions. There is the academic dimension, dominated by theories of causation, and there is the case law aspect, where many judges profess a 'common sense' or 'practical' approach.

Whether or not theory or common sense offers any kind of philosophical insight is a matter that can be decided only by examining the massive case law and doctrine. But what cannot be doubted is that in most systems intuition and social policy have a certain role in the recognition or not of a causal link. Lord Hoffmann illustrated this with an interesting example of a mountaineer, concerned about his knee, who visits a doctor before undertaking a climb. The doctor carelessly passes the man's knee as fit and so the mountaineer sets off up the mountain, only to suffer an injury that has nothing to do with the knee. Assuming that the climber would not have undertaken the climb if the doctor had not been careless, is the doctor to be liable for the injury on the mountain? According to Lord Hoffmann, to impose liability 'offends common sense because it makes the doctor responsible for consequences which, though in general terms foreseeable, do not appear to have a sufficient causal connection with the subject matter of the duty'. As the Law Lord goes on to explain, the 'doctor was asked for information on only one of the considerations which might affect the safety of the mountaineer on the expedition' and thus there 'seems no reason of *policy* which requires that the negligence of the doctor should require the transfer to him of all the foreseeable risks of the expedition' (*Banque Bruxelles Lambert SA v Eagle Star Insurance Co Ltd* (1997), 355–6, emphasis added). Two recent cases, one English and one French, also act as good examples of the importance of morality, justice and factual perception (Cass.ass.plén 17.11.2000 and *Fairchild v Glenhaven Funeral Services Ltd* (2002)).

7.3 Liability for individual acts (2): intentional harm

Most English textbooks on the law of tort approach liability either from the position of particular categories of causes of action – trespass, negligence, nuisance, defamation and so on – or from the perspective of particular interests invaded (physical, economic, reputation, etc) (cf PETL, art 2:102). Given the history of the forms of action and the absence of codification, such an approach is understandable. This cause of action approach to tort means, however, that it is not easy to look at tort strictly from the position of types of behaviour. Moreover, the line between intention and negligence is sometimes difficult, if not impossible, to make (*Wainwright v Home Office* (2003), § 37). Nevertheless, a types-of-behaviour perspective can be useful when it comes to an understanding of how liability functions in a European comparative context, which in turn may provide new insights for analysing litigation problems.

7.3.1 Intention and damage

It would be tempting to say that all intentionally caused damage ought to be actionable by the victim, but a moment's reflection will soon reveal that such a principle would be untenable. The deliberate causing of *physical* injury without legal justification is prima facie actionable, and this includes psychological injury (nervous shock) (*Wilkinson v Downton* (1897); cf *Wainwright v Home Office* (2003), §§ 36–47). Indeed, to put someone in fear of violence can amount to trespass (*Read v Coker* (1853)), as might an indirect act which leads to personal injury (*Fagan v Metropolitan Police Commissioner* (1969)). Maliciously causing someone to be prosecuted can be a tort (*Martin v Watson* (1996)), as can the malicious spreading of false statements about a person and (or) his business. Maliciously abusing the legal process is equally actionable (*Keegan v Chief Constable of Merseyside* (2003)). Creating a noise on one's property with the deliberate intention of annoying a neighbour will amount to a nuisance, since no one has the right to create noise and deliberately causing it will by definition amount to an unreasonable use of land (*Christie v Davey* (1893)). However, intention alone can never constitute a tort since it is not the behaviour that generates liability in English law. Liability is always a matter of a cause of action, and thus a claimant must prove the constituent elements of such a category (*Bradford Corporation v Pickles* (1895)).

The deliberate causing of *economic loss* is more difficult, for if it were made generally actionable capitalism would no doubt grind to a halt. Deliberately caused economic loss will be actionable only in certain circumstances. Thus at common law (but not now under European law) one trader has the right to ruin a competitor by grossly under-pricing his goods or services (*Mogul SS Co v McGregor, Gow & Co* (1892)); only if the trader commits an 'unlawful act' might the loss be actionable. The difficulty in this area of 'economic torts' is to decide what amounts to unlawfulness for the purpose of a claim. The courts have attempted to define liability by requiring the existence of a number of conditional elements, such as an intention directly to injure coupled with some kind of objective wrong (illegal threat, nuisance, etc). But many cases are not free from ambiguity and circularity of reasoning.

7.3.2 Intention and legitimate interest

The main difficulty with these economic torts (a rather specialised area outside of this introductory survey) is to define their limits. Not every intentional injury causing economic loss will be actionable, otherwise all industrial action by ill-treated workers would be tortious (although much of it is) and all calls to boycott a product or service would equally be actionable. One notion developed by the courts is that of *legitimate interest* as related to the behaviour of the defendant. Thus if the defendant is acting to protect a well-estab-lished interest, this may give rise either to the non-existence of any economic tort or to a defence based on justification. For example, a trade association can impose fines on its members and any threat of expulsion for non-payment will not amount to blackmail or an economic tort (*Thorne v Motor Trade Association* (1937)). Even behaviour that is illegal might not be actionable in tort if it was not aimed at the claimant (*Lonrho v Shell Petroleum Co Ltd (No 2)* (1982)). However, if a defendant intentionally damages a claimant in circumstances where he has no interest of his own to protect, it may be that the damage will be actionable even if the behaviour itself does not actually fit into any civil or criminal wrong category (*Gulf Oil (GB) Ltd v Page* (1987); cf *Femis Bank Ltd v Lazar* (1991)).

It is of course these latter cases that make this area so complex, particularly where the remedy sought is an interim (interlocutory) (emergency) injunction rather than damages. But if one was to try to formulate a rule-of-thumb principle it would be based on the idea that the direct, intentional invasion of another's commercial interest might well be action-able if the means used are unlawful and there is an absence of any justification on the defendant's part. What amounts to 'direct', to 'unlawful' or to 'justification' is of course by no means clear, and so if one is able to add a proprietary dimension – the defendant is interfering with the claimant's 'property *right*' – it sometimes gives further conceptual strength to the granting of a remedy (*Ex p Island Records* (1978); cf *Lonrho v Shell*, above).

7.3.3 Intentional torts

The nature of the damage is one important key, then, when it comes to harm intentionally caused. Yet despite movements toward some kind of general principle with respect both to physical and to economic loss, the only safe approach to liability is via specific existing torts (*Wainwright v Home Office* (2003)). Some of the principal torts dealing with intentionally (or maliciously) caused harm thus need to be examined in outline. As there is no common denominator, save a particular state of mind, the torts are arranged alphabetically.

7.3.3.1 Abuse of civil (and criminal) process

Abuse of the criminal process can give rise, as we shall see (at **7.3.3.10**), to the tort of malicious prosecution. Abuse of the civil process is also now a tort, and one that seems to be an extension by analogy of malicious prosecution (see **7.3.3.10**, below). Whereas mali-cious prosecution lies only in respect of criminal proceedings, the tort of abuse of process extends across the whole spectrum of civil proceedings. The foundational modern case is *Speed Seal Products v Paddington* (1985), which in some ways is a rather weak authority being only a striking out action (whether a claimant has an arguable case). Nevertheless, there have been subsequent first instance decisions that fall under this heading of abuse of process, and the whole developmental logic of the law of tort would suggest that this is an established head of liability. One such (relatively) recent decision is *Gibbs v Rea* (1998), which establishes that the malicious procurement of a search warrant is actionable if four conditions are fulfilled. These conditions, set out in a recent case, are: '(1) a suc-cessful application for a search warrant, (2) lack of reasonable and probable cause to make the application, (3) malice and (4) resultant damage arising from the issue or execu-tion of the warrant' (*Keegan v Chief Constable of Merseyside* (2003), § 13, *per* Kennedy LJ).

What is interesting about this tort is that it seems to be a cause of action independent of malicious prosecution, abuse of public office, and even perhaps abuse of civil process (although for convenience it is listed here under this more general heading), thus confirming that an alphabetical list of causes of action is still the approach when it comes to intentional damage.

7.3.3.2 Abuse of public office (misfeasance in public office)

Another 'administrative' tort in some ways analogous to malicious prosecution and abuse of civil process is abuse of public office (or now misfeasance in public office). This tort can be brought by an individual against a public officer who has intentionally or recklessly damaged the claimant. The history and the requirements of the tort have been fully explored recently by the House of Lords in *Three Rivers DC v Bank of England* (2003), where Lord Steyn set out the conditions for liability (at 191ff). These are that there must be an abusive exercise of power by a public officer aimed at the claimant, or a class of persons in which the claimant belongs, and the claimant himself or herself must have a 'sufficient interest' in the claim, which will no doubt be fulfilled if serious economic loss (or other damage) is suffered. The abuse must also be the cause of the claimant's loss. As Lord Millett observed, the 'tort is an intentional tort which can be committed only by a public official' and from 'this two things follow'. The 'tort cannot be committed negligently or inadvertently' and, secondly, the 'core concept is abuse of power', which 'in turn involves other concepts, such as dishonesty, bad faith, and improper purpose' (at 235). This emphasis on abuse of power by a public official means that the victim of abuse may well be able to sue even if he or she cannot prove substantial physical or economic harm; an invasion of a constitutional right might be enough to found a claim which could result in exemplary damages (*Watkins v Home Secretary* (2005)).

7.3.3.3 Conversion

Where one person aims his intention to injure not directly at the claimant but at the claimant's tangible property, there is the possibility of the defendant being liable for wrongful interference with goods. This notion of wrongful interference is possibly not a tort in itself but a statutory creation which includes trespass, negligence and conversion (Torts (Interference with Goods) Act 1977, s 1). Trespass to goods involves a direct interference with *possession*, and thus a defendant will be liable if, for example, he deliberately rides off on the claimant's bicycle simply to annoy him. If the defendant were to sell the bicycle claiming it as his own, the claimant would have a claim in conversion, a tort remedying interference with *title*. Lord Nicholls has recently stated that conversion of goods 'can occur in so many different circumstances that framing a definition of universal application is well nigh impossible'. However, he said that there are in general three basic features to the tort:

(a) that the defendant's conduct was inconsistent with the rights of the owner or other person entitled to possession;
(b) that the conduct was deliberate and not accidental; and
(c) that 'the conduct was so extensive an encroachment on the rights of the owner as to exclude him from the use and possession of the goods'.

Lord Nicholls then added that these requirements are to be contrasted with lesser acts of interference such as trespass or negligence (*Kuwait Airways v Iraqi Airways* (2002), § 39). Conversion, then, can truly be an intentional tort, although it can also be committed even in situations where the defendant is innocent of any fault (see, eg, *Willis & Son v British Car Auctions* (1978)). Finally, it seems that the tort of conversion applies only to goods and cannot be extended to a chose in action (*OBG Ltd v Allan* (2005)).

7.3.3.4 Deceit

'For a plaintiff to succeed in the tort of deceit', said Hobhouse LJ, 'it is necessary for him to prove that (1) the representation was fraudulent, (2) it was material and (3) it induced the plaintiff to act (to his detriment)'. And a 'representation is material when its tendency, or its natural and probable result, is to induce the representee to act on the faith of it in the kind of way in which he is proved to have in fact acted'. And, he added, the 'test is objective' (*Downs v Chappell* (1997), 433). This is an old tort and is the basis of most claims for damages where the loss arises from the defendant's fraud. Accordingly, it can often have a role in situations involving contracts that have been entered into as a result of one party's fraudulent misrepresentation. The main difficulty facing claimants is that they must prove fraud. However, thanks to statute, any misrepresentation that induces a contract will now be actionable in tort without the claimant having to prove fraud; the defendant can escape liability only by proving the absence of fault (Misrepresentation Act 1967, s 2(1)).

7.3.3.5 Defamation

Defamation occurs when one person publishes an untrue statement that is calculated to injure the reputation of another, and it is very easily incurred even in situations where the writer and (or) publisher had no intention of defaming the claimant. It is, therefore, a central tort committed by a person who deliberately sets out to damage another through the publication of statements. Although easily incurred – almost any statement critical of another will be defamatory provided it is published (defamation is strictly a three-party tort) – there are three important defences:

(a) justification (truth);
(b) fair comment; and
(c) privilege.

As a result of the Human Rights Act 1998, the defence of privilege has been extended in recent years to cover the 'reasonable journalist' who reports in good faith a story in the public interest that turns out to be untrue (*Reynolds v Times Newspapers* (1999); cf *Jameel (Mohammed) v Wall Street Journal* (2005)).

7.3.3.6 Harassment

If one moves from the business interest to what might be called the individual interest of freedom from a deliberately caused mental distress, a number of established torts can be relevant. As we shall see below, threats of violence might be a trespass and deliberate harassment of a neighbour can amount to a private nuisance. However, although there is no general tort of harassment (or privacy) at common law (confirmed in *Wainwright v Home Office* (2003)), there is now a statutory one in which damages can be obtained for anxiety and any financial loss arising from the harassment (Protection from Harassment Act 1997, s 3; and see *Majrowski v Guy's & St Thomas's NHS Trust* (2005)). It is possible, in equity, that a court might issue an injunction on the basis of preventing a person from being tempted to commit an existing tort, such as trespass or public nuisance, in situations where the problem is one of harassment and the claimant has a clear interest in need of protection (*Burris v Azadani* (1995)).

7.3.3.7 Human rights

Even if there were no 1997 Act against harassment (see **7.3.3.6**, above), it is possible that certain forms of conduct falling within it would also now amount to an invasion of a right protected by the European Convention of Human Rights and Fundamental Freedoms, now part of English law thanks to the Human Rights Act 1998. The 1998 Act impacts on tort in two main ways. First, it has a vertical effect in declaring unlawful any act by a 'public authority' which is 'incompatible with a Convention right' (s 6) and granting the victim a remedy in damages against such an authority (s 8). Secondly, it has a horizontal effect in introducing into English law some new rights, for example privacy, which were not available at common law. It may be that if these rights are invaded by a private body or individual there will be no claim for damages as such (*Wainwright v Home Office* (2003)). However, equity, whose jurisdiction is wider and encompasses all established legal rights, might well be prepared to grant one of its remedies to the victim of an invasion. It should perhaps be added that, strictly speaking, an action for damages under the 1998 Act is not a claim in the law of tort (*R (Greenfield) v Home Secretary* (2005), § 19).

7.3.3.8 Inducing a breach of contract (economic torts)

Intentionally causing damage in the world of business is, as we have seen, a particularly difficult area for the law of tort since commercial competition is regarded as healthy and justified. This attitude was even extended to trade unions. If, in encouraging its members to go on strike, a union official committed no civil or criminal wrong, then such an official could not be liable in tort (*Allen v Flood* (1898)). However, it had been established earlier in the 19th century that if one person induced another to break his or her contract with a third party, the third party would have an action in tort against the person who induced the breach (*Lumley v Gye* (1853)). In the later 20th century this tort was seemingly extended to include any interference (rather than actual breach) by one person with a contract between two others, and thus the scope of the tort of inducing a breach of contract is now more uncertain (*Torquay Hotel v Cousins* (1969); cf *OBG Ltd v Allan* (2005)).

In addition to this particular tort, the courts have developed others, such as civil conspiracy, that are both separate yet analogous; and one tort, in particular, that is of importance with respect to intention to injure is the tort of intimidation. 'So long as the defendant only threatens to do what he has a legal right to do he is on safe ground', said Lord Reid. Provided that 'there is no conspiracy he would not be liable to anyone for doing the act, whatever his motive might be, and it would be absurd to make him liable for threatening to do it but not for doing it.' However, Lord Reid then asserted 'that there is a chasm between doing what you have a legal right to do and doing what you have no legal right to do, and there seems to me to be the same chasm between threatening to do what you have a legal right to do and threatening to do what you have no legal right to do' (*Rookes v Barnard* (1964), 1168–69).

7.3.3.9 Malicious falsehood

Malicious falsehood is a separate tort from defamation (see **7.3.3.5**, above), although the two may overlap, in that it protects a person's business interest rather than reputation interest (*Joyce v Sengupta* (1993)). It is available where one person maliciously publishes a falsehood about another's trade or business. The claimant does not have to prove loss if the damage to the business was intentional and the publication is in a permanent form (Defamation Act 1952, s 3). More recently the tort has been used in circumstances where one person has deliberately set out to blacken another's name, and although damages may be modest (because the damage must be to a person's business interest rather than reputation), it can be useful to a claimant who wishes to clear his or her name (*Khodaparast v Shad* (2000)).

7.3.3.10 Malicious prosecution

In *Martin v Watson* (1996), Lord Keith, quoting *Clerk & Lindsell on Torts*, said this (at 80):

> In action of malicious prosecution the plaintiff must show first that he was prosecuted by the defendant, that is to say, that the law was set in motion against him on a criminal charge; secondly, that the prosecution was determined in his favour; thirdly, that it was without reasonable and probable cause; fourthly, that it was malicious.

Further, he said, the 'onus of proving every one of these is on the plaintiff'.

One might note here that malicious intention is not enough; the prosecution itself must be unreasonable. However, although the tort is, in practice, one that is used mainly against the police, and is thus an aspect of what a civil lawyer would call administrative liability, it can also be brought against private individuals if such an individual is the person who 'set the law in motion' (Lord Keith).

7.3.3.11 Passing off

Where a defendant interferes with another's intangible property by passing off his goods as those of another, this will also amount to a tort. According to Lord Diplock, five characteristics must be present:

> in order to create a valid cause of action for passing off: (1) misrepresentation, (2) made by a trader in the course of his trade, (3) to prospective customers of his or ultimate consumers of the goods and services supplied by him, (4) which is calculated to injure the business or goodwill of another trader (in the sense that this is a reasonably foreseeable consequence) and (5) which causes actual damage to a business or goodwill of the trader. (*Erven Warnink BV v J Townend & Sons* (1979), 742)

From the defendant's position it is a kind of *deceit* practised on the public, while from the claimant's position it is an invasion of a particular *commercial interest* bordering on a property right. It is, accordingly, a tort that can be put alongside malicious falsehood and the economic torts in as much as it is a claim founded mainly on intentional wrongdoing which invades another's business or professional interests.

7.3.3.12 Private nuisance

Where one neighbour carries out an activity on his land with the sole purpose of intentionally annoying his neighbour, this may amount to the tort of private nuisance if the behaviour is regarded as an unreasonable use of land. Private nuisance is available where a defendant has unreasonably 'used his own land or some other land in such a way as injuriously to affect the enjoyment of the plaintiffs' land' (Denning LJ in *Esso v Southport Corporation* (1954), 196, CA). Intention to injure is important here because this of itself can turn a reasonable activity into an unreasonable one. Thus where one land owner set off shotguns on his land deliberately to cause injury to his neighbour's silver foxes, this amounted to a nuisance (*Hollywood Silver Fox Farm v Emmett* (1936)).

7.3.3.13 Public nuisance

Public nuisance, although it may on some occasions arise out of the same facts as private nuisance, is conceptually a quite distinct tort from private nuisance. It arises out of the crime of public nuisance and generates a claim in tort for any person who suffers special damage, a term which includes pure economic loss. Public nuisance is difficult to define – it 'covers a multitude of sins, great and small' (Denning LJ in *Esso v Southport Corporation* (1954), 196, CA) – but can be summed up as 'any nuisance ... which materially affects the reasonable comfort and convenience of life of a class of Her Majesty's subjects' (Romer LJ in *Att-Gen v PYA Quarrries* (1957), 184). Any person who intentionally intends to cause annoyance or harm through behaviour that injuriously affects a section of the public at large (for example, a demonstration on the highway) risks being sued for damages in public nuisance by any individual who suffers damage over and above the rest of the community. One might also note that indulging in criminal or unsocial activity, such as running a brothel, could well result in a claim for an injunction based on public nuisance brought by an irate neighbour (*Thompson-Schwab v Costaki* (1956)), although no doubt many victims will now seek an Anti-Social Behaviour Order (Crime and Disorder Act 1998, s 1).

7.3.3.14 Trespass

The tort of trespass comes in several forms depending upon the type of invasion. Direct violence to the person is assault and battery, while the unlawful restraint of a person is false imprisonment. Invasion of a person's possession of land or a chattel amounts to trespass to land or to goods. The main requirement is that the defendant directly invades the defendant's person or property without lawful authority.

In theory the mere intentional touching of another is a battery, and thus if D pushes C into a swimming pool and C is badly injured as a result, D will be liable in trespass. But merely bumping into someone in a school playground, supermarket or busy street, even if it causes injury, might be different because there is an implied consent to this type of behaviour ('we live in a crowded world') (*Wilson v Pringle* (1987)).

In false imprisonment, the defendant must be directly responsible for the imprisonment (*Harnett v Bond* (1925)) and there must be no means of escape (*Bird v Jones* (1845)). But technically speaking the claimant does not necessarily have to be aware of the imprisonment (*Murray v Ministry of Defence* (1988)).

Consent is a defence to trespass and this can be implied in, for example, cases of necessity (*In re F* (1990)), or where various persons indulge in sport or even in horseplay (*Blake v Galloway* (2004)).

7.3.4 Intentional torts and methodology

The torts outlined in **7.3.3** above are not necessarily the only ones that can come into play in situations where one person has intentionally caused damage to another (see Rudden, 1991–92). It is not, in other words, a definitive list. However, it does set out the main torts that might be relevant in situations where one person intentionally causes harm to another, and the principal point to emerge from this list is the importance of categorising factual situations around a number of descriptive focal points. These focal points are the nature of the claimant's *harm*, itself often translatable into 'interest' (cf PETL, art 2:101), and the *means used* by the defendant (cf PETL, art 1:101). Where the harm is physical the emphasis tends to shift immediately to the means used, the intensity of the defendant's behaviour and the causal relationship between the two. That is to say, the analysis is relatively straightforward in terms of established legal concepts and institutions. Where acute problems can arise is with respect to invasions of non-physical interests. Here a distinction needs to be made between principles of law and underlying constitutional values. It may well be that English law is guided by underlying principles such as freedom of the press, privacy and so on, but, as Lord Hoffmann has recently asserted, there is a great difference between identifying, say, privacy 'as a value which underlies the existence of a rule of law' and 'privacy as a principle of law in itself' (*Wainwright v Home Office* (2003), § 31). The same is true of freedom of speech. This is a value recognised by the common law (see *Derbyshire CC v Times Newspapers* (1993), yet 'no one has suggested that freedom of speech is in itself a legal principle which is capable of sufficient definition to enable one to deduce specific rules to be applied in concrete cases'. For that 'is not the way the common law works' (*Wainwright v Home Office*, § 31).

8 Liability for Unintentional Harm

If there is one general statement that can be made about liability for intentional harm it is that it is not governed by any general principle. There is no tort of intentionally causing harm (*Bradford Corporation v Pickles* (1895)). In contrast, the obligation to make reparation for harm caused by negligent (careless) behaviour is rather different. Negligence today is not only an independent cause of action but a unifying idea whose influence is dominating the law of torts. It is such a large and complex subject that, in university courses, its study leaves little time for much else in the law of torts. This, no doubt, is another reason for its distorting effect on the category of 'tort'. Yet, that said, within the tort of negligence there is a struggle to control its generality. Control devices, in particular the requirement of a duty of care, have assumed a kind of 'cause of action' category approach to liability.

8.1 Tort of negligence

In English law negligence became an independent cause of action in tort in 1932. Yet even before this date *negligentia* had a very important role in that it 'was one of the range of terms commonly used since the fourteenth century to designate the basis of liability in trespass on the case' and from 'the second half of the eighteenth century "negligence" came more generally to play an increasingly central part in the analysis of tortious liability' (Ibbetson, 1999, 164, 165). This role is still increasing, with the result that many independent torts – such as trespass, nuisance and breach of statutory duty – are being gradually subsumed under its influence; and one reason for this subsuming influence is the notion of 'reasonableness' (see, eg, *Transco v Stockport MBC* (2004), § 96). This notion is used not just to define negligent behaviour itself, but to determine the existence of a duty of care and to act as a means of judging both factual and legal causation. Reasonable behaviour is a vehicle for breaking down the frontiers between different causes (forms) of action.

8.1.1 Definition of negligence

The classic definition of negligence was given by Alderson B in *Blyth v Proprietors of the Birmingham Waterworks* (1856), at 784:

> Negligence is the omission to do something which a reasonable man, guided upon those considerations which ordinarily regulate the conduct of human affairs, would do, or doing something which a prudent and reasonable man would not do.

The point must be made at once that this is a definition of negligence and not the tort of negligence. The distinction is crucial, because the mere causing of harm by a negligent act was, and is, never capable of giving rise to liability in itself; there has to be a pre-existing duty to take care, and it is the breach of this duty – the negligent act or omission – which creates the liability.

Before 1932 the duty might arise as a result of contract (see now Supply of Goods and Services Act 1982, s 13), or as a result of certain clearly established extra-contractual situations such as products dangerous in themselves. Thus in order to establish liability a plaintiff had to show, first, that the defendant owed him a *specific duty* to take care (a question of law for the judge) and, secondly, that the defendant was in *breach* of this duty, that is to say that he was negligent (a question of fact for the jury). A third requirement was that the breach of duty *caused* (factually and legally) the claimant's damage. When juries had more or less disappeared from tort actions by the middle of the 20th century there was no longer any need for a list of specific and fragmented duties of care (Ibbetson, 1999, 188–9). Nevertheless, the idea of negligence as a 'breach of duty' survived.

8.1.2 Breach of duty

This breach of duty question is a useful place to start since it is the central factual issue (see PETL, art 4:102(1)). Was the defendant actually negligent? The absence of any duty of care or sufficient causal link can be as fatal to a victim's claim as the absence of any carelessness (breach of duty); however, the duty and remoteness of damage questions are regarded as control devices. They limit as a pure question of law the scope of liability even in situations where actual carelessness can be proved (see, eg, *Spartan Steel & Alloys Ltd v Martin & Co* (1973)) (**6.3.2.6**, above). Of course, the distinction between fact and law becomes blurred at the level of conceptual analysis because concepts themselves – even so-called descriptive concepts – are rarely normatively neutral. Thus the application of the 'reasonable man' test, rather than sharply differentiating 'is' (descriptive) from 'ought' (normative), tends to merge the two by analysing a factual situation in terms not just of how the defendant actually behaved but how he ought to have behaved. 'Is' becomes subsumed under 'ought' because deciding whether someone has been careless in any particular situation involves the court in measuring the actual behaviour of the defendant with some idealised behaviour (in turn determined with reference to a constructed individual such as the 'reasonable man').

For example, it might not be careless (unreasonable) to fail to supply goggles to workers with normal sight in a vehicle repair shop. Yet it might be careless for the same employer not to supply a pair of goggles to a one-eyed worker since the loss of the good eye in an industrial accident would, for him, be catastrophic (*Paris v Stepney BC* (1951)). More controversially, perhaps, the learner driver's act of driving will be measured not against the reasonable learner driver, but against the reasonably competent and experienced driver (*Nettleship v Weston* (1971)). The same objective test is applied to the do-it-yourself householder. If he or she does carpentry work around the house, he or she must show the degree of care and skill of a reasonably competent carpenter, although this is not to be judged by reference to a professional carpenter doing work under a contract (*Wells v Cooper* (1958)).

The reason why the law of tort takes this approach is because it has a mixture of aims (cf **6.2.3**, above). On the one hand, it wants to provide an arena in which entrepreneurs can act without fear of oppressive liabilities; on the other hand, the law of tort wants to remain partly true to its compensatory aim and to a commitment to risk. It does not want to see victims of road accidents go uncompensated on the basis of the vagaries of types of behaviour dictated by chance.

8.1.2.1 Breach of duty and precedent

The reasonable man test is in theory, then, a test of fact, and thus one which once belonged to the jury rather than to the judge. Juries may have disappeared (*Ward v James* (1966)) but the distinction remains vital, because decisions of juries never formed part of the precedent system; indeed juries never gave reasons for their verdicts. This means that breach of duty cases are not in themselves precedents. The point has been well put by Lord Somervell in a leading case on breach of duty. 'A judge naturally gives reasons for the conclusion formerly arrived at by a jury without reasons,' he said, 'but if the reasons given by a judge for arriving at the conclusion previously reached by a jury are to be treated as "law" and citable, the precedent system will die from a surfeit of authorities' (*Qualcast (Wolverhampton) Ltd v Haynes* (1959), 758). Care must be taken, then, when deciding the factual question of whether or not a person was negligent. This is a question of *fact* and not law, and therefore precedent is, or ought to be, irrelevant.

8.1.2.2 Reasonable behaviour

The test for breach of duty is not therefore one that can be found in the law reports. It all depends upon the circumstances. Nevertheless, there are cases which act as guidelines, and sometimes these guidelines can produce propositions that can be expressed as principles (see eg PETL, art 4:102(1)).

The leading case here is *Bolton v Stone* (1951), which was an action for damages by a bystander in the street against a cricket club for an injury sustained by the bystander when she was struck on the head by a cricket ball hit out of the ground by a batsman. Cricket balls had been hit out of the ground before, and so if one were to apply the foreseeability test it could be said that the accident was foreseeable. Did this mean that the cricket club did not behave reasonably in failing to provide a system of fencing that would ensure that cricket balls never reached the street? The House of Lords held that the cricket club had not been negligent and their judgments establish very clearly two propositions. First, that the test of breach of duty is not foreseeability; it is *reasonable behaviour*, and this is not the same thing. Secondly, that some risk is acceptable. The reasonable man does not have to guard against every conceivable risk, particularly with respect to activities that are socially acceptable; indeed in cases of emergency the degree of acceptable risk may be higher (*Watt v Hertfordshire CC* (1954)). Thus employers are not bound to sack an employee rather than expose her to some risk of dermatitis (*Withers v Perry Chain Co Ltd* (1961); but cf *Coxall v Goodyear Great Britain Ltd* (2003)); nor are they expected to shut down their factory when the floors become slippery as a result of a severe storm (*Latimer v AEC Ltd* (1953)). They are expected to act reasonably in the circumstances, and in judging this behaviour the cost of precautions as measured against the gravity of the risk can be taken into account. Foreseeability can of course re-enter by the back door; and so those dig up the streets must foresee that blind, as well as normally sighted, people will use ∂ pavement, and thus must erect suitable barriers (*Hayley v LEB* (1965)).

8.1.2.3 Special skills and proof of breach

Two further general points need to be made. First, that professional defendants (eg, doctors) are not judged by the ordinary reasonable man test but by the ordinary reasonably professional person (eg, reasonable doctor) professing those skills (*Bolam v Friern Hospital* (1957)). In medical negligence cases the courts have traditionally judged the behaviour in the light of prevailing medical opinion without ever subjecting the opinion to legal review (*Sidaway v Bethlem Royal Hospital* (1985)); yet this attitude might now be changing (*Bolitho v City and Hackney HA* (1998)). The difficulty, of course, is that judges are not doctors, architects or engineers, and thus they have to rely on the expert evidence. In addition, they worry about defensive medicine.

Secondly, that although it is normally the claimant who must prove negligence, there are some situations where 'the thing speaks for itself' (*res ipsa loquitur*), putting an onus on the defendant to provide at least some explanation other than carelessness for the accident (cf PETL, art 4:201)). If the defendant can provide an explanation, that will put the onus back on the claimant (*Roe v Minister of Health* (1954)). Yet some cases seem to go further and virtually presume negligence, effectively reversing the burden of proof (see *Henderson v HE Jenkins & Sons* (1970); *Ward v Tesco Stores Ltd* (1976)).

8.1.3 Duty of care

It has already been stated that it is not the negligent act itself that generates liability in tort (see **8.1.1**, above); it is the breach of a pre-existing duty of care owed by the careless actor to the person or class of persons damaged by the act. And thus, perhaps in contrast to French law, one can in theory talk of the formation of a non-contractual pre-existing obligation in respect of careless behaviour.

8.1.4 *Donoghue v Stevenson* (1932)

The starting point for the modern UK tort of negligence is *Donoghue v Stevenson* (1932). Despite being a Scottish case, it is equally an English precedent, because the House of Lords stated that they were declaring the law of England as well as that of Scotland. Mrs Donoghue brought an action for damages against the manufacturer of a bottle of ginger beer which, so she alleged, had caused her personal injury damage as a result of containing a decomposed snail. She had drunk the beer in a café after it had been bought for her by a friend. The manufacturer sought to have her claim struck out on a preliminary point of law: even if he had been careless in allowing the snail to get into the beer, he owed no duty of care to Mrs Donoghue. A majority in the House of Lords held that a duty did exist. Why is the case so important? The answer is to be found in a number of factors.

8.1.4.1 Extension of 'contract'

The immediate facts were (and to some extent still are) important in that they extended the structural symmetry of consumer protection. Before the decision, a consumer injured by a defective product could normally sue only if he or she had actually purchased the product (Sale of Goods Act 1893 (now 1979), s 14); the advantage of such a contract claim, however, is that a consumer did, and does, not have to prove fault (*Frost v Aylesbury Dairy Co Ltd* (1905)). *Donoghue* establishes that a consumer, even one who did not buy the product, injured by a defective product can sue the manufacturer. The seeming disadvantage is that the consumer must prove fault, but this is less of a burden than it might seem thanks to a later case establishing that the defect itself is prima facie evidence of negligence (*Grant v Australian Knitting Mills Ltd* (1936)). Legislation has further improved the position of the third-party consumer in that he or she *may* (it is not entirely clear) now be able to sue in contract (Contracts (Rights of Third Parties) Act 1999). A separate statute, anyway, allows consumers suffering personal injury and property damage to sue for damages without having to assert negligence (Consumer Protection Act 1987, Pt I) (see **9.1.2**, below).

8.1.4.2 Neighbour principle

Normally a case is rarely an authority beyond its own material facts, and thus it was argued in *Grant v Australian Knitting Mills* (1936), which involved defective underpants, that underpants were materially different from a bottle of ginger beer. Not surprisingly the argument was rejected (but was it such a daft argument for a lawyer to make?), and this was not just because both pants and ginger beer are 'products'. Lord Atkin in *Donoghue* famously said (at 580):

> The rule that you are to love your neighbour becomes in law, you must not injure your neighbour; and the lawyer's question, who is my neighbour? receives a restricted reply. You must take reasonable care to avoid acts or omissions which you can reasonably foresee would be likely to injure your neighbour. Who, then, in law is my neighbour? The answer seems to be – persons who are so closely and directly affected by my act that I ought reasonably to have them in contemplation as being so affected when I am directing my mind to the acts or omissions which are called in question.

This is what lifts negligence liability out of its imprisonment within specific factual categories and establishes the tort as a general cause of action prima facie applicable, seemingly, to any set of facts where damage is caused, by a careless act, to anyone within the 'neighbour' range of 'proximity'.

8.1.4.3 Proximity

A key limiting factor, then, is the notion of 'proximity', a term used and developed by Lord Atkin himself in *Donoghue*. Yet if 'duty' is based on 'proximity', what is the actual difference between these two notions? First, the former is *normative*, that is to say a concept that expresses a pure *ought* situation. To say that someone is under a 'duty' to do something is a moral and legal way of expressing what he ought to do. Proximity, in contrast, is purely *descriptive*; to say that one person is proximate to another is simply to describe a factual (an 'is') situation and implies in itself no 'ought' dimension (cf *Caparo Industries Plc v Dickman* (1990), 633).

Secondly, the two terms are not synonymous even when viewed from the standpoint of liability; there can be situations of proximity but no duty (*Marc Rich & Co v Bishop Rock*

Marine Co Ltd (1996)). Where 'proximity' and 'duty' are valuable is that the former can be used within a factual situation to organise the facts in such a way that the imposition (or non-imposition) of a duty becomes almost a natural consequence; it is, in other words, a valuable reasoning tool since it functions within the facts (see, eg, Lord Lloyd's dissent in *Marc Rich*). Duty, in contrast, functions only in a world of normative rules.

8.1.4.4 Damage

However, the neighbour principle was not to be as abstract as it might first have appeared. One material fact was the damage suffered by Mrs Donoghue: the decomposed snail made her physically ill, and it was for this damage that Stevenson might potentially have been liable. But this was not the only harm suffered by Mrs Donoghue; she had also 'lost' the value of a bottle of ginger beer. Later cases, citing earlier ones, identified the 'interest' forming the object of manufacturer's duty as the threat to health, not the threat to the pocket (see Consumer Protection Act 1987, s 5(2)). Put another way, the physical injury suffered by Mrs Donoghue and her economic loss are two quite different types of 'damage' (*Birse Construction Ltd v Haiste Ltd* (1996)). And thus the 1932 case is important in establishing (if retrospectively) the financial loss rule in the tort of negligence (see **8.2**, below).

8.1.4.5 Procedure

It is often said that it was never proved whether or not there was a snail in the ginger beer bottle (*Freeman v Home Office (No 2)* (1984), 555–6), and this is because the case never went to trial. The appeal that reached the House of Lords was a 'striking out' action; that is to say, the defendant asked the court on a preliminary question of law to strike out the case as disclosing no cause of action. Even if, argued the defendant, all the facts, including negligence, were proved by the claimant, these facts would still not make him liable since they disclosed no duty of care. What the House of Lords had to decide, then, was whether they did disclose a duty of care and, in order to decide this question, it was assumed that there was a snail in the bottle. Having lost the preliminary question of law action, Stevenson settled the case. Many subsequent duty of care cases are striking out claims; thus to say, for example, that the Home Office was found liable in negligence in *Home Office v Dorset Yacht Co* (1970) is not exactly true. These striking out claims have proved problematic from a human rights position since they can appear arbitrarily to deny the claimant a remedy if not a fair trial (see *Barrett v Enfield LBC* (1999); *Z v UK* (2001)).

8.1.4.6 General remarks

From a comparative law position, *Donoghue* can be linked to art 1382 of the *Code civil* and art 4:101 of the PETL in the way it lays down a general principle based on negligence. Indeed, when put beside intentional physical damage to the person, it is now possible to talk in terms of a general *culpa* liability (*Letang v Cooper* (1965)). However, given the limitation on liability imposed by the duty of care control device, the case is really closer to § 823 of the German Civil Code, which requires, in addition to fault, cause and damage, the invasion of a specific interest ('life, body, health, freedom, ownership or any other right'). Duty of care, therefore, is in practice more than an abstract rule in that it is the means by which the tort of negligence protects only certain interests (cf PETL, art 2:102).

8.1.5 *Hedley Byrne v Heller* (1964)

The next major development in the tort of negligence was the decision in *Hedley Byrne & Co v Heller & Partners Ltd* (1964). The case itself involved a favourable credit reference letter gratuitously given by a bank in respect of a company that subsequently proved unable to pay its debts. The recipient of the reference, who had extended credit to the company on the strength of the letter, lost heavily when the company went into liquidation, and it brought an action in negligence for its loss against the bank. Although the claimant lost its action because of a disclaimer in the credit reference letter, the House of Lords indicated that a duty of care could in principle exist between the bank and the claimant. This decision thus extended liability to damage done by careless words (misrepresentation); and although it looks at first sight a major extension of *Donoghue v Stevenson*, it is probably more accurate to see the case as a development in the area of the tort of deceit (*Peek v Derry* (1887, CA); cf (1889, HL)) (cf **7.3.3.4**, above), perhaps with the idea of filling gaps in the law of contract rather than in extending *Donoghue* as such (cf Supply of Goods and Services Act 1982, s 13). Those suffering loss as a result of a misstatement need no longer prove fraud provided they can establish a *special relationship*. In the words of Lord Steyn, 'the rule was established that irrespective of contract, if someone possessed of a special skill undertakes to apply that skill for the assistance of another person who relies upon such skill, a duty of care will arise' (*Arthur JS Hall & Co v Simons* (2002), 676).

What makes the case particularly special is that it appears to be a major exception to the established idea that *Donoghue v Stevenson* was concerned with physical rather than economic interests. However, the key to the case is a *voluntary assumption* of responsibility by the defendant together with *reliance* by the claimant (see, eg, *Lennon v Comr of Police of the Metropolis* (2004)). Yet it may be that 'reliance' will be interpreted quite generously when the duty problem is closely associated, directly or indirectly, with a contractual relationship, and thus liability can attach to a reference from an ex-employer (*Spring v Guardian Assurance Plc* (1995)) and to a breach of contract by a solicitor where only a third party (and not the contracting party) suffers loss as a result of the breach (*White v Jones* (1995)). What is particularly important about *Hedley Byrne* is its central place in the law of obligations in as much as it both straddles the divide between contract and tort, and acts as one starting point for recovering pure economic loss through the tort of negligence.

8.2 Particular interests (1): economic loss

Negligence, then, is not just about behaviour but also about interests, and these interests need to be examined in a little more depth since they form some of the key areas of difficulty within the tort of negligence (see also Lord Rodger in *D v East Berks Community Health NHS Trust* (2005), §§ 100–3). Two areas have proved to be particularly problematic: liability for pure economic loss, and liability for causing what used to be called 'nervous shock' (psychiatric damage; see **8.3**, below). An added complication is the fact that many defendants in these damage cases are public bodies, often local authorities or the police (see **8.4**, below). These defendants create complications for two reasons:

(a) because they are often not the direct cause of the damage in issue; they are bodies that have allegedly failed to do their job properly, and thus who have failed to prevent the claimant's damage (for example, it was not the prison staff who damaged the yacht in *Dorset Yacht* (1970)). This failure to act (mere omission) has, for duty of care purposes, been treated differently from positive acts;

(b) being public rather than private bodies, they have raised what might be called special policy problems. This, in turn, has propelled the courts into creating what might be called an extra requirement of negligence (besides duty, breach, causation and remoteness): is it fair and reasonable to impose a duty of care?

8.2.1 Methodological considerations

Behind these duty and interest questions lay a problem of reasoning method. Is the *ratio decidendi* in *Donoghue* to be treated and applied as an abstract principle (the 'neighbour principle') like some continental code provision? Or is it a matter of moving more cautiously (incrementally) through reasoning by analogy, that is to say from factual situation to factual situation? In *Anns v Merton LBC* (1978), Lord Wilberforce said that it was no longer necessary to bring the facts of any new case within those of previous situations in which a duty of care had been held to exist. One applied only the proximity test and then asked whether there were any considerations which ought to negative liability. However, this two-stage principle approach has now been comprehensively rejected; 'the most that can be attempted is a broad categorisation of the decided cases according to the type of situation in which liability has been established in the past in order to found an argument by analogy' (Lord Oliver in *Caparo Industries Plc v Dickman* (1990), 635; and see Lord Rodger in *D v East Berks Community Health NHS Trust* (2005), § 100).

The facts of duty of care cases thus remain a fundamental part of the law itself; and what the lawyer must do is to compare the facts of any new problem with those in the precedents (see, eg, *Goodwill v British Pregnancy Advisory Service* (1996)). Of course, whether or not one situation is analogous to another is itself a matter of some choice, as we have seen. And thus behind this form of reasoning are often to be found other forms of argument. Reference may be found to policy, certainty, reasonableness, 'practical justice', fairness and so on (see **6.3.2**, above).

8.2.2 Damage and loss

We have already seen that in *Donoghue v Stevenson* the plaintiff suffered not just 'damage' but also 'loss' (see **8.1.4.4**, above). This distinction became a fundamental one in the case law following the landmark decision of 1932. A defendant who had caused harm through a careless act owed a duty of care only to those who had suffered physical injury as a result of the act; those suffering pure economic loss had no claim. This rule applied even to claimants who had suffered some physical injury (two-party situations); if the court could make a clear distinction between *damnum emergens* (consequential loss) and *lucrum cessans* (failure to make a gain), the latter could be excluded as a head of damages (*Spartan Steel & Alloys Ltd v Martin & Co* (1973)) (see **6.3.2.6**, above).

However, care must be taken here. Economic loss could, and can, always be recovered in the tort of negligence as part of the loss *consequential* to the physical harm. Thus in *Spartan*, damages were recoverable in respect of the loss of profits on the ruined 'melt' because this was an economic 'interest' that attached to damaged tangible property. It was only the 'pure' economic loss that attached to no item of damaged property – the loss of an expectation – that could not be recovered. Equally, economic interests attaching to the claimant as a person can be recovered if the claimant has suffered personal injuries, and this economic loss will include loss of earnings past, present and future; indeed damages are sub-divided into non-pecuniary and pecuniary. The so-called economic loss rule – which, it must be noted, applies for the main part only to the tort of negligence plus, on occasions, to breach of statutory duty (see, eg, *Merlin v British Nuclear Fuels plc* (1990)) – has been justified in a number of ways. Lord Denning has said it is a matter of policy (*Spartan Steel*), while Weir argues that people and tangible things are more important interests than money (2004, 6–7). The PETL gives some support to the Weir approach (art 2:102).

Whatever the justification, the rule is breaking down, and at one point nearly disappeared (*Junior Books Ltd v Veitchi Co Ltd* (1983)). What one can say, then, is this. The causing of physical damage has universally to be justified, whereas the infliction of pure economic loss does not (*Murphy v Brentwood DC* (1991); PETL, art 2:102(4)). Yet even though the logic of the rule suggests that where a defendant does carelessly cause physical damage to property there must, almost by definition, be a duty of care, it may be that a duty will be denied if policy and (or) fairness demand such a denial, say, because of the insurance position or because the physical loss is analogous to economic loss (*Marc Rich & Co v Bishop Rock Marine Co Ltd* (1996)). One can still talk of an economic loss rule in negligence, but one is forced back, these days, to the circumstances of each case. The rule is subject to exceptions, if only, sometimes, because the distinction between the physical and economic is not always an easy one (*Murphy*).

8.2.3 Negligent misstatement and economic loss

The first important major exception to the economic loss rule was, as we have seen, the decision in *Hedley Byrne v Heller* (1964) (**8.1.5**, above). After this decision it was clear that a duty of care could be owed in respect of pure economic loss arising out of a misstatement. However, the plaintiff had to show a *special relationship* based upon an *assumption of responsibility* by the defendant and *reliance* by the plaintiff. Thus the case, and its duty of care, could be placed in a category of its own: it was more an extension of the tort of deceit (where pure economic loss can always be recovered) within a relationship 'close to contract' (cf Misrepresentation Act 1967, s 2(1)). And even within this special category it has not always been easy for a plaintiff to recover (see eg *Mutual Life Citizens Assurance Co v Evatt* (1971): *Caparo Industries plc v Dickman* (1990)). Nevertheless, *Hedley Byrne* was to have far-reaching consequences in the realm of professional liability, in that breaches of contract that caused loss to third (non-contractual) parties might result in liability in tort to the third party (see in particular *Smith v Eric Bush* (1990); *White v Jones* (1995)).

Moreover, as with *Donoghue v Stevenson*, the effect of *Hedley Byrne* is to redefine tortious liability in general, in as much as both cases cut across the old categories of liability approach. Thus factual situations thought to be confined to a particular cause of action (eg, defamation) have now been redefined in terms of duty of care (*Spring v Guardian Assurance Plc* (1995)). This has attracted criticism (Birks, 1996, 5–6). However, it has to be remembered that when seen from an *interests* viewpoint the position turns out to be complex; a reference letter that contains a serious misstatement will invade not just the reputation interest of the subject of the reference (cf defamation), but also his or her economic interest (cf duty of care). The point to be made about both *Donoghue* and *Hedley Byrne* is that they are continually, if only slowly, redefining the notion of tortious liability (Weir, 1998). This redefinition means that even the scope of notions like 'misstatement' and 'reliance' are open to reinterpretation, with the result that the 'misstatement' (does it include silence or inaction?) and even 'reliance' itself are continually being reassessed where, say, 'practical justice', 'fairness' or 'policy' require it (*White v Jones* (1995)). The close relationship with contract does, however, raise another issue inherent in *Hedley Byrne* itself: a defendant always has the right expressly to exclude any duty of care, although this may fall foul of exclusion clause legislation (see *Smith v Eric Bush* (1990)) (cf **5.2.4**, above).

The development of duty of care to cover misstatement in situations close to contract creates a zone where the boundary between contract and tort becomes unclear. In French law, the rule of *non cumul* once excluded any tort liability where the facts were governed by contract, but such a rule has been specifically rejected in English law (*Henderson v Merrett Syndicates Ltd* (1995)). Nevertheless, the existence of a contract can impact upon the existence or non-existence of a duty of care. The courts may well refuse to allow a third party to avoid a contractual risk structure even if the party is outside the contract (*Norwich CC v Harvey* (1989)). But much will depend upon the facts, and this is why Lord Woolf made it clear in *Spring v Guardian Assurance* (1995) that cases are confined to their own factual classes.

8.3 Particular interests (2): shock and omissions

Psychological damage, or nervous shock as it was once called, and mere omission cases, together with on occasions those involving pure economic loss, often share a common structure. They involve three-party situations. This is often because serious accidents impact not just upon the victim but upon the victim's family as well. This impact is usually financial, but may be physical in the form of mental distress or worse (see, eg, *Best v Samuel Fox & Co Ltd* (1952)). To what extent should such family members be able independently to sue the tortfeasor? In particular, to what extent should they be able to sue for mental (nervous) shock? A general response to these questions has recently been given by Lord Rodger: for the most part, 'the policy of the law is to concentrate on compensating the victim for the effects of his injuries while doing little or nothing for the others' (*D v East Berks Community Health NHS Trust* (2005), § 101)

Alternatively, the victim of an accident may find that the cause of his misfortune can be attributed not just to a primary defendant but also to a secondary defendant, such a secondary defendant having usually carelessly failed to prevent the first defendant from acting the way he did. Often these secondary defendants are public bodies like local authorities, who, for example, might negligently have failed to check, when it was being built, the foundations of the claimant's house (*Murphy v Brentwood DC* (1991)), or the police who might carelessly have failed to catch a dangerous criminal (*Hill v Chief Constable of West Yorkshire* (1989)). The family and public bodies thus form two central focal points in this area of duty of care.

8.3.1 Psychiatric illness (nervous shock)

Nervous shock is the old name given to psychiatric damage suffered by a vic
rise to several types of problem in law. The first is one of definition; the law
between different types of actionable mental harm, ranging from mental di
psychiatric harm via pain and suffering (*Heil v Rankin* (2001)) and bere
Accidents Act 1976, s 1A). These different mental 'interests' are protected differently in the
law of obligations. Thus mental distress *may* be recoverable in contract (*Jarvis v Swans
Tours* (1973)), but not in the tort of negligence; only psychiatric illness ('nervous shock') can
be recovered in negligence (*Alcock v Chief Constable of South Yorkshire* (1992)).

The second problem is structural. Where the psychiatric illness is suffered by the primary
victim (two-party situations) the problem is not really one of duty, because the defendant
is already under a duty not to cause personal injury, but one of legal causation, that is to
say remoteness of damage (*Page v Smith* (1996)). In this situation the question of psychiatric illness can be seen as part of the general problem of defining personal injury
damage, although it may even attach to property damage (*Attia v British Gas Plc* (1988)).
But sometimes it is not easy to determine whether the psychiatric illness victim is primary
or secondary. Where, however, the claimant is a secondary victim (three-party situations)
the problem becomes one of duty of care.

8.3.1.1 Unforeseeable claimant

The starting point is that a third party (C) who witnesses an accident in which a victim (V)
is injured or killed by the careless act of the defendant (D), will not have a claim in negligence for psychiatric illness (*Bourhill v Young* (1943)). C is said to be too remote and owed
no duty of care (the unforeseeable claimant). There were, however, exceptions to this rule
based upon a relationship between V and C. The most important of these relationships
was, and remains, a family one, now described as 'a close tie of love and affection' (Law
Comm Report No 249, Draft Negligence (Psychiatric Illness) Bill, cl 1(3)(b)). Thus if V is
badly injured by D's negligent act and the accident is witnessed by C, his mother (or probably any family member in the Law Comm Bill category cl 3(4)), then D will be liable to C
for C's psychiatric illness. And this will be true even if C does not witness the actual accident but sees the victim in a bad state in the hospital shortly (but how long?) after the
accident (*McLoughlin v O'Brian* (1983)).

Two other relationships were once (but probably no longer) of importance. If V and C
were co-employees, and C witnessed an accident at the workplace attributable to the
employer's negligence, there was some authority that this might allow C to sue for psychiatric illness (*Dooley v Cammell Laird* (1951); cf *Hunter v British Coal* (1998)). Equally if C
was a rescuer who intervened to help after an accident caused by D's negligence, it
seemed that C would have an action against D for psychiatric damage (*Chadwick v British
Railways Board* (1967)). The symmetry once seemed fairly clear: a psychiatric illness
claimant would no longer be 'unforeseeable' if there existed some relationship between
the victim and claimant that brought him or her into the range of proximity and thus duty.

8.3.1.2 Hillsborough tragedy

The structure and symmetry of the law regarding psychiatric illness was quite radically
modified in two important cases arising out of the dreadful Hillsborough stadium tragedy,

which the police were negligent in opening gates to a pressing crowd outside a football ground resulting in many deaths by suffocation. In the first case, relatives and friends of those killed who witnessed, either directly or indirectly on television or radio, the events claimed damages for psychiatric illness; their claims were dismissed on the ground that they were outside the scope of proximity (*Alcock v Chief Constable of South Yorkshire* (1992)). Either there was not a sufficient close tie of love and affection, or, if there was, the claimants were too far removed from the accident. Basically secondary claimants (three-party situations) must:

(a) have a close tie of love and affection with victims;
(b) be close to the incident; and
(c) witness the accident *directly* (sight and sound), although there might be some *very limited* exceptions.

In the second case, police officers who had been present at the stadium brought claims for psychiatric injury on the basis that they were both rescuers and employees of the police force. The Court of Appeal allowed their claims, but in the House of Lords this was reversed by a majority (*Frost v Chief Constable of South Yorkshire Police* (1999)). One reason for this reversal was based upon public perception: it would not be fair to allow police officers to recover (especially as it was the police who had been negligent) but not the relatives of those killed and injured (Lord Steyn, at 495). In giving effect to this public perception, however, the House of Lords has now discarded the employment and rescuer relationships as capable, in themselves, of giving rise to a foreseeable claimant in nervous shock cases. This is not to say that fellow employees or rescuers will never be able to claim for psychological damage; but they will have to show more than the mere relationship to bring themselves within the duty range. They will, for example, have to show that the tortious act threatened their personal safety.

8.3.1.3 Primary and secondary victims

One of the structural aspects of psychiatric illness problems that has come into focus thanks to *Alcock* and *Frost* is the dichotomy between two-party and three-party situations. This dichotomy arose out of the nature of the damage itself; because mental injury has been treated differently from actual physical injury, claimants were treated as being outside the immediate accident event (and in one sense they often are of course). Nevertheless, if psychiatric injury were to be treated as physical injury, all claimants would be primary victims, and all could bring claims for their damage in the normal way against the tortfeasor. The law does not take this view, except when the shock claimant was present at the scene of the accident and either suffered some physical injury or was immediately threatened (see *Page v Smith* (1996)). Rescuers are on the whole secondary victims, and thus must prove the three *Alcock* conditions before they can recover (see **8.3.1.2**, above). However, if their lives were immediately threatened by, say, falling masonry or whatever, they will be treated as primary victims (*Chadwick* (1967), as reinterpreted). In *Frost*, the police were not so threatened and thus had to prove the *Alcock* conditions, which they could not do. These *Alcock* conditions mean, however, that factual analysis in nervous shock cases is now complex and the law 'a patchwork quilt of distinctions which are difficult to justify' (Lord Steyn in *Frost*, 500). Note again, with regard to this complexity, that bereavement has its own rule (Fatal Accidents Act 1976, s 1A).

8.3.2 Mere omissions

Another complex area of duty of care is where a defendant's negligence consists not in a positive act which causes damage, but in a failure to act. Here the direct cause is either an event of nature (eg, flood or landslide), or the act of a person other than the defendant (eg, thief, or a builder whose incompetence is not noticed by local authority inspector). In principle there is no liability for such a mere omission on the basis of an absence of duty (*East Suffolk Rivers Catchment Board v Kent* (1941)). In other words, there is no duty to be a Good Samaritan (*Stovin v Wise* (1996)). As with psychiatric illness, though, there are exceptions, usually based upon some pre-existing relationship between the claimant (C) and the person failing to act (D). For example, if D owed a clear and defined pre-existing duty to C, there might be liability (*Reeves v Comr of Police for the Metropolis* (2000)); equally, once D has intervened he may be liable if he makes matters worse (*Barrett v Ministry of Defence* (1995)). On the whole such defendants are usually public bodies, and much may depend upon the nature of the statutory duty that D has failed to perform. Sometimes a range of factors may point one way or the other: the nature of the damage, the status of the defendant, the insurance position, the contractual relations and so on (see *Marc Rich* (1996); but cf *Capital & Counties plc v Hampshire* CC (1997)).

8.4 Particular liabilities: public bodies

The fact that many defendants in mere omission cases have been local authorities is not surprising since their job is often to supervise. Now, in French law, a fundamental distinction is made between civil liability (*la responsabilité civile*) and administrative liability (*la responsabilité administrative*). Claims for compensation for damage caused by a public body or public agent usually have to be pursued in a quite different set of courts than claims against private persons or bodies. In the common law world no such formal distinction exists. In principle the law of tort applies equally to all persons, public and private; in substance, however, the position turns out to be more complicated.

8.4.1 Policy problems

The starting point for the liability of public bodies is simple enough: local authorities and central government bodies can be sued for damages where they wrongfully cause damage. Thus, for example, local authorities have been held liable in trespass, negligence, nuisance and so on. Indeed, occasionally one finds one government body suing another in tort. The same is true for central government: they can be sued in tort where they damage citizens. Damages claims in negligence against NHS hospitals (or Area Health Authorities) have become a specialist area of tort law (medical negligence).

However, the courts recognise that subjecting public bodies to tort liability can raise difficult questions of policy, in that a claim for damages might not always be an appropriate vehicle for investigating the efficiency of the police force or a local government social services department. In negligence claims this issue is dealt with as a duty of care problem; thus if the courts think a claim for damages is inappropriate, they deny the existence of a duty between public body defendant and claimant. This denial in turn can be based on a number of more formal notions. For example, the absence of a duty might be justified on the mere omissions rule, or upon the fact that the damage is pure economic loss. More generally the judges often now refer to the idea that it is not 'fair, just and reasonable' to impose such a duty (see, eg, *Elguzouli-Daf v Comr of Police of the Metropolis* (1995)). And behind all these formal notions lie policy considerations: 'In a wide range of cases', said Lord Browne-Wilkinson, 'public policy has led to the decision that the imposition of liability would not be fair and reasonable in the circumstances, eg some activities of financial regulators, building inspectors, ship surveyors, social workers dealing with sex abuse cases'. And he continued, in 'all these cases and many others the view has been taken that the proper performance of the defendant's primary functions for the benefit of society as a whole will be inhibited if they are required to look over their shoulder to avoid liability in negligence'. For in 'English law the decision as to whether it is fair, just and reasonable to impose a liability in negligence on a particular class of would-be defendants depends on weighing in the balance the total detriment to the public interest in all cases from holding such class liable in negligence as against the total loss to all would-be plaintiffs if they are not to have a cause of action in respect of the loss they have individually suffered' (*Barrett v Enfield LBC* (2001), 559).

These words might seem convincing enough. But one can reflect upon whether they have any foundation in social reality; certainly the judgments themselves are often completely devoid of any sociological evidence, and this exposes a serious problem with legal reasoning in the common law. Admirable as it may be that the judges are prepared to go beyond mere rule application, functional reasoning does actually require something more than mere armchair philosophy (a point now perhaps recognised: *Transco v Stockport MBC* (2004), § 105). There may well be very pertinent reasons why the liability of local authorities ought not to be open-ended (for example, it might seriously threaten the viability of public liability insurance); but the judgments sometimes read like tabloid newspaper editorials. This is, perhaps, an area where comparative law might well be able to make a contribution (Markesinis et al, 1999).

8.4.2 Statutory framework

A particular problem encountered with respect to local authorities is that they are statutory creations whose duties and powers are determined by the legislator. They discharge statutory functions operating within a statutory framework. The view of the courts is that because the will of the legislator is paramount when it comes to such functions, a 'common law duty must not be inconsistent with the performance by the authority of its statutory duties and powers in the manner intended by Parliament, or contrary in any other way to the presumed legislative intention' (*Stovin v Wise* (1996), 935).

What has made matters difficult is the question of discretion often conferred upon public authorities, and what the courts have attempted to do is to distinguish between a policy decision (eg, not to build a new sports centre) and an operational decision (eg, making a careless decision about the safety of a building). 'The greater the element of policy involved,' said Lord Slynn, 'the wider the area of discretion accorded, the more likely it is that the matter is not justiciable so that no action in negligence can be brought' (*Barrett v Enfield LBC* (2001), 571). The result is that a:

claim of negligence in the taking of a decision to exercise a statutory discretion is likely to be barred, unless it is wholly unreasonable so as not to be a real exercise of the discretion, or if it involves the making of a policy decision involving the balancing of different public interests; acts done pursuant to the lawful exercise of the discretion can, however, in my view be subject to a duty of care, even if some element of discretion is involved. (Lord Slynn, at 572)

Subsequent to this statement, Lord Slynn and his colleagues have held that educational psychologists and teachers, working for a local authority, might owe duties of care to pupils in their care, and that the local authority would be vicariously liable for breach of such a duty (*Phelps v Hillingdon LBC* (2001); and see *D v East Berks Community NHS Trust* (2005)).

8.4.3 Human Rights Act 1998

A whole new dimension has been added to the public bodies liability question with the incorporation of the Convention for the Protection of Human Rights and Fundamental Freedoms by the Human Rights Act 1998. The effects of the incorporation of the Convention go much further than establishing a statutory remedy against public bodies. Many of the leading negligence cases (including *Donoghue v Stevenson* itself) are what are called striking out claims (see **8.1.4.5**, above). This is where the defendant, as a preliminary question of law, asks the court to put an end to the whole case because of the absence of a duty of care and thus a cause of action in negligence. If the court agrees, the claimant is in effect left with no right to proceed. One such case was *Osman v Ferguson* (1993), where a claim for damages against the police was struck out on policy grounds; however, the European Court of Human Rights ruled that this striking out fell foul of the right to a fair trial as set out in Article 6(1) of the Human Rights Convention (*Osman v United Kingdom* (1999)). Although academics and judges were critical of this Strasbourg ruling, the House of Lords has appeared to retreat from the position it had formerly adopted in cases like *X (Minors) v Bedfordshire County Council* (1995). There is now a reluctance to strike out cases on a preliminary motion. This development is important because it means that the courts have had to be more generous in holding that a public body is under a duty of care (*Barrett v Enfield LBC* (2001); *Phelps v Hillingdon LBC* (2001)), and thus the 1998 Act has had an important impact on substantive questions within the tort of negligence.

In fact, since these decisions, the *X (Minors)* case has been heard by the Strasbourg Court, which has changed its position from the one adopted in *Osman*. The Court admitted that it was wrong to regard the striking out procedure as a breach of Article 6 since the striking out cases clearly went into substantive detail with respect to the policy issues behind the duty of care question. However, the Strasbourg Court went on to say that it was nonetheless the case that the interpretation of domestic law by the House of Lords resulted in the applicants' case being struck out. Yet the experiences of the claimants, according to the evidence, were 'horrific'; this meant that, in preventing the applicants from suing, there was a gap in the UK domestic law and 'one that gives rise to an issue under the Convention, but in the Court's view it is an issue under Article 13, not Article 6 § 1' (*Z v United Kingdom* (2002), § 102; and for a full history see now Lord Bingham in *D v East*

Berkshire Community Health NHS Trust (2005)). However, as Article 13 of the Convention has not been incorporated into UK law by the 1998 Act (see s 1), it would seem that the effect of *Z v UK* could be limited.

8.4.4 Equality and inequality

Before leaving the topic of liability of public bodies, mention should be made of one of the disadvantages, at least from a victim's point of view, of failing to develop a thesis of administrative liability. In French law the *Conseil d'État*, the highest administrative court, with the help of academic doctrine, has developed a whole field of liability without fault. The court has been able to do this through the application of constitutional ideas in the area of what an English lawyer would see as tort liability. One such idea is the principle of equality (*égalité*). This principle has been used, alongside that of risk, to justify the imposition of strict liability in a number of situations where, in English law, given the same facts, negligence would have to be proved.

Take, for example, the situation that arose in one English case. In order to recapture a dangerous criminal who had barricaded himself into the claimant's gun shop, the police fired CS gas into the building, with the result that the shop caught fire and was destroyed. The owner of the shop (or perhaps his insurance company) brought an action against the police in tort, and the judge made it clear that in order for the action to succeed negligence would have to be proved. Any strict liability claim would fail because of the defence of necessity. In fact the plaintiff was able to show negligence and so damages were awarded (*Rigby v Chief Constable of Northants* (1985)). But what if there had been no carelessness? The logic seems to be that the owner of the destroyed building would be left to carry the loss himself (although in truth the loss may fall on the building insurer). French administrative lawyers would regard such a result as both unjust and unconstitutional since the community has benefited while a single individual has been left with the burden. Consequently, in French law, damages would have been awarded to the shop owner, without proof of fault, on the basis of the principle that equality demands the sharing of burdens suffered in the pursuit of the public interest.

This strict liability (no fault) principle flows naturally from public lawyers who are continually having to balance the community interest against the interests of individuals. Private lawyers, at least in the UK, find such thinking more difficult. Indeed, the idea of community benefit has been used to arrive at the opposite conclusion from the French one; negligence must be proved before a public body supplying a community benefit like gas, water or electricity can be liable to a citizen injured by, for example, a gas explosion. 'Gas, water and also electricity services are well-nigh a necessity of modern life', said Sellers LJ in *Dunne v NW Gas Board* (1964), 'or at least are generally demanded as a requirement for the common good'. He concluded from this premise that it 'would seem odd that facilities so much sought after by the community and approved by their legislators should be actionable at common law because they have been brought to places where they are required and have escaped without negligence by an unforeseen sequence of mishaps' (at 832).

8.4.4.1 Risk and public bodies

In addition to this equality principle, administrative lawyers in France take the view that public authority activities involving risk should equally give rise to no fault liability.

However, in English law, the fact that the injured claimant is a civil servant (or public service employee) injured in the exercise of her duties in a situation involving danger is irrelevant. If such a person is injured during the course of his or her duties, fault or the unlawful breach of a statute must be shown (*Read v J Lyons & Co* (1947)). Indeed, those involved in dangerous public service jobs are deemed to have gone some way in accepting the risks involved (*Watt v Hertfordshire CC* (1954)). Equality appears, at least traditionally, to be neither a constitutional nor a private law principle. Risk also appears to be a principle with only a limited direct influence on liability theory; indirectly, of course, it can find expression through maxims such as *res ipsa loquitur*.

8.4.4.2 Human rights

Has the position been modified by the Human Rights Act 1998? In a recent nuisance case involving noise from military jet aircraft, Buckley J observed that the 'problem with putting the public interest into the scales when deciding whether a nuisance exists, is simply that if the answer is no, not because the claimant is being over sensitive, but because his private rights must be subjugated to the public interest, it might well be unjust that he should suffer the damage for the benefit of all' (*Dennis v MOD* (2003), § 46). And he continued:

> If it is to be held that there is no nuisance, there can be no remedy at common law. As this case illustrates, the greater the public interest, the greater may be the interference. If public interest is considered at the remedy stage and since the court has a discretion, the nuisance may continue but the public, in one way or another, pays for its own benefit. ... Allowing a human rights claim but denying a remedy in nuisance would, of course, be another solution, but it would be one that reflected adversely on the flexibility of the common law...

One might hope that the 1998 Act would equally impact on another administrative liability case. In *Elguzouli-Daf v Comr of Police for the Metropolis* (1995), two plaintiffs brought an action against the Crown Prosecution Service (CPS) claiming that they had been held in prison on remand as a result of the negligence of the defendants. The Court of Appeal dismissed their claims on the basis of an absence of a duty of care, Steyn LJ asserting 'that the interests of the whole community are better served by not imposing a duty of care on the CPS' because 'such a duty of care would tend to have an inhibiting effect on the discharge by the CPS of its central function of prosecuting crime'. Imposing a duty, he continued, 'would in some cases lead to a defensive approach by prosecutors to their multifarious duties'. Steyn LJ offered no evidence whatsoever to support the claim that the 'CPS would have to spend valuable time and use scarce resources in order to prevent law suits in negligence against the CPS' (at 349). And even if it did involve some extra work, it is by no means clear that the interests of the community are served in depriving individuals of recourse against the administration in situations where they have suffered horrifying invasions of their family life, private life and (or) other human rights as a result of the careless exercise of state power (and one might note on this point Lord Steyn's dissenting judgement, based on a point of principle rather than political functionalism, in *Birmingham CC v Oakley* (2001)). And thus Steyn LJ's judgment stands as a warning. It is all very well for him to say that we now live in 'a less formalist age' (*Watts v Aldington* (1993)), but if judges are to rely on functional approaches, rationalism demands that the functions envisaged be supported by empirical evidence. However, the rule that the police do not owe a duty of care to victims in an *Elguzouli-Daf* situation has now been reconfirmed by the House of Lords in *Brooks v Comr of Police for the Metropolis* (2005).

8.5 Unlawful acts

Another complication is the existence of two sets of remedies in respect of public bodies: there are the 'private law' claims for damages and the 'public law' actions for judicial review. As Lord Browne-Wilkinson has observed (in (*X (Minors) v Bedfordshire County Council* (1995), 730–31):

> It is important to distinguish such actions to recover damages, based on a private law cause of action, from actions in public law to enforce the due performance of statutory duties, now brought by way of judicial review. The breach of a public law right by itself gives rise to no claim for damages. A claim for damages must be based on a private law cause of action.

And he continued:

> Private law claims for damages can be classified into four different categories, viz: (A) actions for breach of statutory duty simpliciter (ie irrespective of carelessness); (B) actions based solely on the careless performance of a statutory duty in the absence of any other common law right of action; (C) actions based on a common law duty of care arising either from the imposition of the statutory duty or from the performance of it; (D) misfeasance in public office, ie the failure to exercise, or the exercise of, statutory powers either with the intention to injure the plaintiff or in the knowledge that the conduct is unlawful.

8.5.1 Breach of statutory duty

Besides negligence (and nuisance, etc), then, the torts of breach of statutory duty and misfeasance in public office (see **7.3.3.2**) have a role to play in the liability of public bodies or officials. Lord Browne-Wilkinson in *X (Minors)* went on to summarise the main principles of breach of statutory duty (at 731):

> The principles applicable in determining whether such statutory cause of action exists are now well established, although the application of those principles in any particular case remains difficult. The basic proposition is that in the ordinary case a breach of statutory duty does not, by itself, give rise to any private law cause of action. However a private law cause of action will arise if it can be shown, as a matter of construction of the statute, that the statutory duty was imposed for the protection of a limited class of the public and that Parliament intended to confer on members of that class a private right of action for breach of the duty. There is no general rule by reference to which it can be decided whether a statute does create such a right of action but there are a number of indicators.

And he continued:

> If the statute provides no other remedy for its breach and the Parliamentary intention to protect a limited class is shown, that indicates that there may be a private right of action since otherwise there is no method of securing the protection the statute was intended to confer. If the statute does provide some other means of enforcing the duty that will normally indicate that the statutory right was intended to be enforceable by those means and not by private right of action: *Cutler v Wandsworth Stadium Ltd* [1949] AC 398; *Lonrho Ltd v Shell Petroleum Co Ltd (No 2)* [1982] AC 173. However, the mere existence of some other statutory remedy is not necessarily decisive. It is still possible to show that on the true construction of the statute the protected class was intended by Parliament to have a private remedy. Thus the specific duties imposed on employers in relation to factory premises are enforceable by an action for damages, notwithstanding the imposition by the statutes of criminal penalties for any breach: see *Groves v Wimborne (Lord)* [1898] 2 QB 402.

In fact this tort of breach of statutory duty is of particular importance in one of the great sources of tort claims, accidents at work. In one sense, of course, it is a liability arising out of an individual act and therefore deserves to be classified alongside negligence. However, in reality many cases involve defective industrial plant, machinery, buildings or other things. It is a cause of action, then, that might be better categorised under a 'liability for things' heading (see **Chapter 9**).

9 Liability for Things and for People

Article 1384 of the *Code civil* declares that one is 'liable not only for the damage which one has caused by one's own act, but also for that which is caused by the act of persons for whom one is responsible, or by things which one has in one's keeping'. The French private law courts have, during the 20th century, used this article as the basis for the construction of a major area of no fault civil liability. English law has no such general principle. Nevertheless, it does have pockets of no fault liability, some of which can be analysed in terms of a liability attaching to things that cause damage. Indeed, even aspects of fault liability can be seen in terms of damage done by things under the control of another. In addition, English law also recognises a principle of vicarious liability, whereby an employer is automatically liable for a tort committed by his employee acting in the course of his employment.

9.1 Liability for moveable things

Article 1384 of the *Code civil* imposes a liability for damage done by a thing under the control (*sous sa garde*) of another. For well over a century this statement was thought to be simply a general introduction to arts 1385 and 1386, and thus restricted to damage resulting from dilapidated buildings and from animals. However, during the 20th century the *Cour de cassation* used this principle to develop a liability for things in general, and one particular landmark was the application of this strict liability article to motor vehicles in the famous *Jand'heur* decision in 1930. Such a general liability is to be found in few other systems (cf PETL, art 5:102)), although many do now have special traffic accident regimes (including France since 1985). Instead the tendency is to create specific areas of liability, one of the most important being the EU inspired liability for defective products.

9.1.1 English law: general overview

In English law, liability without fault attaches to dangerous animals and, in certain circumstances, to non-dangerous ones as well. In addition there are one or two other strict liabilities. The tort of private nuisance can make a landowner liable for damage arising from the unreasonable use of his land (see **7.3.3.12**, above), and 'unreasonable' in this context is not confined to fault. Public nuisance can be used in respect of dangerous structures that injure members of the public on the highway, and it can equally extend to vehicles parked on the highway (*Benjamin v Storr* (1874); and see **7.3.3.13**, above). A landowner or an occupier may also be liable under the rule in *Rylands v Fletcher* (below, **9.3.5**) for the escape of a dangerous thing brought onto the land, although it seems that this rule has to some extent been subverted by the torts of negligence and nuisance (*Transco plc v Stockport MBC* (2004)). Factory machinery and other things that are dangerous may well entail an employer in liability through the tort of breach of statutory duty or negligence (see **Chapter 8**), and there are a number of statutory strict liability regimes (on which see, eg, *Transco*, above, §§ 42, 45, 108). Contract also has a central role to play in respect of a liability for things. Thus the victim of defective goods may well have a contractual claim and, even if he does not, all EU systems now have, or should have, delictual liability regimes in place.

9.1.2 Dangerous products

Products liability is central to the tort of negligence in as much as the foundational case of *Donoghue v Stevenson* was of course a products case (see **8.1.4**, above). Damage arising from a defective product also transcends the contract and tort divide in that a purchaser of goods that are not reasonable fit for their purpose and (or) not of satisfactory quality can sue the professional seller for damages without having to prove fault (Sale of Goods Act 1979, s 14). Similar provisions apply where goods are hired. In addition to these existing claims there is now a statutory regime, itself the result of a European Directive (Council Directive of 25 July 1985), in respect of dangerous products. The key provision states that 'where any damage is caused wholly or partly by a defect in a product' the producer 'shall be liable for the damage' (Consumer Protection Act 1987, s 2). The Act goes on to lay down that 'there is a defect in a product ... if the safety of the product is not such as persons generally are entitled to expect' (s 3). The statutory regime follows the common law negligence position with respect to the type of damage remedied. The regime does not apply to pure economic loss, and thus the defective product must cause either personal injury or physical damage to property (s 5(1)) other than to itself (s 5(2)) (cf *Murphy v Brentwood DC* (1991)).

The main question here is likely to focus upon what consumers are 'entitled to expect'. This is not as simple as it may seem, for several reasons. First, because some products are themselves controversial; one thinks here not just of tobacco and alcohol but of complex and/or potentially dangerous mechanical products such as microwave ovens, lawnmowers, mobile telephones and the like. If such products come without adequate warnings, are they defective? Or what if a consumer fails to warn his or her hairdresser of an undue sensitivity with respect to a particular product that can be dangerous for some people (cf *Ingham v Emes* (1955))? Secondly, some products, such as chicken, pork and (possibly) eggs, have at some time or another been food items that have properly to be cooked for them to become safe to eat. What if a customer fails to cook pork properly (cf *Heil v Hedges* (1951))? Thirdly, much will depend upon whether the court puts the emphasis on the product itself – does the public expect it to be 100% perfect? – or whether account is also taken of the producer's manufacturing processes: did the manufacturer have in place a system of safety that meets public expectations? With respect to infected blood it has been held that one looks at the product rather than the system (*A v National Blood Authority* (2001)); this approach is valuable for the claimant since strict liability becomes less 'strict', so to speak, the moment one begins to take account of the defendant's 'act' (of producing).

Indeed, here one must mention another ambiguous point in the legislation. To what extent does it take consumer protection beyond the existing position at common law, that is to say beyond the protection offered by the tort of negligence and the law of contract? One point of contention is s 4(1)(e), whose wording can be compared with the words in the Directive. The Directive states that the 'producer shall not be liable ... if he proves: ... that the state of scientific and technical knowledge at the time when he put the product into circulation was not such as to enable the existence of the defect to be discovered' (Article 7(e)). The Act, however, says 'that the state of scientific and technical knowledge at the relevant time was not such that a producer of products of the same description as the product in question might be expected to have discovered the defect if it had existed in his products while they were under his control'. The European Commission took the view that s 4(1)(e) was not compatible with Article 7(e), but the European Court of Justice held that the two were not necessarily incompatible (*European Commission v UK* (1997)). The European Court stated that it is not just a matter of the wording in the text but how national courts actually interpret the legislation, and on this point the Court noted s 1(1) of the 1987 Act, which states that the Act 'shall have effect for the purpose of making such provision as is necessary in order to comply with the product liability Directive and shall be construed accordingly'. In other words, the European Court is looking less at the words in s 4(1)(e) and more at the interpretative leeway given to the judges to read the text in conformity with the Directive.

9.1.3 Defective equipment

One of the great sources of personal injury is the workplace, and many accidents are caused by dangerous things such as machinery, plant, tools and other equipment. As a result the workplace is covered by detailed safety legislation the breach of which, if it leads to injury, will be actionable via the tort of breach of statutory duty (see **8.5.1**, above) and (or) the tort of negligence. Breach of statutory duty is very much a liability for things, in that emphasis is put on the thing rather than on the behaviour of the defendant; if a piece of dangerous machinery must be fenced and, in breach of statute it is not, the employer will be strictly liable (*John Summers v Frost* (1955); *Millard v Serck Tubes Ltd* (1969)). The problem for claimants is when an employee is injured by a thing that does not fall within any statutory definition. If the court is not prepared to give a wide definition to the statutory term (see, eg, *Haigh v Charles W Ireland* (1973); cf *Coltman v Bibby Tankers* (1988)), then a claimant will have to rely on the tort of negligence, always assuming that this tort has been pleaded (*Morris v NCB* (1963)).

Where an employee is injured by equipment dangerous as a result of a manufacturing defect, the employer who supplied the equipment will be liable, at common law, only if he himself is in breach of a duty of care towards the employee (*Davie v New Merton Board Mills* (1959)). This in effect meant that the employer would often not be liable since he would on the whole be unaware of any latent manufacturing defect in a piece of equipment. This position came in for criticism and Parliament stepped in with the Employers' Liability (Defective Equipment) Act 1969, which deems the employer liable where 'the defect is attributable wholly or partly to the fault of a third party (whether identified or not)'. What is interesting from a liability for things point of view is that 'fault' 'means negligence, breach of statutory duty *or other act or omission which gives rise to liability in tort*' (emphasis added). Logically, therefore, it would seem that the employer will now be deemed liable for any liability that would attach to the manufacturer of the defective equipment under the Consumer Protection Act 1987.

9.1.4 Animals

Liability for damage done by animals is also the subject of a statutory regime and, with respect to a dangerous animal, there is a strict liability which attaches, via the animal, to the keeper (Animals Act 1971, s 2(1)). Much more difficult is the strict liability that can attach to non-dangerous animals. This will be the case only if the damage was of the type that the animal was 'likely to cause' or, if caused, 'was likely to be severe', and 'the likelihood of the damage or of its being severe was due to characteristics of the animal which are not normally found in animals of the same species or are not normally so found except at particular times or in particular circumstances'. Moreover, these characteristics had to be known to the keeper (s 2(2)). Not surprisingly, this section has been described by the judiciary, on several occasions, as 'opaque', and it is, for example, by no means clear that if a cat eats a neighbour's canary the keeper of the cat will be strictly liable.

In a major House of Lords decision on s 2(2), a bare majority held that the keeper of a horse that escaped from a field, without any negligence on the part of its owners, and caused a serious car accident was to be strictly liable, and this suggests that the judiciary are prepared to give a generous interpretation to the difficult section (*Mirvahedy v Henley* (2003)). The position is not entirely clear, of course, given the two dissenting opinions, and in consequence much will depend on the facts of each case. But, as things stand, the majority have established a genuine liability for things regime on the basis of an ambiguous legislative section. In addition, the case is valuable for the background depth it gives both to the Animals Act 1971 in general and to s 2 in particular. However, one should add that the 1971 Act goes on to deal with further types of damage done by other types of animal; and thus strict liability attaches to dogs which injure livestock (s 3) and for livestock which stray on to the land of another and cause property damage (s 4). The Act, in other words, is, as a French Professor once observed, more an exercise in animal character studies than legal principle, a view that seems to be confirmed by the Court of Appeal, who once devoted pages to the study of a dog's character (*Curtis v Betts* (1990)).

9.1.5 Motor vehicles

It may seem odd that animals are subjected to a statutory regime at a time when their importance in terms of transport had been completely eclipsed by motor vehicles. One might, instead, have expected a 'Motor Vehicles Act', perhaps along the lines of the French Law of 1985 which aimed to 'ameliorate' the legal position of victims injured on the roads (see Zweigert and Kötz, 1998, 665–6). For, alongside accidents at work, traffic accidents are the other great source of personal injury litigation. Yet English law has, on the whole, refused to establish a no fault liability of things regime for motor vehicles, with the result that civil liability for accidental harm is almost entirely dependent on the tort of negligence. Indeed, even the tort of breach of statutory duty – applicable to things in the workplace – was largely excluded from things on the road (*Phillips v Britannia Hygienic Laundry Co* (1923); but cf *Monk v Warbey* (1935)). Thus a victim must usually prove fault before damages can be obtained (*Mansfield v Weetabix Ltd* (1998)).

However, two points do need to be noted. First, there is a kind of liability for things that can apply to motor vehicles when a car owned by one person is driven by another and when a taxi, owned by one person, is directed to customers by another firm (see **9.4.5**, below). Secondly, there is one case which suggests that those who put commercial vehicles on the road which cause damage through a defect in, for example, the brakes, might be put into a position where they virtually have to disprove fault (*Henderson v HE Jenkins & Sons* (1970)); but such a principle, if in fact there is such a principle, probably does not in general extend to private vehicles. Despite these two exceptional situations, the civil liability position is controversial when compared with France. Victims of traffic accidents in France do not, on the whole, have to prove fault and, in addition, they can use the criminal proceedings to obtain civil compensation. It is, arguably, much less of a lottery in an area of personal injury where statistics are able fairly accurately to predict how many will be killed or injured on the roads in any one year.

9.1.6 Aircraft

A statutory strict liability regime does apply, however, to 'material loss or damage' that 'is caused to any person or property on land or water' by things falling from an aircraft (Civil Aviation Act 1982, s 76(2)). The 'cost' to the individual is that the same statute limits the right to bring a claim for nuisance in respect of annoyance caused by aircraft (ss 76(1), 77) and prohibits any claim in trespass (s 76(1)). Nevertheless, the courts seem to take the view that a claim in nuisance is not completely excluded, and in one recent decision it was held that the Ministry of Defence could be liable in private nuisance for the considerable noise caused to an occupier of land over which military jets flew. Such over-flights are no doubt in the public interest, said the judge, but 'it might well be unjust that he [the claimant] should suffer the damage for the benefit of all' (*Dennis v MOD* (2003)).

The judge also thought that the over-flights constituted an invasion of the claimant's human rights under the Human Rights Act 1998. However, it has recently been held by the Grand Chamber of the European Court of Human Rights that night flights at Heathrow would not amount to an invasion of Article 8 provided that the Government had seriously weighed the interests of the individual against the general economic interest of the country. The Court concluded that it:

> does not find that, in substance, the authorities overstepped their margin of appreciation by failing to strike a fair balance between the right of the individuals affected by those regulations to respect for their private life and home, and the conflicting interests of others and of the community as a whole, nor does it find that there have been fundamental procedural flaws in the preparation of the 1993 regulations on limitations for night flights (*Hatton v UK* (2003), § 129; and see *Marcic v Thames Water Utilities Ltd* (2003), § 41).

9.2 Liability for land and buildings (1): harm on the premises

Where damage has been caused by things on land, the position becomes complex because the sources of such liability are complex. Statute plays a fundamental role; yet not only are several different statutes to be considered, but the common law continues to have a background role as well (*Gwilliam v West Herts NHS Trust* (2002), §§ 35–44). It might be useful, therefore, to approach this area from the viewpoint of the formal source of liability, that is to say the various relevant statutes. However, one fundamental starting point must always be kept in mind, the actual premises (land, buildings and natural objects on the land) themselves.

9.2.1 Occupiers' Liability Act 1957

Where damage was caused by things on or done to land the position at common law was, before 1957, particularly complex because of the differing kinds of status of all those connected with the land. Occupiers might well have to be differentiated from landlords, and those coming on to land might enter under a contract (eg, football spectators), or because they were invited (guests) or because they were given an implied licence to enter (eg, travelling salesman). The common law once had different levels of duty attaching to these different classes of people. The aim of the Occupiers' Liability Act 1957 was to simplify the position, and it did this by reducing all the duties owed by an 'occupier' to a 'visitor' to a 'common duty of care' (s 2(1)).

The duty itself is one of taking such care as in all the circumstances of the case is reasonable to see that the visitor will be reasonably safe in using the premises (s 2(2)). This is, therefore, negligence liability, but a particular liability because it attaches to the state of the premises and extends to omissions (failure to make safe). Thus if the visitor is injured by a dangerous product on the premises the source of any liability might be outside of the Act (cf *Ward v Tesco Stores Ltd* (1976)) (but what about a collapsing stack of chairs?). The Act specifically mentions certain relevant circumstances: an occupier must be prepared for children to be less careful than adults (s 2(3)(a)), but he can expect that those who enter 'in the exercise of a calling' will guard against any risks attaching to this calling (s 2(3)(b)). Thus an occupier who calls in a specialist to deal with a defective installation can reasonably expect the specialist to appreciate and guard against the dangers arising from the defect (*Roles v Nathan* (1963)).

The statutory 'common duty' exists, however, only between an 'occupier' and a 'visitor', which gives rise to two questions. Who is an 'occupier'? And who is a 'visitor'? The occupier is a person who has *sufficient degree of control* over the premises (*Wheat v E Lacon & Co* (1966)) – and thus there might be two occupiers of the same premises (landlord and tenant) – while a visitor covers the old invitee (guest) and licensee (permitted to enter).

9.2.2 Occupiers' Liability Act 1984

What the term 'visitor' in the 1957 Act did not cover was the uninvited person who enters land as a 'trespasser' (see Law Comm Report No 75, Cmnd 6429, 1976). Thus, in principle, it would seem that no duty of care was owed to trespassers, save a duty not intentionally to injury them (*Edwards v Railway Executive* (1952); *Revill v Newbery* (1996)). The position was modified at common law mainly in respect of the problems caused by children: trespassers were owed a duty of common humanity, a much more limited duty than the ordinary duty of care (*Herrington v British Railways Board* (1972)).

Today uninvited persons are covered by the 1984 Act. An occupier owes a duty to 'persons other than his visitors in respect of any risk of their suffering injury on the premises by reason of any danger due to the state of the premises or to things done or omitted to be done on them' (ss 1(1)(a), 1(3)). However, the occupier must be *aware* both of the *danger*, or have reasonable grounds to believe that it exists, and of the *uninvited person* being 'in the vicinity of the danger' (s 1(3), emphasis added). Moreover, the risk must be such that it is *reasonable* in all the circumstances for the occupier to offer to the other some protection (s 1(3)(c), emphasis added). As to the duty itself, it is only 'to take such care as is reasonable in all the circumstances ... to see that he does not suffer *injury* on the premises by reason of the danger concerned' (s 1(4), emphasis added), the definition of 'injury' being confined to personal injury (s 1(9)). The duty is thus a very limited one (and note the interest protected), and much will depend upon the age of the trespasser and whether the danger was an obvious one or not. Indeed it may well be that it is only on rare occasions that an occupier will be liable to adult trespassers injured by obvious dangers, even at night (*Ratcliff v McConnell* (1999); *Tomlinson v Congleton BC* (2004)). Children might be treated with more sympathy, especially if the occupier is a large enterprise (*Herrington*) and (or) there is an allurement on the land (*Jolley v Sutton LBC* (2000)). But again it may be that an occupier is entitled to assume that parents will not normally allow their little children to go out unaccompanied (*Phipps v Rochester Corporation* (1955)). The occupier owes no duty to those with a statutory 'right to roam' in respect of natural features of the landscape (s 1(6A)).

9.2.2.1 *Tomlinson v Congleton BC* (2004)

In *Tomlinson v Congleton BC* (2004), a major case to reach the House of Lords on the 1984 Act, a teenager entered land owned by a local authority and dived into a lake on the property, suffering severe injury when his head struck the bottom. The defendant local authority was aware that people were attracted by the lake, but prominent notices declared that swimming was prohibited. The defendants were equally aware that these notices were often ignored and they intended, when finances permitted, to plant vegetation around the lake that would physically prevent people from entering the water. However, at the time of the accident the vegetation plan had not been executed. A majority of the Court of Appeal gave judgment for the teenager, but this was reversed by the House of Lords. There were a number of reasons put forward as to why the occupier should not be liable, but perhaps the general policy basis was expressed by Lord Hoffmann (at § 45):

> I think it will be extremely rare for an occupier of land to be under a duty to prevent people from taking risks which are inherent in the activities they freely choose to undertake upon the land. If people want to climb mountains, go hang-gliding or swim or dive in ponds or lakes, that is their affair. Of course the landowner may for his own reasons wish to prohibit such activities. He may think that they are a danger or

inconvenience to himself or others. Or he may take a paternalist view and prefer people not to undertake risky activities on his land. He is entitled to impose such conditions, as the Council did by prohibiting swimming. But the law does not require him to do so.

One problem with this observation of Lord Hoffmann is that it appears to be propounding a policy that actually conflicts with the careful wording of, and thus possibly the intention behind, the 1984 Act. The Law Lord seems to be envisaging that the risk is almost entirely on the trespasser, yet the language of the Act does not fully confirm this view. Where there is a danger attaching to land and premises there is some obligation that in turn attaches to the occupier.

9.2.3 Defective Premises Act 1972

The two occupiers' liability statutes are concerned with the duties owed by occupiers. But it is also necessary to consider the position of landlords where the latter are not occupiers (cf *Wheat v Lacon* (1966); *Harris v Birkenhead Corporation* (1976)), and this is where the 1972 Act is relevant. It puts a landlord under a duty of care 'to *all persons* who might reasonably be expected to be affected by the *defects* ... to see that they are *reasonably safe* from personal injury or from damage to their property caused by a relevant defect' (s 4(1), emphasis added; and note again the interests protected). However, this duty exists only in respect of let premises where the landlord is under an obligation to the tenant for the maintenance or repair of the premises. This of course means that where a third party (C) is injured as a result of defective premises, any claim against the landlord (D) might well depend not on the legal relationship between C and D, but upon the exact nature of a tenancy contract between D and tenant, reducing liability to a matter of chance (*McCauley v Bristol CC* (1991)). No doubt the tenant might well be liable if the landlord is not, but if the person was off the premises when injured by the defect (eg, a collapsing wall), the 1957 and 1984 Act will not apply (see s 1(7) of the 1984 Act). The question then is whether there is liability of occupier and (or) landlord at common law for public (*Mint v Good* (1951)) or private (*Brew Brothers Ltd v Snax Ltd* (1970)) nuisance.

9.2.4 Unfair Contract Terms Act 1977

The Occupiers' Liability Act 1957 specifically allows an occupier to 'extend, restrict, modify or exclude his duty' (s 2(1)). Thus, before 1977 all occupiers could potentially exclude liability by erecting a notice containing an exclusion provision; provided the notice was clear the occupier would not be liable (*White v Blackmore* (1972)). However, the 1977 Act now renders void any attempt to exclude liability for personal injury (s 2(1)) arising out of a 'business liability' (s 1(3)(a)); in the case of damage to property the exclusion will have to pass the reasonableness test (s 2(2)). The non-business occupier can therefore continue to exclude liability through a general notice (s 1(3)(b)). One anomaly is that a visitor may be in theory be a worse position than a trespasser, although it is unlikely that the judges will be over-impressed with such logic (see *Tomlinson v Congleton BC* (2004)). Note also that a notice, if ignored, might turn a visitor into a trespasser, although much will depend here on the actual facts (*Tomlinson*, above). However, it is difficult to imagine that a notice would be held to be binding against a young child.

9.3 Liability for land and buildings (2): harm off the premises

Occupiers' liability, as expressed in legislation, is primarily (although not exclusively) concerned with the liability of an occupier to those on the land under his control. However, dangerous premises can equally injure or damage people off the premises. A collapsing wall might fall onto a passer-by, or an activity carried out by the occupier might seriously annoy, if not physically damage, a neighbour. An activity attached to or associated with a particular piece of land can, of course, physically spread itself beyond the premises and spill onto the public highway. And this can cause problems for neighbours if not the community in general.

9.3.1 General overview

Several specific torts are of importance when it comes to the liability of an occupier and (or) owner of premises to those off the land. The most important are trespass, private nuisance, public nuisance and the rule in *Rylands v Fletcher*. One must not, of course, forget negligence, since one foundational case involved injury to a person on the highway (ie, public road) as a result of an activity (cricket) carried on by an occupier (*Bolton v Stone* (1951)). This case also raised the difficult issue of the relationship between the torts of nuisance and negligence. In many ways it is a sterile exercise to try to compare the so-called strict liability torts like nuisance with negligence at the formal level; it is more often a question of the nature of the damage suffered and the activity producing this damage, not forgetting, either, the remedy and interests (public or private) in issue (see now, eg, *Transco plc v Stockport MBC* (2004)). The actual requirements of many of these torts were set out by Denning LJ in *Esso Petroleum Ltd v Southport Corporation* (1954).

In addition to these torts one must not forget public law. There is now a range of statutes empowering public authorities, such as a local authority or the police, to act in situations where a person or commercial enterprise is carrying out an anti-social activity. For example, the Environmental Protection Act 1990 gives to local authorities the power to serve abatement notices where a statutory nuisance exists (ss 79–80) and the Noise Act 1996 empowers a local authority to issue a warning notice where noise which exceeds the permitted level is being emitted from a dwelling during the night hours (s 3). An unsocial occupier of land might also find himself the subject of an Anti-Social Behaviour Order (Crime and Disorder Act 1998, s 1). It must be remembered, in addition, that a severe interference with family life might well amount to an invasion of a human right. Some of these statutory protections are not as effective as one might at first think. The European Court of Human Rights has expressed the view that the rights of individuals are to be balanced against the economic interests of the community as a whole (*Hatton v UK* (2003)) and the Environmental Protection Act allows a firm that is prima facie committing a statutory nuisance the defence of 'best practicable means' in countering the nuisance (s 80(7); cf *Hounslow LBC v Thames Water Utilities Ltd* (2003), § 52).

9.3.2 Trespass to land

An occupier of land can be liable for trespass to a neighbour if he directly invades the land of the latter (cf **7.3.3.14**, above). Thus, if he builds a garage on his land that by several inches transgresses onto the land of his neighbour there will liability; however, the victim probably does not have the right to destroy that part of the garage that transgresses the boundary (*Burton v Winters* (1993)), although in principle a victim can abate a nuisance (self-help remedy). He can seek damages and (or) an injunction. The same trespass principle applies to a crane jib that transgresses the air space of a landowner (*Anchor Brewhouse Developments Ltd v Berkley House Ltd* (1987)); but merely to photograph a person's house without actually entering the premises or airspace will not be a trespass (*Bernstein v Skyviews and General Ltd* (1978)), although it might amount to a contravention of Article 8 of the European Convention of Human Rights. The damage must normally be direct if it is to constitute trespass (see Denning LJ in *Esso Petroleum Ltd v Southport Corporation* (1954), 195), but a person who deliberately sets a pack of dogs in pursuit of, say, a stag or a fox, knowing that there is a real risk that the dogs will enter on another's land without permission of the landowner, will be liable in trespass (*League Against Cruel Sports v Scott* (1986)). One could also talk here of a liability for animals.

9.3.3 Private nuisance

Trespass is about direct invasions of a person's land, while nuisance is about indirect invasions (cf **7.3.3.12**, above). However, these indirect invasions must result from an activity carried out by a landowner that amounts to an *unreasonable use of land*. The essence of the tort is not so much the behaviour of one person vis-à-vis the damage suffered by another person; the essence is the activity, or state of affairs, associated with one piece of land and its effect on a neighbouring property, with the result that the damage arising from nuisance is damage to *land* (*Hunter v Canary Wharf Ltd* (1997)). Accordingly, the claimant must have an *interest* in the land affected. The use of the word 'unreasonable' means that the behaviour of the defendant *might* be relevant on occasions; encroaching tree roots or direct damage often requires an 'unreasonableness' that is close to the Lord Atkin neighbour formula (see *Delaware Mansions Ltd v Westminster CC* (2001), 1017–18; *Transco plc v Stockport MBC* (2004), § 96; *Morris v Network Rail* (2004)). Moreover, if an occupier deliberately indulges in an activity with the sole purpose of irritating his neighbour he will be liable (*Hollywood Silver Fox Farm v Emmett* (1936)). Equally a failure to remedy a dangerous state of affairs – a mere omission in the eyes of the tort of negligence but not in the tort of private nuisance – could result in liability (*Goldman v Hargrave* (1967); *Delaware Mansions Ltd v Westminster CC* (2001)).

Nevertheless, the type of damage is important. If the damage is *intangible* (noise, smell etc) the nature of the locality and the activity will play a vital role in determining liability; if it is *tangible* – physical damage to persons or property – then locality will be irrelevant (*Halsey v Esso Petroleum & Co Ltd* (1961)). Often this distinction is reflected in the type of the remedy in issue: intangible damage is usually the subject of an injunction claim, and here the public interest might be balanced against the private (*Miller v Jackson* (1977)). The remedy of damages in contrast usually focuses on where the loss should fall, which in turn tends to emphasise interference, activity and causation (*Holbeck Hall Hotel Ltd v Scarborough CC* (2000)).

An important defence to nuisance is its authorisation by statute; indeed the tort may be inapplicable where a statutory scheme is in place (*Marcic v Thames Water Utilities Ltd*

(2003)). However, the mere granting of planning permission is not a licence to commit a nuisance (*Wheeler v JJ Saunders Ltd* (1996)). Another defence was undue sensitivity with respect to the claimant's own activity on his land, but this has possibly now been subsumed by the more general requirement of foreseeability and may no longer be relevant in the 21st century (*Morris v Network Rail* (2004) per Buckley LJ). It is, it must be added, no defence that the claimant came to the nuisance (but cf *Miller v Jackson* (1977)).

9.3.4 Public nuisance

Private nuisance involves a claim by one land user against another and is concerned with private interests; public nuisance – whose origins are conceptually different – usually involves a claim for interference with a person's use and enjoyment of a public highway (including waterways, etc), and thus must involve an invasion of the public interest (cf **7.3.3.13**, above). The interference must amount to the crime of public nuisance, and to sue in tort the claimant must suffer *special damage* over and above other members of the public. Here, however, it is important to note that pure financial loss will suffice. Consequently, a claim in public nuisance could succeed where the tort of negligence would fail (*Tate & Lyle v GLC* (1983)).

What the court does, according to Edmund Davies LJ in a case involving personal injury on the road, in a claim for public nuisance is not to look at the conduct of the defendant and ask whether he was negligent. What it does is to look at the actual state of affairs as it exists in or adjoining the highway, without regard to the merits or demerits of the defendant's act; and if the state of affairs is such as to be a danger to persons using the highway it will amount to a public nuisance. Once it is held to be a danger, the person who created it is liable unless he can show sufficient justification or excuse (*Dymond v Pearce* (1972), 506–07). This tort can thus be used to gain damages for injury, damage or loss suffered by public highway users as a result of dangerous buildings and structures which adjoin the highway (ie, public road, path or waterway: see, eg, *Tarry v Ashton* (1876); *Wringe v Cohen* (1940); *Mint v Good* (1951); and note also Defective Premises Act 1972, s 4). Even an activity that is prima facie a private nuisance – that is to say where private interests are affected – can become a public nuisance if the effects are wide enough to affect the community as a whole, for in such a situation the public interest comes into play. And in such cases the Attorney-General (and now the local authority thanks to legislation) can seek an injunction to restrain the nuisance (*Att-Gen v PYA Quarries Ltd* (1957)).

9.3.5 Rule in *Rylands v Fletcher*

If one was looking for one single authority that appears closest, in spirit at least, to the idea of a liability for a thing under the control of another (cf CC, art 1384) it is the mid-19th century decision of *Rylands v Fletcher* (1866–68)). This case is not just a precedent but has traditionally been considered as the basis of an independent cause of action in tort. 'We think', said Blackburn J in his Court of Exchequer Chamber judgment (1866), 'that the true rule of law is, that the person who for his own purposes brings on his lands and collects and keeps there anything likely to do mischief if it escapes, must keep it in at his peril, and, if he does not do so, is *prima facie* answerable for all the damage which is the natural consequence of its escape' (at 279). In the House of Lords (1868), Lord Cairns added the requirement of 'non natural use' (replacing 'not naturally there'). Whether the judges and Law Lords thought they were laying down new law is open to question (see now *Transco plc v Stockport MBC* (2004)). But the case became separated from nuisance in that it involved a single escape rather than a state of affairs. Its potential was huge; in the United States it has become the basis for 'extra hazardous liability'.

However, in the United Kingdom later cases severely restricted its scope by focusing on one or more of what are three basic requirements. These are:

(a) that the thing must be dangerous (thus bringing in an element of foreseeability: *Cambridge Water Co v Eastern Counties Leather Plc* (1994));
(b) that the dangerous thing must escape from D's land (and so no liability under the rule to someone injured on the premises: *Read v J Lyons & Co* (1947)); and
(c) that the accumulation on the land must be a non-natural use.

The last requirement has now been subsumed to some extent under the foreseeability principle (*Cambridge Water*), which means that the focal point is now the 'dangerousness' of the thing brought onto land. The escape rule is a serious restriction in that a person injured *on the premises* will not, it seems, have a claim under the rule and will have to prove a breach of a common duty of care. Moreover, if the escape of the thing results from the act of a stranger (*Perry v Kendricks Transport Ltd* (1956)) or an 'act of God' (*Nichols v Marsland* (1876)), the landowner may have a defence; and it is unlikely that the rule now applies to personal injury (*Read v Lyons*; *Transco plc v Stockport MBC* (2004)). In Australia the rule has been absorbed into the tort of negligence.

9.3.5.1 *Transco v Stockport MBC* (2004)

The rule in *Rylands v Fletcher* has recently been comprehensively reviewed by the House of Lords in the case of *Transco plc v Stockport MBC* (2004). In this case the owner of a gas-pipe damaged by water escaping, without negligence, from the defendants' land unsuccessfully brought a *Rylands v Fletcher* claim in respect of the damage. Lord Hoffmann summarised (at § 39) the relevance of the rule in contemporary tort law:

> I pause at this point to summarise the very limited circumstances to which the rule has been confined. First, it is a remedy for damage to land or interests in land. As there can be few properties in the country, commercial or domestic, which are not insured against damage by flood and the like, this means that disputes over the application of the rule will tend to be between property insurers and liability insurers. Secondly, it does not apply to works or enterprises authorised by statute. That means that it will usually have no application to really high risk activities. As Professor Simpson points out ([1984] 13 J Leg Stud 225) the Bradfield Reservoir was built under statutory powers. In the absence of negligence, the occupiers whose lands had been inundated would have had no remedy. Thirdly, it is not particularly strict because it excludes liability when the escape is for the most common reasons, namely vandalism or unusual natural events. Fourthly, the cases in which there is an escape which is not attributable to an unusual natural event or the act of a third party will, by the same token, usually give rise to an inference of negligence. Fifthly, there is a broad and ill-defined exception for 'natural' uses of land. It is perhaps not surprising that counsel could not find a reported case since the second world war in which anyone had succeeded in a claim under the rule …

Whatever the success of the strict liability principle in the United States (ultra-hazardous activity), in the English common law *Rylands v Fletcher* has been largely subsumed by private nuisance and negligence. As Lord Hoffmann concluded: 'It is hard to escape the conclusion that the intellectual effort devoted to the rule by judges and writers over many years has brought forth a mouse' (at § 39). This may be so.

9.3.6 Liability for fire

Dangerous animals and fire might seem to be covered by *Rylands v Fletcher*. However, liability for damage done by animals is, as we have seen (cf **9.1.4**, above), now governed by a separate statutory regime. With respect to damage caused by fire, there is a statutory defence 'against any person in whose house, chamber, stable, barn or other building, or in whose estate any fire shall *accidentally* begin' (Fires Prevention (Metropolis) Act 1774, s 86, emphasis added). The word 'accidentally' has been construed narrowly, with the result that spreading fire can give rise to liability under a number of heads: *Rylands v Fletcher* (*Mason v Levy Auto Parts* (1967)); private nuisance (*Goldman v Hargrave* (1967)); and of course negligence. If the fire has been caused by a trespasser, the occupier from whose land the fire spreads may be able to escape liability in negligence provided he has not allured the trespasser onto the property (*Smith v Littlewoods Organisation Ltd* (1987)). Fire also brings into play fire insurance and contractual structures in complex commercial situations, and this may lead to the following question often posed implicitly, if not explicitly, by the judges. Upon which insurance policy should the fire risk fall? Certainly damage done to property by water can now attract this kind of insurance analysis (*Transco plc v Stockport MBC* (2004), § 46, but cf § 60) and the same is no doubt true for damage by fire (*Photo Production v Securicor* (1980)).

9.3.7 Occupiers' liability: methodological considerations

Before leaving the topic of occupiers' liability something should perhaps be said about the methods involved in handling problems arising in this area. The supposed strength of the 1957 Act was that it was designed to simplify the situation with respect to liability and duty. Instead of differing duties at different levels, the Act imposed a common duty of care. Yet it should be obvious that the plethora of duties that attach to an occupier have not in general been simplified. If a wall collapses harming three different persons – one on the land on which the wall was constructed, another on the public highway and one living next door whose property is damaged – the situation will be complex. The owner of the wall will find that he owes three quite different duties. To the person on the highway the duty is strict, or almost strict (*Mint v Good* (1951)); to the person next door, the duty might be quite strict (*Wringe v Cohen* (1940)); while to the person on the land the duty will be one where the injured person has to prove fault (Occupiers' Liability Act 1957, s 2). Such a difference of duties will also be found where, for example, a shed full of fireworks explodes and causes all kinds of damage to property both on and off the premises. To those off the premises the duty will probably be strict, whereas to the owners of property parked on the premises the duty will be the common duty of care. Indeed, if a trespasser has left property on the premises, there will be no duty owed by the occupier.

All these differing duties result, of course, from different kinds of causes of action. To those off the premises the duties will be determined by the torts of public nuisance, private nuisance and *Rylands v Fletcher*; to those on the premises the duties will be defined by statute, and much will depend upon whether the claimant is a 'visitor' or a 'trespasser'. Yet even where the duty is fixed by statute complexity can still resurface. If the occupier brings onto to his land an independent contractor to provide entertainment for his visitors, the occupier may remain under some residual duties, perhaps to check the contractor's insurance if the activity is a risky one (*Gwilliam v West Herts NHS Trust* (2002)). Over and above the statutory regime, it may well be that the occupier continues to owe a duty at common law in respect of the kind of safety system that is in operation; and thus in one case a woman injured in a supermarket when she slipped on a pot of spilt yoghurt was able to recover damages when she indicated that the supermarket might have a faulty system for handling such spillages (*Ward v Tesco Stores* (1976)).

When faced, therefore, with a set of facts involving land and (or) buildings it remains important to identify exactly where the accident took place, the nature of the damage and how it occurred. Was the claimant injured on or off the premises? If the latter, then the Occupiers' Liability Acts 1957 or 1984 will not be applicable; one will need to look at one of the strict liability torts and the common law tort of negligence. What was the nature of the damage? If it was intangible (smell, noise), locality might be relevant. If it was economic or damage to property, the status of the claimant could be vital. If a trespasser, the occupier will owe him a duty only in respect of personal injury.

How did the damage occur? If it was of a continuing nature then the tort of nuisance might be relevant; if a single event, like an explosion or escape, then *Rylands v Fletcher* would be the cause of action (although this cause of action probably will not apply to personal injury: *Transco plc v Stockport MBC* (2004)). Was the damage caused by an activity started and operated by the defendant, or did it arise from a situation of which he was not the immediate cause? If a neighbour suffers damage as a result of a commercial activity, it may well be that the occupier will be liable in nuisance even if he is not at fault; the mere causing of damage by the activity could well deem it an unreasonable use of land vis-à-vis the person who individually suffers as a result of the defendant's activity (*Bamford v Turnley* (1862); *Dennis v MOD* (2003); but cf *Marcic v Thames Water Utilities Ltd* (2003)). However, if the damage is caused by some process of nature, or some activity reasonable in itself, then the occupier will probably be liable only if he *adopted* the nuisance, that is if he was aware, or ought to have been aware, of the danger (*Delaware Mansions Ltd v Westminster CC* (2002); and see *Lippiatt v South Gloucestershire Council* (1999)). In this latter situation nuisance and negligence to some extent merge via the notion of *unreasonable*. If the activity causes annoyance to more than just one or two neighbours, it may be that the local authority will be able to seek an injunction since the interests of the community are in play; in other words, public nuisance might provoke a community remedy whereas private nuisance is actionable only by the person affected (*Att-Gen v PYA Quarries* (1957)). If the activity is governed by a statutory scheme there may be no scope for a liability at common law (*Marcic v Thames Water Utilities Ltd* (2003)). However, if injury occurs as a result of a breach of some safety statute, perhaps the tort of breach of statutory duty might come into play.

The intervention of statute in 1957 has, admittedly, probably not exacerbated the duty complexity which attaches to an occupier. Yet it has not really simplified the overall picture either. Nor, perhaps, could, or should, statute do this. The situation is complex because the activities carried out on land are complex and give rise to a range of different types of problem. The advantage of the forms of action approach – trespass, public nuisance, private nuisance, *Rylands v Fletcher* and negligence – is that it forces legal problem-solvers to operate at the level of fact and to distinguish between different types of damage, causes, actors and activities (compare eg *Hussain v Lancaster CC* (1999) with *Lippiatt v South Gloucestershire Council* (1999)). Or, put another way, it offers a range of possibilities when it comes to categorising the facts in order to apply the law. The difficulty is, of course, that the forms of action are not watertight; concepts from one can infect others, and this immediately gives rise to a conceptual problem of boundaries. What is the difference between nuisance and negligence? Why does Baron Bramwell in *Bamford v Turnley* seem to be applying a criterion that is different from, say, the one used by Lord Hoffmann in *Transco v Stockport MBC*? One reason, perhaps, is that a commercial brick factory is not quite the same as a statutory concern charged with supplying water and sewerage facilities (although privatisation has 'muddied the waters' to use an apt metaphor). Judges do not always openly say such things, but the concepts they apply can reflect differences in social fact and in historical outlook (see *Transco plc v Stockport MBC* (2004); *Hounslow LBC v Thames Water Utilities Ltd* (2003); *Marcic v Thames Water Utilities Ltd* (2003)).

Perhaps, however, the biggest challenge in the area of occupiers' liability is to fashion a methodology suitable for dealing with the new environmental concerns, no doubt more challenging than those that had to be faced in former times. How does the public interest, or the interest of future generations, get recognised, for example, in a private nuisance claim? In addition to all of this, one must not forget the Human Rights Act 1998, which might impose even further duties on an occupier (*Dennis v MOD* (2003); but cf *Marcic v Thames Water Utilities Ltd* (2003)). One thing is certain, merely applying a 'common duty of care' across the whole spectrum of liability for things would be far too simplistic, and possibly rather dangerous for local, national and international environmental interests.

9.4 Liability for people

The idea of a liability for things is balanced, symmetrically speaking, in art 1384 of the *Code civil* by the further idea of a liability for people. We have seen that English law does give *some* expression to the idea of a liability based on the control of a thing. Does it also give expression to the idea of a liability arising out of the control of a person? As with liability for things, the answer is not entirely negative by any means, but the conceptual structure of English tort law can make comparison with French law complex (compare eg *Hussain v Lancaster CC* (1999) with *Lippiatt v South Gloucestershire Council* (1999)).

9.4.1 General overview

As one might expect, there is no general principle in English law similar to the liability for persons in art 1384 of the *Code civil*. Instead there is a number of specific situations where one person will be liable for a tortious act committed by another person. These specific situations fall broadly into three categories:

(a) the liability of an employer for torts committed by an employee (vicarious liability);
(b) certain direct liabilities arising out of torts committed by persons who might or might not be employees; and
(c) the specific liability of an owner of car for the careless driving of another using the car when the owner has an interest in the journey.

These categories are not scientific creations, particularly the second; they are simply designed to orientate the researcher towards the main groups of cases where one person can be held liable for the tortious act of another. One complicating factor, of course, is the notion of legal personality, since such an 'abstract' person (or *personne morale* as the French say, developing an idea first found in medieval Roman law scholarship) can act only through human persons. Where an employee or other contractor causes damage to a third person the latter is immediately confronted with two possible defendants, the corporation and the individual actor (on which see Lord Hoffmann in *Meridian Global Funds v Securities Commission* (1995)).

9.4.2 Vicarious liability

The starting point of liability for another's tort is the well-established principle of vicarious liability, whereby an employer ('master') is liable for torts committed by an employee ('servant') acting in the course of his ememployment. The liability is based on three sub-rules:

(a) there must be a tort;
(b) committed by a servant;
(c) acting within the course of his employment.

All of these rules have given rise to case law.

9.4.2.1 Tort

The claimant injured by an employee must establish a tort, that is to say he must establish that the employee's act that has caused the damage amounted to trespass, negligence, conversion, defamation or whatever. If there is no tort there is no employer's liability (*Staveley Iron & Chemical Co v Jones* (1956)). The claimant might be able to derive some help from the maxim *res ipsa loquitur*; and so if someone goes into a hospital operating theatre for a minor operation on his hand and comes out minus his arm, there will be a prima facie assumption that this is due to a tort committed by the hospital (*Cassidy v Ministry of Health* (1951)). But such an aid does not amount to a reversal of the burden of proof (*The Kite* (1933)); all that the defendant need show to put the burden of proving negligence back onto the claimant is that the accident could have happened without fault (*Roe v Minister of Health* (1954).

9.4.2.2 Servant (employee)

The individual who has committed a tort must be a 'servant', that is to say an employee and not an independent contractor (*Rowe v Herman* (1997)). Thus a business enterprise will be liable for the careless driving of a driver on the payroll, but not for a taxi driver who drives some of the managers to the station. There are some ambiguous situations how-ever. Some firms hire out not just vehicles but also drivers: thus if the driver carelessly injures a third person it may not always be clear whether it is the owner or hirer of the vehicle who is to be vicariously liable (*Mersey Docks & Harbour Board v Coggins & Griffiths Ltd* (1947)). An added difficulty is that some contracts of employment specifically state that employees are not 'servants' but independent contractors; here the courts may or may not be influenced by form (*Ready Mixed Concrete v MOP* (1968); cf *Ferguson v John Dawson & Partners* (1976)).

In *Hall v Lorimer* (1992), the judge (ultimately supported by the Court of Appeal) had to decide if a person was an employee or in business on his own account. The judge said this (at 944):

> In order to decide whether a person carries on business on his own account it is necessary to consider many different aspects of that person's work activity. This is not a mechanical exercise of running through items on a check list to see whether they are present in, or absent from, a given situation. The object of the exercise is to paint a picture from the accumulation of detail. The overall effect can only be appreciated by standing back from the detailed picture which has been painted, by viewing it from a distance and by making an informed, considered, qualitative appreciation of the whole. It is a matter of evaluation of the overall effect of the detail, which is not necessarily the same as the sum total of the individual details. Not all details are of equal weight or importance in any given situation. The details may also vary in importance from one situation to another.

In *Market Investigations Ltd v Ministry of Social Security* (1969), Cooke J broadly adopted this approach but by asking two questions. The first was 'whether the extent and degree of the control exercised by the company, if no other factors were taken into account, be consistent with her being employed under a contract of service'. And the second question was, 'whether when the contract is looked at as a whole, its nature and provisions are consistent or inconsistent with its being a contract of service' (at 185). The question that he had to decide was whether a woman interviewer employed from time to time to carry out interviews was acting as an employee (contract of service), or as an independent con-tractor in business on her own account (contract of services). After weighing up a number of considerations – including the degree of *control* exercised by the employer over her work, plus the fact that there was nothing in the contracts that was actual *inconsistent* with it being a contract of service – Cooke J decided that she was an employee.

9.4.2.3 Course of employment

The third requirement is perhaps the most difficult since there is a large grey area between acting for one's employer and acting for oneself (a 'frolic of one's own'). For example, the company van driver who carelessly injures another road user while delivering his employer's goods will involve the employer in liability. However, if the driver was using the company van to take his family out to a picnic one Sunday, the employer will probably not be liable. The test used to be summed up in this question: was the actor doing something he was employed to do? Thus in one case a bus company was held not liable for an assault by a bus conductor on a passenger since assaulting passengers was not what he was employed to do (*Keppel Bus Co v Sa'ad bin Ahmad* (1974)). But in another case the House of Lords insisted that an employer of a security guard would have been liable (but for an exclusion clause) for his criminal act in deliberately burning down the premises of a client whose factory he had been sent to guard (*Photo Production Ltd v Securicor* (1980)).

The leading case is one involving the theft of a valuable mink stole by an employee of a firm of cleaners: the firm was held liable to the owner of the stole because he was employed to 'handle' it, and thus his theft was an extension of doing what he was employed to do (*Morris v CW Martin & Sons Ltd* (1966)). If the stole had been stolen by a secretary or night porter, presumably there would have been no liability. In fact the case is complicated because there was a direct bailment duty between owner and cleaners, and this makes it more of a property than an obligations case (cf **1.3.8**, above). Nevertheless, it acted as the basis for the most recent major decision in this area: the law ought not to protect property owners better than human victims. Thus the employers of a warden who abused children in his care were held to be vicariously liable since he abused his position of trust (*Lister v Hesley Hall Ltd* (2001)). The test now is the 'connection' between employment duty and tortious act, and thus an employer has been held liable for a doorman who took violent revenge on a member of the public leaving him severely handicapped (*Mattis v Pollock* (2003)). The connection test has has also been applied to the statutory tort of harassment commited in the workplace (*Majrowski v Guy's & St Thomas's NHS Trust* (2005)).

9.4.2.4 Theory of vicarious liability

Just why an employer is, in English law at least, automatically liable for torts committed by employees is not that easy to determine. Of course at first sight one can fashion a number of seemingly convincing theories based, for example, on the idea of those who profit from another's work should take the risk, or on the thesis that the employer is in the best position to insure (*Morris v Ford Motor Co* (1973)). On closer examination many of these theories do not stand up to scrutiny. Thus the insurance argument breaks down because liability is joint; the victim has the choice of suing either the servant or the employer, and even if the employer is sued the insurance company, subrogated to the rights of the employer, is entitled in law to recoup the money from the employee who committed the tort (*Lister v Romford Ice & Cold Storage Co Ltd* (1957)). Indeed, the insurance company could also do this as a matter of contribution (Civil Liability (Contribution) Act 1978).

Possibly vicarious liability was once an extension of the principle of agency: *qui facit per alium facit per se* (he who acts through another acts for himself). But recently Lord Millett has stated that it 'is best understood as a loss-distribution device' whose 'theoretical underpinning of the doctrine is unclear'. He went on to suggest that the employer 'is liable only if the risk is one which experience shows is inherent in the nature of the business' (*Lister v Hesley Hall Ltd* (2001), § 65). Again Lord Millett's thesis is open to attack on the ground that it is the person at fault who is, in theory, ultimately liable to pay. Yet if he is reflecting what most judges believe then one further valuable reform that they might undertake is to remove the right of the employer (or in effect its insurance company) to reclaim from the employee an indemnity. In practice insurance companies do not do this, and so any reform by the judiciary would have the added advantage of mirroring social practice. French judges have not been frightened to pursue such reforms, but it is arguable that this is because French judges in both the private and the public systems have a very clear sense of social justice. English judges, it is sometimes said, are more in favour of individualism.

9.4.3 Non-delegable duty

Vicarious liability cannot apply where an *independent contractor* commits a tort since he is not a 'servant' (*Salsbury v Woodland* (1970); and see also *A (A Child) v Minister of Defence* (2004)). Yet there appear to be cases that contradict this logic; there are decisions where an employer of an independent contractor is seemingly held liable for the tort committed by the contractor. For example in *Rylands v Fletcher* (1866–68), the owner of land, who hired a firm of independent contractors to build a reservoir on the property, was held liable for the negligent work carried out by the contractors. However, the liability of the employer in these exceptional cases is not vicarious; it is based on the breach of a direct *non-delegable* duty between victim and employer. In addition to any statutory duties, such a duty can arise from the keeping of a dangerous thing (*Rylands*), an extra-hazardous act (*Honeywill & Stein Ltd v Larkin Bros Ltd* (1934)), a bailment relationship (*Riverstone Meat Co v Lancashire Shipping Co* (1961)), a public nuisance (*Tarry v Ashton* (1876)) and, of course, a contractual relationship between victim and employer (*Wong Mee Wan v Kwan Kin Travel Services Ltd* (1996); and see *Photo Production Ltd v Securicor* (1980)).

This last relationship is of particular importance because it so clearly indicates how the law of obligations can become distorted by the relationship between legal personality and liability. When a company contracts to do something it can perform the contract *only* through its employees and thus vicarious liability is irrelevant. If an employee fails to perform his employer's contractual promise the employer cannot claim that the employee's act (or failure) is not *their* act; it is they, the employer, who have promised and thus it is they who will be in breach of contract. In other words, the contractual performance and duty cannot be delegated, in the sense of freeing the employer of his contractual responsibility, to an employee.

Land can also give rise to a non-delegable duty attaching to the owner or occupier. In one recent case a local authority was held liable for a nuisance caused by a group of travellers who had occupied land belonging to the council; as one judge pointed out, this was not a matter of vicarious liability, but a matter of whether the council had *adopted* the nuisance in as much as it was connected with its land (*Lippiatt v South Gloucestershire Council* (2000)). If there were no local authority land to which the nuisance could attach the result would be different (*Hussain v Lancaster CC* (2000)). The key question for the employer, contractor or landowner is whether he can use the person who actually commits the tort to isolate himself from liability. Thus the householder who hires a reputable firm of contractors to build, say, a garage will probably not be liable if the contractors commit a public nuisance (*Rowe v Herman* (1997)). But the employer cannot always isolate himself from a general duty to provide safe premises simply by hiring a firm of independent contractors (see, eg, *Gwilliam v West Herts NHS Trust* (2002)).

9.4.4 Duty of care

Thus another form of non-delegable duty is where the employer himself owes a direct duty of care to the victim. Take the case of *Home Office v Dorset Yacht Co* (1970), where the claimant's yacht was damaged by borstal boys out on a supervised camping trip. There is no doubt that this actual case was a vicarious liability decision in that the House of Lords had to decide if the warders themselves owed a duty of care to supervise borstal boys; if they did, and were in breach of it, the Home Office would be vicariously liable for the warders' tort. Yet the facts raise further issues. Could the Home Office itself, as a legal person, owe a direct duty of care to the population living close to a prison in respect of supervising inmates? This question is not the same as the vicarious liability one, in that the court would have to examine the security *system* that operated in prisons. If the system itself was found wanting then the Home Office might be in breach of a direct duty of care if a prisoner had escaped, due to the faulty system, and had harmed a nearby resident (cf *Ward v Tesco Stores* (1976)). Another interesting question, of course, is whether the Home Office might be vicariously liable for torts committed by prisoners. One could immediately respond by saying that prisoners are not servants. But what if they were out doing prison work in return for payment by the Home Office?

This systems point is well brought out by *McDermid v Nash Dredging and Reclamation Co* (1987). This case involved an accident on a tug which arose out of the negligence of the captain, who was not actually an employee of the defendants. The House of Lords nevertheless held the defendants liable not on the ground of vicarious liability, but on the basis that an unsafe system of work was being operated on the tug. The defendants were liable, in other words, for the breach of a *direct* duty of care owed to the claimant. Again, more recently, the House of Lords has stated that in these kind of cases it is important to identify the correct basis of liability (*Phelps v Hillingdon LBC* (2001)), and of course this is what was at the heart of the pleadings difficulty in *Esso Petroleum Ltd v Southport Corporation* (1953–56)).

In French law vicarious liability extends to parents for torts committed by their children. This is not true of English law; a parent cannot be vicariously liable for the tort committed by a child unless, perhaps, the child is acting as an 'employee' (child doing a paper round for his parents' newsagent business?). However, parents can be liable for torts if they are in breach of a direct duty of care to supervise, or if their children were committing a nuisance said to have been adopted by the parents. Thus in one case a local authority was held in breach of its duty of care when a child ran into the road from one of its nursery schools and caused a serious accident (*Carmarthenshire CC v Lewis* (1955)).

9.4.5 Liability with respect to motor vehicles

One apparent extension of the principle of vicarious liability beyond the employment relationship is where an owner of a car is held liable for the negligent driving of the car by another person. The liability is based on a form of 'agency' (*qui facit per alium facit per se*) and thus the owner must have a real interest in the journey; that is to say, the driver must be undertaking a specific task for the owner (*Morgans v Launchbury* (1973)). If there is no interest – the owner is just lending the car as a favour – then there will be no liability under this principle. However in *Morgans*, where the husband was using a car owned by his wife and, when he got too drunk, handed over the keys to a friend so that he could drive, it was held that the husband was *vicariously liable* for the friend's negligent driving (see *Nottingham v Aldridge* (1971)). Most insurance policies will, however, extend to drivers named by the owner, so in practice this form of vicarious liability is less important than it may seem.

Non-delegable duty can also play a role. In one case, where a taxi customer was injured as a result of the defective condition of the taxi, the customer was able to obtain damages not from the owner of the taxi, but from the mini-cab firm who had supplied a radio to the taxi, used to direct the owner towards customers (*Rogers v Night Riders* (1983)). The mini-cab firm was in breach of a direct non-delegable duty that the taxi was reasonable fit for its purpose. This decision has attracted criticism, but it can be justified on the basis that taxi customers direct their 'offers' towards the mini-cab firm seemingly to be 'accepted' or rejected by the firm. It is not necessarily unreasonable that such a relationship, even if not actually contractual, should contain a guarantee of safety.

10 Escaping Liability

Devoting a chapter to escaping from liability might at first sight appear somewhat cynical. In addition, it is probably not a fully comprehensive term vis-à-vis everything that will be covered in this chapter. Nevertheless this perspective has a number of strengths, the most important of which is to shift the emphasis off claimants, and off things, and onto the defendant. What means are open to a defendant, faced with a possible liability, to mount a fully or partial defence against damages, or some other remedy, demanded by the claimant?

If one was to look for one single notion that would more or less cover most of the possible defences, it might be 'causation'. Now it has to be said at once that this is not readily obvious from most contract and tort textbooks, or even from the cases themselves. But that is because 'causation' is something of a term of art in itself and, as a specific legal notion, is relatively narrow in scope. Yet if one takes a wide view of causation it can be seen to cover many areas that do not appear in the causation chapter to be found in many of the textbooks. For example, self-induced frustration (see *Maritime National Fish Ltd v Ocean Trawlers Ltd* (1935)) or consent is not normally dealt with as a matter of causation, even although each functions as a means for cutting the connection between cause (or intervention) and effect. This chapter will, accordingly, interpret causation in its widest sense, and as a result it will include many of the main defences available to a defendant in a law of obligations claim.

10.1 Causation

In the tort of negligence, in addition to establishing that a defendant was under a duty of care to the claimant and that he was in breach of this duty, a claimant must prove that the breach of duty (the negligence) *caused* the damage incurred. In fact this requirement is to be found across the whole spectrum of the law of obligations, and thus a defendant will escape liability for a breach of contract, a breach of a statutory duty and a breach of a strict liability duty if he can prove that he was not the cause of the claimant's damage (see **7.2.3**, above). Indeed causation problems can even arise in conversion (*Kuwait Airways v Iraqi Airways* (2002)). This causal requirement in turn usually sub-divides into two questions: Was the defendant's wrongful act the *factual* cause of the claimant's damage? And was it the *legal* cause? However, as we have mentioned, causation as a topic stretches beyond these two sub-questions. It is a requirement in all torts (and of course in contractual liability), and it finds expression in other tort notions such as the defences of contributory negligence and mitigation of damage.

10.1.1 General overview

Causation, when viewed generally in the law of obligations, is not a unitary subject since it tends to be split up into different rules and concepts. It can be found as part of the definition of some torts (actionability), or as a defence in others (measure of damages). It is of course a substantive requirement in all torts where damage has to be specifically proved (factual causation), in that if the defendant is able to show that the damage has no causal connection with the tort or breach of contract, he will escape liability for this particular damage. Thus in one case the employers of a lorry driver escaped liability in public nuisance for a dangerously parked lorry, into which a motor cycle crashed, because the accident was actually caused by the motorcyclist looking at girls on the pavement (*Dymond v Pearce* (1972)).

A defendant can still escape liability, even if a factual cause can be shown, if he establishes that the damage is too remote (legal causation). Here the court is not actually saying that the defendant was not the cause of the damage; it is allowing the defendant to escape liability in whole or in part because the connection between breach and damage is too weak. The damage is *too remote* from the breach of duty. This rule is to be found in systems other than the common law and so, for example, the *Code civil* contains an article in its section on contract which lays down that a defendant 'is held liable only for damages which were *foreseen* or which *could have been foreseen* at the time of the contract, when it is not by his *wilfulness* that the obligation is not executed' (art 1150, emphasis added). What remoteness adds to causation is, supposedly, a subjective element, and this is as true for English law as it is for French. However, whereas causation in fact is a question of fact (in the sense that it was once a question for the jury), remoteness is a question of law; it is for the judge to decide upon the subjective element.

Causation can also function at the level of the remedy of damages. A claimant who is partly responsible for his own damage may find his damages reduced by a percentage that reflects his share of the blame (Law Reform (Contributory Negligence) Act 1945). Equally, a claimant who fails to take reasonable steps to mitigate his damage may have to face a reduction in his damages deemed caused by his own unreasonableness. Here, of course, one is not taking a strictly objective approach to causation since one has moved from the connection between breach and damage to the subjective notion of blame. Thus much could depend upon the behaviour of the defendant. One tort writer (Tony Weir) fashioned the adage that 'bad people pay more', and this moral maxim has now seemingly been openly adopted by the House of Lords (*Smith New Court Securities v Vickers Ltd* (1997)).

Given these different levels of causation – actionability, fact, law and damages – it will be useful to approach causation across the whole spectrum of tort and contract law, especially as the different levels have their own conceptual expressions and requirements. Indeed, even when focusing only on the tort of negligence, causation is to be found in areas other than just the 'causation and remoteness' question. As has been mentioned, it often has a role in the duty question (actionability) and is an issue in many defences to negligence (see, eg, *Tomlinson v Congleton BC* (2004)). However, before looking at these different levels something must be said about the various theories of causation.

10.1.2 Theories of causation

The literature on causation is massive, but its existence has done nothing to make the subject any easier or clearer in the law of obligations. Indeed, according to Honoré, the 'theories tend to induce a feeling of frustration, because they either have little empirical content and so fail to point the way, or are clear-cut but apply to only a segment of the circle of problems which present themselves' (Honoré, 1969, § 1).

The idea of competing theories starts with the Roman jurists, one of whom famously repeated a problem posed by an earlier jurist. Several persons were playing with a ball near a place where a barber had set up his chair. One of the players hit the ball rather hard and it knocked against the hand of a barber, who was in the process of shaving a slave, with the result that the barber cut the throat of his client. Who is causally to blame? The jurist poses the problem as if the choice is between ball-player and barber, one jurist, we are told, suggesting that the liability is with the barber for setting up his chair in a place where people were accustomed to play ball. The jurist who posed the problem, however, adds a third possibility: anyone who allows himself to be shaved under such circumstances only has himself to blame (D.9.2.11pr). In this practical problem a number of theory points seem to lie under the surface; there are ideas about directness of cause, about foreseeability, about blame, about contributory negligence, about last opportunity and so on. What is interesting, of course, is that the Roman jurists do not appear to have a definitive answer to the actual problem.

Little has changed today. One problem is that causation itself has never been properly defined and thus can mean a range of different things, depending upon whether the term, at one extreme, is purely objective or, at another extreme, embraces notions of fault, harm, policy and imputability. Common law judges like to avoid these theory questions by claiming that the law adopts a 'common sense' approach. But, as Lord Hobhouse has pointed out,

> causation as discussed in the authorities has been complicated both by conflicting statements about whether causation is a question of fact or of law or, even, 'common sense' and by the use of metaphor and Latin terminology, eg, *causa sine qua non*, *causa causans*, *novus actus* and *volenti*, which in themselves provide little enlightenment and are not consistently used. (*Reeves v Comr of Police for the Metropolis* (2000), 391)

These Latin terms and metaphors seem at first sight scientifically impressive but, as Honoré has pointed out, they are largely empty of content. They do not directly relate to facts. 'But in any case', says Honoré, 'the problems to be answered are so various that they cannot be solved by a single formula which remains at all meaningful' (1969, § 105).

10.1.3 Principles of European tort law

Instead of examining, then, all the various theories, it might be better to state those that have received some practical application as reflected in the recent *Principles of European Tort Law* (PETL) drawn up by the European Tort Law Group. The relevant principles concerning causation are stated in the following terms:

Art 3:101. *Conditio sine qua non*
An act or omission (hereafter: activity) is a cause of the victim's damage if, in the absence of the activity, the damage would not have occurred.

Art 3:102. Concurrent causes

In case of multiple activities, where each of them alone would have caused the damage at the same time, each activity is regarded as a cause of the victim's damage.

Art 3:103. Alternative causes

(1) In case of multiple activities, where each of them alone would have been sufficient to cause the damage, but it remains uncertain which one in fact caused it, each activity is regarded as a cause to the extent corresponding to the likelihood that it may have caused the victim's damage.
(2) If, in case of multiple victims, it remains uncertain whether a particular victim's damage has been caused by an activity, while it is likely that it did not cause the damage of all victims, the activity is regarded as a cause of the damage suffered by all victims in proportion to the likelihood that it may have caused the damage of a particular victim. Regard is to be had to the background risk and the specific circumstances of each victim.

Art 3:104. Potential causes

(1) If an activity has definitely and irreversibly led the victim to suffer damage, a subsequent activity which alone would have caused the same damage is to be disregarded.
(2) A subsequent activity is nevertheless taken into consideration
    (a) if it has led to additional or aggravated damage, or
    (b) if it has led to continuous damage, but only starting from the time that it also would have caused it.

Art 3:105. Minimal causation

In the case of multiple activities, when it is certain that none of them has caused the entire damage or any determinable part thereof, those that are likely to have minimally contributed to the damage are presumed to have caused equal shares thereof.

Art 3:106. Alternative and potential causes within the victim's sphere

If an activity, occurrence or other circumstance, including natural events, within the sphere of the victim may have caused the damage, the victim has to bear his loss to the extent that the cause may lie within his own sphere.

With regard to remoteness of damage, the PETL state:

Art 3:201. Scope of liability

Where causation has been established under Section 1 of this Chapter, whether and to what extent damage may be attributed to a person depends on factors such as

(a) the foreseeability of the damage to a reasonable person at the time of its occurrence, taking into account in particular the closeness in time or space between the damaging activity and its consequence, or the magnitude of the damage in relation to the normal consequences of such an activity;
(b) the nature and the value of the protected interest (Art 2:102);
(c) the basis of liability (Art 1:101);
(d) the extent of the ordinary risks of life; and
(e) the protective purpose of the rule that has been violated.

Now it must be stressed that it is not being suggested that these principles necessarily reflect English law. What they do is to give expression to some theory ideas that are to be found not just in the case law of various continental legal systems but, to some extent, in the English case law and judgments as well. Thus these principles can act as a reference point for understanding the way causation and remoteness function in English contract and tort law; they suggest various categories under which causal problems might be classed. However, rather than focus on these categories directly, it might be easier, as has been suggested, to look at the levels at which causation can operate in the English law of obligations.

10.1.4 Actionability

The first level where causation can function is 'actionability'. This is to say, it can function as a requirement for getting certain tort claims off the ground; if the required causal relationship between harm and act is not present then the tort itself will not be present. Thus trespass will not normally lie where damage results from the indirect act of the defendant; accordingly, in false imprisonment, the defendant must have *directly* imprisoned the claimant and not be just part of a causal chain of events (*Harnett v Bond* (1925)). This trespass requirement emerges out of the old distinction between the writ of trespass and the action on the case; and so in the past causation could play a role in determining whether a plaintiff had brought the right form of action (*Scott v Shepherd* (1773)). Historically, then, actionability was a question of procedure (and to an extent jurisdiction), yet the point can return today as one of substantive law. For example, in *Esso Petroleum v Southport Corporation* (1954, CA), Denning LJ said that he was 'clearly of opinion that the Southport Corporation cannot here sue in trespass' because the 'discharge of oil was not done directly on to their foreshore, but outside in the estuary'; and it 'was carried by the tide on to their land, but that was only consequential, not direct' (at 196). Similar requirements apply to malicious prosecution, and in a tort such as inducing breach of contract the causal link between the 'inducing' and the 'breach' probably needs to be strong before there can be liability. Thus merely furnishing the means by which others can break a contract will not be enough (*CBS Songs Ltd v Armstrad Consumer Electronics* (1988)).

10.1.4.1 Duty of care and causation

Causation issues can also emerge in duty of care cases. For example, the cause of psychological harm is a vital ingredient in the establishing of a duty of care; if the victim has suffered the shock by indirect means – through seeing a disaster in which a loved one is involved on television, or learning of it by word of mouth – the required causal connection will not be enough (see **8.3.2**, above). The mere omission rule can be viewed in similar terms. In *East Suffolk Rivers Catchment Board v Kent* (1941), the defendants were held not to owe a duty of care because their carelessness had not actually caused the claimant's flooding damage. That was an act of nature. All that the defendants could be accused of was not making it better. Similarly in *Tomlinson v Congleton BC* (2004), the decision can be viewed as one in which the claimant was the cause of his own misfortune in diving into such shallow water (see **9.2.2.1**, above).

10.1.4.2 *Volenti non fit injuria*

A claim can fail to get off the ground if the defendant can show that the claimant consented to the damage (PETL, art 7:101(1)(d)). Thus the surgeon is not liable in trespass for the invasion of the patient's body because the patient will have consented to the operation; equally the victim of a legitimate tackle in sport will be taken to have consented to the injury, and this may even extend to horseplay (*Blake v Galloway* (2004)). Of course, just what amounts to consent can on occasions be difficult, and one old case which suggests that submission can amount to *volenti* is probably no longer good law (*Latter v Braddell* (1881)). Equally the surgeon who fails to inform a patient of the full risks associated with any operation can undermine any consent. But such a situation may not result in a trespass claim, for the law takes the view that the patient consented to the invasion so to speak; it may give rise, instead, to liability in negligence if a risk materialises. A particular difficulty arises in this area of medical law where the patient, perhaps through unconsciousness, is unable to give consent. Here the courts have applied the notion of the patient's 'best interests', adding also the presumption that the medical profession is under an obligation to save life. However, despite the clear public policy presumption, where absence of consent is very clear, the doctors cannot act.

One distinction that is fundamental is that between knowledge and consent: mere knowledge of a risk will not act as defence (*Smith v Baker & Sons* (1891)). The risk has to be 'willingly accepted' (Occupier's Liability Act 1957, s 2(5)). In contract, the defence of consent will normally operate as a contractual promise, often in the form of an exclusion or limitation clause, or perhaps even via a notice; but these clauses are not automatically valid thanks to restrictive interpretation or consumer legislation (cf **5.2.4**, above).

10.1.4.3 Necessity

Another defence that, in medical law, is often associated with consent is necessity. 'That there exists in the common law', said Lord Goff, 'a principle of necessity which may justify action which would otherwise be unlawful is not in doubt' (*Re F* (1990), 74). The emergency treatment of a patient without his or her consent can be justified as a matter of necessity if such treatment is reasonable and in the best interests of the patient; and such a defence will extend to, for example, a sterilisation operation on a mentally weak person provided it is reasonable and in her own best interest (*Re F*). More difficult is the problem that arose in one case where the police, in order to recapture a dangerous criminal, ended up by destroying, through the use of CS gas, the shop in which the criminal had barricaded himself. If the police had not been negligent – for necessity is not a defence to negligence – the owner of the shop would not have succeeded in any of the strict liability torts because the police would have had the defence of necessity (*Rigby v Chief Constable of Northants* (1985)). One can speculate if such a defence will today always be valid in such situations now that the Human Rights Act 1998 is in force; for it seems hard that an individual should have to suffer an invasion of his property and perhaps family life for the benefit of the community (cf *Dennis v MOD* (2003); cf **8.4.4**, above).

10.1.4.4 External causes

The PETL provide that a strict liability claim 'can be excluded or reduced if the injury was caused by an unforeseeable and irresistible (a) force of nature (*force majeure*), or (b) conduct of a third party' (art 7:102). This article represents English law as well, since there is authority that both an 'Act of God' (*Nichols v Marsland* (1876)) and an act of a third party (*Perry v Kendricks Transport* (1956)) can be defences to a claim under the rule in *Rylands v Fletcher* (reconfirmed in *Transco plc v Stockport MBC* (2004)). But it may be that these defences will be interpreted more strictly where the thing brought onto land creates a serious risk to surrounding neighbours (*Cambridge Water Co v Eastern Counties Leather* (1994)).

10.1.4.5 Illegal behaviour

A defendant may also escape liability if it can be shown that the claimant was engaged in an illegal activity when he sustained the damage The maxim here is the one that applies in contract: *ex turpi causa non oritur actio* (no action arises out of an illegal cause) (cf **4.3.2.2**, above). In contract such a defence functions more at the level of the remedy rather than the right – the contract is unenforceable rather than void – but in tort one can say that it is a matter of actionablity. The courts will not enforce a right if such enforcement can be regarded 'as sufficiently anti-social and contrary to public policy' (*Pitts v Hunt* (1991)).

10.1.5 Cause in fact

The second level at which causation can operate is the level of fact (and thus was originally a question for the jury). Did the defendant's tortious act cause the claimant's harm? In one famous case a night-watchman, who had been drinking some tea with co-employees, became very ill and went to a hospital for treatment; the duty doctor sent him home without proper examination and the man later died. The doctor was found to have been negligent in sending him home without examination, but the hospital was held not liable because the cause of the illness was poisoning by arsenic. Even if the night-watchman had been admitted for treatment he still would have died since, by the time he had arrived at the hospital, it was too late to save his life (*Barnett v Chelsea and Kensington Hospital Management Committee* (1969)). Similarly, in *McWilliams v Sir William Arrol & Co* (1962), Lord Devlin stated curtly that the 'courts below have held that the employers were in breach of their duty in failing to provide a safety belt, but that was not the cause of the deceased's death since he would not have worn it if it had been provided' (at 308). The general test said to apply in these factual causation cases is the 'but for' test (see PETL, art 3:101, above **10.1.3**). Yet this does not always work since causation problems often prove too complex for such a simple test. Thus the other causation tests set out in the PETL can become relevant. One must add, of course, that policy issues do play a role at this level of 'fact'.

A similar causal rule applies in the tort of breach of statutory duty (cf **8.5.1**, above). It must be the breach of the statutory regulation that actually causes the claimant's injury; and so even where an employer is in breach of a statute, there will be no liability if the employer can prove that the damage would have occurred despite the breach (*Bailey v Ayr Engineering Co Ltd* (1958); *McWilliams v Sir William Arrol & Co* (1962)). Similarly, in *Gorris v Scott* (1874) the defendant shippers were able to avoid liability in breach of statutory duty (see **8.5.1**, above) for the loss of a cargo of sheep washed overboard in a storm, by arguing that their breach of statute did not cause the loss. The object of the statute, which required ships carrying sheep to be divided into pens, was not to protect sheep from being washed overboard; it was to protect against the spread of disease.

10.1.5.1 Loss of a chance

The facts of the *Barnett* and *McWilliams* cases appear, at first sight, as clear examples of the absence of cause and connection between careless act and damage suffered. Yet there is another way such facts can be envisaged, at least in cases where there is more uncertainty as to the effects (or lack of them) of the careless act. What if there had been some chance, however remote, of saving the out-patient's life had the doctor acted without negligence? If such a chance were to exist then the doctor's negligence would have led to some loss, even if the careless act cannot be deemed the actual cause of the death. The out-patient would have lost the chance of having his life saved. Loss of a chance has been recognised as a head of damage in the English law of obligations (*Chaplin v Hicks* (1911); *Allied Maples Group v Simmons & Simmons* (1995)), and there is even a Court of Appeal decision in a medical negligence case in which the careless diagnosis and treatment of an accident victim was held to have caused the loss of a chance of avoiding a serious physical handicap (negligent act → loss of a chance). However, this Court of Appeal decision was overturned by the House of Lords, who insisted on seeing the damage not as the loss of a chance, but as the actual handicapped condition (*Hotson v East Berks AHA* (1987)). This latter structure (negligent act → physical condition) allowed the Law Lords to deny a causal link between negligent treatment and final handicap; the physical handicap was the result of the *accident* not the medical negligence (original accident → physical condition).

The idea of a loss of a chance can be extended to embrace risk. An employer fails to provide washing facilities to employees working in a dirty and dusty brick kiln, and one of the employees contracts dermatitis. The failure to supply the facilities amounts to a tort, but what if the employee cannot actually establish cause and connection between absence of facilities and the dermatitis (negligent omission → ? → physical condition)? Expert medical evidence says only that there is a chance (? in the diagram) that the washing facilities might have prevented the dermatitis. One way around this problem is to focus on the loss of this chance and hold the employers liable for in effect creating an enhanced risk of dermatitis (negligent omission → loss of a chance of avoiding dermatitis; or negligent omission → risk of contracting dermatitis). And this is exactly what the House of Lords did in *McGhee v NCB* (1972), Lord Wilberforce asserting that 'the employers should be liable for an injury, squarely within the risk which they created and that they, not the pursuer, should suffer the consequence of the impossibility, foreseeably inherent in the nature of his injury, of segregating the precise consequence of their default' (at 7). However, in *Hotson v East Berks AHA* (1987) the Law Lords distinguished, and seemingly marginalised, *McGhee*, and although the decision was rehabilitated in *Fairchild v Glenhaven Funeral Services Ltd* (2002) (see **10.1.5.2**, below), the force of the *Hotson* case (together with *Wilsher v Essex AHA* (1988)) has by no means disappeared. A majority of the House of Lords has recently reaffirmed the need for a claimant to prove beyond the balance of probabilities (50%) that the negligence of the defendant has caused the adverse consequences suffered; if the statistical probability of the wrong causing the damage is less than 50% the claim will fail (*Gregg v Scott* (2005)). As Baroness Hale observed, almost 'any claim for loss of an outcome, could be reformulated as a claim for loss of a chance of that outcome' (§ 224) and the 'complexities of attempting to introduce liability for the loss of a chance of a more favourable outcome in personal injury claims have driven me, not without regret, to conclude that it should not be done' (§ 226). In short, it is not enough for a claimant to show that the defendant's negligent act *might possibly* (less than 50% chance) have caused the claimant's loss of a chance for a more favourable medical outcome; it must be shown that it *probably* (more than 50% chance) did cause it.

10.1.5.2 *Fairchild v Glenhaven Funeral Services Ltd* (2002)

In *Fairchild* the causation problem turned out to be rather different from a loss of a chance one, since the causation difficulty arose not from the inexistence of causal relation between fault and disease, but from uncertainty about where to locate the relation in respect of the negligent actor. The claimant was negligently exposed to asbestos dust by two employers but, on contracting mesothelioma, he was not able to establish which workplace exposure had actually triggered the disease; accordingly, the Court of Appeal dismissed his claim against the employers on the ground of failing to prove causation. They rejected in effect the rule expresses in art 3:103 of the PETL. The House of Lords allowed an appeal, Lord Bingham stating (§ 33):

> It can properly be said to be unjust to impose liability on a party who has not been shown, even on a balance of probabilities, to have caused the damage complained of. On the other hand, there is a strong policy argument in favour of compensating those who have suffered grave harm, at the expense of their employers who owed them a duty to protect them against that very harm and failed to do so, when the harm can only have been caused by breach of that duty and when science does not permit the victim accurately to attribute, as between several employers, the precise responsibility for the harm he has suffered. I am of opinion that such injustice as may be involved in imposing liability on a duty-breaking employer in these circumstances is heavily outweighed by the injustice of denying redress to a victim. Were the law otherwise, an employer exposing his employee to asbestos dust could obtain complete immunity against mesothelioma (but not asbestosis) claims by employing only those who had previously been exposed to excessive quantities of asbestos dust. Such a result would reflect no credit on the law.

What is clear, of course, from this observation is that factual causation is not just a question of fact (a point discussed in some detail by Lord Hoffmann). Policy and axiological considerations equally have their role. Interestingly, in *Fairchild* the judges asked counsel to cast their net wider than common law precedents; they wanted to know how such problems were handled in the civil law, and Lord Hope even spent time examining the Roman jurists. As Lord Bingham explained, this was not a question of finding out the law but of discovering where justice lay. Yet in the end much comes down not to some theory or other about causation, but to how one views, or perhaps one should say constructs, the facts. Two hunters carelessly fire their guns at the same time and wound someone out for a walk. One can either accept the mutually exclusive causal defence based on the argument 'it is not me, it is him'; or one can see the two hunters as a single 'actor' and hold both liable. Escaping liability, in other words, becomes something of an ontological (what exists) question; it depends on how one 'sees' the world (do forests exist, or are there only trees?)

10.1.5.3 *Chester v Afshar* (2004)

The *Fairchild* case has been followed by a further decision of the House of Lords that could be said to modify the normal causation rule in the tort of negligence. The claimant underwent surgery which resulted in significant nerve damage that left her partially paralysed. The trial judge held that the surgeon had not been negligent in the performance of the operation, but he had failed in his duty adequately to warn the claimant of the risks which attached to such surgery. What made the case difficult was that the claimant did not argue that had she known the risks she would never at any time have consented to surgery, and this resulted in the judge not being able to state as a fact that the claimant would never have had the operation. Could it be said, therefore, that the absence of the warning was the cause of her partial paralysis?

Two of the Law Lords thought that that the causal test had not been satisfied; the claimant had 'not established that but for the failure to warn she would not have undergone surgery' (Lord Bingham, §8). In other words, she had not proved that she 'would have taken the opportunity to avoid or reduce that risk' (Lord Hoffmann, § 29). However, the majority thought there was sufficient causal connection. Lord Steyn asserted that 'in the context of attributing legal responsibility, it is necessary to identify precisely the protected interests at stake'. And that the duty to warn not only 'tends to avoid the occurrence of the particular physical injury the risk of which a patient is not prepared to accept' but 'also ensures that respect is given to the autonomy and dignity of each patient' (§ 18). Accordingly, 'policy and corrective justice pull powerfully in favour of vindicating the patient's right to know' (§ 22).

This last point made by Lord Steyn has to be appreciated in the context of the particular facts of the case. Failure to warn can of course be seen (and normally is seen) as a 'negligent act'; yet it also reaches beyond negligence and into the tort of trespass, in that it is the patient's informed consent to surgery that prevents the surgical operation amounting to a trespass. Trespass, of course, is a tort that protects constitutional as well as health interests, and thus it is not unreasonable to bring into play interests other than the ones protected by the tort of negligence. As Lord Hope pointed out, the 'function of the law is to protect the patient's right to choose' (§ 56). And 'if the application of logic is to provide the answer, the consequences ... are stark', in as much as there is duty, breach of duty and injury within the scope of the duty but 'the patient to whom the duty was owed is left without a remedy' (§ 73). Causation in the tort of negligence is, accordingly, normally applied as between negligent act or omission and actual injury sustained (act/omission → partial paralysis). But an omission to warn brings into play a mediating 'law of persons' (dignity) interest, which allows a weaker form of causation to function as between the omission and the ultimate injury on the basis that there was a clear invasion of the patient's *right* to choose (omission → absence of right to choose → physical injury). If this *right* were ignored it would, as Lord Hope observed, leave the *duty* 'useless in the cases where it may be needed the most' (§ 87). *Chester v Afshar* indicates once again how the law of tort often has to protect a range of quite different interests, which in turn can reflect themselves in the relationship between a defendant's 'duty' and a claimant's 'right'.

All the same, much will depend upon the actual facts and the way the damage is envisaged (physical outcome or loss of a chance). If the defendant had argued that the claimant had simply not proved beyond the balance of probabilities (ie, more than 50% chance) that the failure to warn had caused her physical injury, the result might have been different, as a later House of Lords decision indicates (*Gregg v Scott* (2005)). Indeed, in his dissenting judgment in *Afshar*, Lord Hoffmann denounced the whole decision as being 'about as logical as saying that if one had been told, on entering a casino, that the odds on the number 7 coming up at roulette were only 1 in 37, one would have gone away and come back next week or gone to a different casino' (§ 31).

10.1.6 Overlapping causes and overlapping damage

Another difficulty to be encountered in factual causation is where damage is aggravated, or indeed just incurred again, by a second independent cause (cf PETL, art 3:104)). C's car is involved in two separate accidents both the fault of the other party (D1 and D2 respectively), and each accident, if viewed independently, necessitates a re-spray of the vehicle; C sues D1 for the re-spray and, although successful, does not get satisfaction (D1 is bankrupt). It would seem that C cannot sue D2 for the re-spray since D2 takes the car as he finds it, that is to say already damaged (*Performance Cars Ltd v Abrahams* (1961); *Halsey v Milton Keynes General NHS Trust* (2004)). D damages C's ship and temporary repairs are effected to make her seaworthy; but the damage is such that the ship will need to return to the USA for more long-term repairs. While crossing the Atlantic she suffers further damage from a storm and again becomes unseaworthy. Both sets of repairs are carried out in the USA, which means that the ship is in dry dock for a longer period than would have been the case if there had been no storm; the owners cannot recover their loss of profits from D for any part of the period while in dry dock (*Carslogie SS Co v Royal Norwegian Government* (1952)).

There were grounds for thinking that personal injury might have been treated differently. D damages C's leg and is sued by C for this damage; just before the trial C is shot in the damaged leg by robbers, and this results in C having his leg amputated. D's argument that C has literally lost the cause of his damage (ie, his leg) will, it seems, be unsuccessful; D must pay for the original damage (*Baker v Willoughby* (1970); and see also *Rahman v Arearose Ltd* (2001)). Yet the position is not clear. In 1973, C suffered a back injury at work due to the negligence of D his employer; in 1976, C became totally disabled owing to an illness that was completely independent of the employment accident; D was liable for C's damage only up to 1976 (*Jobling v Associated Dairies Ltd* (1982)). More recently the decision in *Performance Cars v Abraham* (1961) has been directly applied to a personal injury claim (*Halsey v Milton Keynes General NHS Trust* (2004)), where the earlier precedent was described as 'still good law' and as 'a matter of logic and common sense, it is clearly correct'. The judgment of the court continued (at § 70):

> The claimant is entitled to recover damages from the first defendant for the losses inflicted by him; and from the second defendant for any additional losses inflicted by him. It is true that, if the first defendant is not before the court or is insolvent, the claimant will not be fully compensated for all the losses that he has suffered as a result of the two accidents. But that is not a reason for making each defendant liable for the total loss. In *Baker*, the issue was whether the tortfeasor who had caused the first injury was liable for its consequences after they had arguably become merged in the

consequences of the second injury. In the present case, the question is whether the second tortfeasor is responsible for the consequences of the first injury. To that question, the answer can only be: no. It is true that, but for the first accident, the second accident would have caused the same damage as the first accident. But that is irrelevant. Since the claimant had already suffered that damage, the second defendant did not cause it. This is not a case of concurrent torfeasors.

The situation seems to be, then, that if two hunters both carelessly fire off a shot and a passer-by is hit by a single bullet, both hunters will be liable to the victim, if it can be proved that the bullet came from one or other of the guns (*Fairchild v Glenhaven Funeral Services* (2002)). However, if one hunter carelessly fires a shot which smashes the passer-by's right knee and, a few minutes later, a second hunter fires a shot that would have smashed the victim's right knee if it had not already been smashed, the second hunter will not be liable (*Halsey v Milton Keynes General NHS Trust* (2004)). But if one hunter fires off a shot which hits the passer-by's right knee and a second hunter fires off a shot that hits the passer-by's left knee, each hunter will, apparently, be liable for one knee each (*Rahman v Arearose Ltd* (2001)). The position will of course become complicated if the victim is hit in one knee by one hunter and in the other knee by another hunter and, as a result of the cumulative effect of both injuries, suffers very severe psychological shock. One possibility is to treat the different injuries as a single form of personal injury damage and make one or other hunter liable for all this damage, the hunter held liable then being able to claim contribution from the other hunter (Civil Liability (Contribution) Act 1978). It is, however, uncertain, thanks to the *Rahman* case, how this last situation might be analysed. Matters will become even more complicated if the hunters carelessly injure one knee each with their shots and, subsequently, the victim is run over in the street, losing both legs by amputation that would not have been necessary if the knees had not already been smashed by bullets. Will each hunter be liable for (i) just one injured knee; (ii) the loss of one leg; (iii) the loss of both legs; (iv) the loss of a chance of not having to lose one leg; or (v) the loss of a chance of not having to lose two legs? Do the PETL help answer this question (see **10.1.3**, above)?

10.1.7 *Novus actus interveniens*

Some of these cases can be approached from the position of a supervening event that can then be characterised as a new intervening act (*novus actus interveniens*). In fact new intervening acts can be of different kinds. First, the intervening act can be that of a third party (including an 'Act of God'). D's ship negligently collides with a ship on which C is a sailor; the captain of C's ship decides to set out in a small boat, with a crew including C, to liaise with the captain of D's ship. While crossing between the two ships in a rough sea, the small boat capsizes and C is drowned; the act of the captain in deciding to set out in the small boat does not break the chain of causation (it is a 'natural consequence' of the accident) and D is liable to C (*The Oropesa* (1943)). D, a decorator, working in C's house goes out for lunch leaving the front door unlocked; a thief slips in and steals C's goods. D is liable to C (*Stansbie v Troman* (1948)) (but one might note the contractual relationship).

Secondly, the intervener can be the claimant himself. D negligently injures V, which causes such depression that V subsequently commits suicide; the chain of causation is not necessarily broken and D may be liable for the death (*Pigney v Pointers Transport Services Ltd* (1957)). This is particularly so if D is under an actual duty to guard against V's suicide, and thus the police have been held liable, although subject to a reduction for contributory negligence, where they have failed to prevent V from killing himself (*Reeves v Comr of Police for the Metropolis* (2000)). However, where D has carelessly injured C, the latter must conduct himself with care and must not take unreasonable risks which may result in him suffering further injury; if he does then D will not be liable for the second injury (*McKew v Holland & Hannen & Cubitts Ltd* (1969)). But much depends on the nature of the risk and the situation of the claimant. Some judges try to answer the question by asking whose fault caused the accident (*Ginty v Belmont Building Supplies Ltd* (1959)), but this tends to extend factual causation into the realm of duty which, of course, might be unavoidable on occasions (see *Reeves*, above, and Lord Hoffmann in *Fairchild*, at **10.1.5.2**).

Thirdly, there is the intervention by a rescuer. Here the chain of causation is not broken in situations where a rescuer intervenes to save life and limb; such an intervention is not deemed unreasonable (*Haynes v Harwood* (1935)). A rescuer who intervenes just to save property might not be treated so generously (*Cutler v United Dairies Ltd* (1933); and psychological damage suffered by a rescuer causes particular difficulties (cf **8.3.1**, above).

The general test to emerge from these situations is that of 'reasonableness'. However, it is important to stress that this test is to be understood in a causal sense and thus must not be confused with the reasonable test in breach of duty cases. For example, objectively, suicide might be unreasonable, but in the context of causation things are different (but cf Lord Hobhouse in *Reeves*); there are situations where suicide might not break the chain of causation (see generally *Reeves v Comr of Police for Metropolis* (2000)). Yet care must be taken. In *Fairchild v Glenhaven Funeral Services Ltd* (2002), Lord Hoffmann was of the opinion that (§ 54):

> ... the essential point is that the causal requirements are just as much part of the legal conditions for liability as the rules which prescribe the kind of conduct which attracts liability or the rules which limit the scope of that liability. ... [O]ne is never simply liable, one is always liable for something – to make compensation for damage, the nature and extent of which is delimited by the law. The rules which delimit what one is liable for may consist of causal requirements or may be rules unrelated to causation, such as the foreseebility requirements in the rule in *Hadley v Baxendale* (1854) 9 Exch 341. But in either case they are rules of law, part and parcel of the conditions of liability. Once it is appreciated that the rules laying down causal requirements are not autonomous expressions of some form of logic or judicial instinct but creatures of the law, part of the conditions of liability, it is possible to explain their content on the grounds of fairness and justice in exactly the same way as the other conditions of liability.

Escaping liability on grounds of factual causation must now, it seems, be considered within the whole context of the legal obligation itself, and what 'theory' is to be applied depends, at least in part, upon policy and axiological considerations (cf **6.3.2**, above). Indeed this point has been specifically re-affirmed recently by Lord Steyn (*Chester v Afshar* (2004), § 22).

10.2 Remoteness of damage

The third level at which causation operates is that of law in the full sense of the meaning. That is to say, it was once a question for the judge rather than for the jury. The point to stress here is that one is not applying a factual-orientated concept like 'reasonable' because the problem is not one of making sense of fact as such. The question is one of limitation of liability; a defendant is not to be liable for every consequence flowing from the wrongful behaviour. As a legal question, therefore, the concepts in play are much more normative in nature and try to reflect policy issues as much as causal. There are of course plenty of cases that, not surprisingly (now the jury has gone), confuse factual and legal causation (see, for example, Lord Hoffmann in *Fairchild*, at **10.1.5.2** above), but the starting point for legal causation is the test to be applied, and this test has varied. Being a legal issue this is a matter of precedent, yet, while it is true to say that the test formulated in the 19th century has been replaced by one laid down in 1961, the older test(s) cannot be completely ignored.

10.2.1 Direct damage

The test of liability for a particular head of damage formulated in the 19th century was founded upon the principle of directness. A defendant would be liable for all damage directly and naturally flowing from the negligent act. Thus a railway company was held liable for the destruction of the plaintiff's cottage by fire; the company had negligently caused a fire on its embankment, and the fire spread across a field and then a road and finally arrived at the cottage. The company was liable because the link between fire destruction and negligent act was one of directness (*Smith v L & SW Ry* (1870)). This test was subsequently confirmed in a leading Court of Appeal decision. An employee of a company that had chartered a ship carelessly allowed a plank to fall into the hold of the vessel; the falling plank caused a spark which ignited some petrol vapour in the hold, leading to an explosion that completely destroyed the ship. The charterer was held liable for the destruction even although such extensive damage was an unforeseeable result of a falling plank (*Re Polemis* (1921)).

10.2.2 Foreseeable damage

The directness test, which had come under some criticism, was, formally speaking, abandoned in 1961. Oil was carelessly discharged from a ship during its bunkering operations in Sydney harbour, and it spread to the plaintiff's wharf some 200 yards away where another ship was being repaired. The plaintiff halted its welding operations until assured by scientific opinion that oil on water would not ignite; subsequently, when a spark from the plaintiff's welding fell onto a piece of floating rag, the oil did ignite and the plaintiff's wharf was destroyed in the ensuing fire. The Australian courts, applying the directness test, held the charterers of the ship liable to the plaintiff, but an appeal was allowed by the Privy Council on the ground that the damage was unforeseeable (*The Wagon Mound (No 1)* (1961)). Foreseeability replaced the directness test.

The shift effected by the Privy Council is an interesting one from a methodological point of view. The directness test was one that put the emphasis on the relation between tortious act and damage; if unbroken in the 'directness' sense, there would be liability irrespective of any subjective element on the part of the tortfeasor. The test was genuinely causal in its method. However, the foreseeablity test introduced a whole new approach, in that the facts were now to be reconstructed in terms of an *actor* whose subjective view of the world was to determine the limits of liability. In a sense this has introduced a more 'contractual' flavour into the analysis, in as much as the link between tortious act and damage will depend partly upon what the constituted actor (the reasonable man) had in mind when any particular activity is undertaken. In other words, the 'reasonable man', so central to the breach of duty question (see **8.1.2**, above), has moved to a new stage where duty, breach and causation become, at least in part, merged within the idea of foreseeability. This in turn will affect the other tests, including that of breach of duty, which, it may be recalled, was originally one of reasonable behaviour. In *Tomlinson v Congleton BC* (2004), Lord Hoffmann states (§ 44) that the reason Miss Stone failed in her claim was that she was owed no duty of care by the cricket club. This analysis must be wrong since all occupiers owe a duty of care (if not a higher duty) to highway users not to cause physical injury. The club was not liable because it was not *in breach* of the duty. Yet what seems to be creeping into the analysis is foreseeability; but even this is wrong, since the cricket ball accident, according to Lord Radcliffe, was quite foreseeable. An 'actor' approach to liability thus becomes all-consuming in a *functional* way. Is it the function of the tort of negligence (or any other tort) for this *actor* to remedy this particular *damage*? Here, of course, one is effecting a shift, via the 'subjective actor', off the idea that tort consists of rules or definable structures and onto the aims and objectives of tort (cf **6.2.3**, above; and see also *Morris v Network Rail* (2004)). Decisions are to be justified by reference to social history, economic theory or whatever (see, eg, *Transco plc v Stockport MBC* (2004), § 29 and § 39).

10.2.3 Remoteness in contract

This emphasis on the actor might well be seen as the remoteness test that has always operated in contract, for the *Code civil* (and now the PECL and UNIDROIT) states that a contractor who fails to perform – or who is in breach, to use the common law language – is liable only for damage that was foreseeable at the time of entering the contract (CC, art 1150). This rule was incorporated into English law in the 19th-century decision of *Hadley v Baxendale* (1854), although the term employed was 'contemplation' rather than 'foreseeable'. Thus the actual remoteness rule in contract is that a contractor is liable only for damage that was in his contemplation. In a bailment contract what is contemplated, according to *Hadley*, unless the bailee is made aware of some greater risk, is the value of the thing bailed.

In terms of aims and objectives of contract this contemplation rule can, however, be more generous than the tort rule in that damages for failure to gain a profit are not automatically excluded under a financial loss rule. Thus if *Spartan Steel* (see **6.3.2.6**, above) had been a contract case, the claimant would probably have recovered damages under all of the heads claimed, since it is not difficult to hold that a contractor acting under a contract with the claimant who negligently cuts through a cable will contemplate both stoppage and loss of profits. One also has to add the more general damages rule in contract that the aim is to put the contractor in the position he would have been in had the contract been performed (expectation interest). Nevertheless, the effect of *Hadley v Baxendale*, according to the French analysis that attaches to art 1150 of the *Code civil*, is that it is an implied limitation clause. The aim is to shield a contractor from liability when, say, an object sold is put to an unsuitable and unforeseeable use by the buyer, resulting in serious damage. In other words, a contractor must be able to assess the risk of entering into the contract. Thus a swimming pool contractor who constructs a pool that is not in accordance with the contract will not be liable for the whole cost of a new pool if this is way outside the economic risk (*Ruxley Electronics Ltd v Forsyth* (1996)). A surveyor will, in contrast, be liable for the mental distress caused by over-flying aircraft when this kind of harm was the central risk in the surveying contract of which he was in breach (*Farley v Skinner* (2002)).

10.2.4 Remoteness in tort

Is the same true of tort? Is the foreseeability test one whereby the actor can assess the risk of entering into some course of conduct like driving or manufacturing ginger beer? It has been authoritatively stated that the contemplation (contract) and foreseeability (tort) tests are different, the latter being wider in terms of probability or likelihood (*The Heron II* (1969)). This analysis was viewed with a sceptical eye by Lord Denning MR in *Parsons v Uttley Ingham* (1978), who preferred to emphasise a more general law of obligations rule based on the distinction between physical damage and pure economic loss; but this distinction was not accepted by the other two judges in the case. The present law seems to be, then, that foreseeability is wider in scope and thus encompasses a greater degree of risk.

10.2.5 Untypical damage

Nevertheless, foreseeability can be deceptive here, in that this test can end up excluding certain types of harm for reasons that are not strictly relevant in terms of risk. This point is well illustrated by a particular difficulty that arose after the adoption of the foreseeability test. A farmer carelessly allowed his farm to become infested with rats, with the result that a farm worker became infected with a very rare disease contracted from rats' urine (Weil's Disease). The farmer was held not liable since this particular damage was unforeseeable; had the worker been infected through a rat's bite, he would have recovered (*Tremain v Pike* (1969)). What foreseeability (of the actor) has done here is to introduce a problem of genus and species: one must foresee not only damage (genus) but also the particular species of harm. Breach of duty (reasonableness) becomes intertwined with remoteness (see, eg, *Doughty v Turner Manufacturing Co* (1964)). The courts had begun to grapple with this genus and species problem in a case where a small boy entered a shelter erected by the defendants over a manhole in the street, and started to play with a paraffin warning lamp; the lamp fell down the manhole and exploded, causing the boy serious burns. The defendants argued that while injury by fire was foreseeable, injury by explosion was not, but the House of Lords rejected this defence on the ground that the harm was of a recognised type (*Hughes v Lord Advocate* (1963)). The problem surfaced again more recently when two friends decided to repair an old boat which had been left on local authority land. The boat collapsed on one of the boys, causing him very serious injury, yet his damages claim was rejected in the Court of Appeal on the ground that it was unforeseeable that the boys would jack up and prop up the boat; in other words, the species of *accident* was unforeseeable. This decision was overturned in the House of Lords: the 'foreseeability is not as to the particulars but the genus', said Lord Hoffmann (*Jolley v Sutton LBC* (2000), 1091). Such an approach is clearly right in that foreseeability of the species of damage becomes relevant only if one wishes to exclude particular *interests* (*Spartan Steel* (1973); and see the nuisance case of *Morris v Network Rail* (2004)).

One area which seemingly remained untouched by the foreseeability test was the principle that a tortfeasor must take his victim as he finds him. A worker was burnt on the lip by some molten metal, an injury that might have been prevented had the employer not been negligent; however, the burn turned cancerous owing to the plaintiff's special susceptibility to cancer and he died. The employer was held liable for the death (*Smith v Leech Brain & Co Ltd* (1962); and see also *Robinson v Post Office* (1974)). Again, as with the genus and species issue, this kind of damage simply cannot be excluded by reference to the foreseeability test. If it is to be excluded it should be on the basis of a more structured and objective relationship between the category of damage suffered and the risk attaching to the actor.

10.3 Causation and damages

The fourth level at which causation operates is at the level of damages as a remedy. At this level causation tends to operate not to deny liability but to exclude certain heads of damage. D negligently cut the power supply to C's factory and this caused three types of harm: (i) damage to valuable molten metal in the furnaces when they cooled; (ii) loss of profit on this ruined melt; (iii) loss of profits that the factory could have made during the period it was closed through lack of power. The Court of Appeal held that C was entitled to damages under heads (i) and (ii) but not for head (iii) since this damage, being pure economic loss, was, *inter alia*, too remote (see **6.3.2.6**, above). In this example the exclusion of head (iii) was a question of legal causation; however, factual causation can also be used at this level to limit the extent of liability in damages (*The Liesbosch* (1933)). In addition to this general operation of causation and remoteness to limit liability, several specific defences now operate at this level of damages.

10.3.1 Contributory negligence

The first defence is contributory negligence. Before 1945, if the claimant (C) had causally contributed to his own damage this was regarded as a *novus actus interveniens* isolating the defendant (D) from liability; contributory negligence, in other words, was once a matter of factual causation. In 1945 the law changed. The courts now have a power to apportion responsibility between C and D, and thus if C is 40% to blame for his damage his damages from D will be reduced by this amount (Law Reform (Contributory Negligence) Act 1945). Contributory negligence is mainly now a question of damages. Nevertheless, the courts can still have recourse to factual causation so as to deny any liability where C himself is the cause of his own damage (see, eg, *Dymond v Pearce* (1972)). The 1945 Act does not, it seems, apply to contract unless the facts giving rise to the contractual claim also disclose a cause of action in tort.

10.3.2 Mitigation

The second defence is mitigation. This has been expressed as follows: 'a plaintiff suing for breach of contract or, for that matter, for tort cannot call upon a defendant to pay the full direct consequences unless he himself has acted reasonably to mitigate the loss'. The judge went on to comment that it 'is sometimes loosely described as a plaintiff's duty to mitigate' (*Thomas v Countryside Council for Wales* (1994), 860). But in a 1983 case, Sir John Donaldson MR stated that a 'plaintiff is under no duty to mitigate his loss, despite the habitual use by the lawyers of the phrase'. The claimant 'is completely free to act as he judges to be in his best interests'. However, 'a defendant is not liable for all loss suffered by the plaintiff in consequence of his so acting'; he 'is only liable for such part of the plaintiff's loss as is properly to be regarded as caused by the defendant's breach of duty' (*The Solholt* (1983), 608).

This assertion by Sir John Donaldson is helpful in as much as it clearly locates mitigation in the realm of causation and links it to the interests in play. Moreover, it makes clear that failure to mitigate is not a wrong in itself. Yet it remains an odd comment, in that from the claimant's viewpoint mitigation is dependent upon how he acts and this can be explained in normative terms. For example, in one leading case, a plaintiff was not allowed the full cost of restoring his motor car written off by the defendant's negligence; he could only claim the cost of a similar car on the second-hand market (*Darbishire v Warran* (1963)). Of course in having his car, something of a collector's item, restored he could be said to be acting in his own best interests; yet the judges in the case did not focus on this interest aspect. The test they applied was one focused on the plaintiff as an actor: did the plaintiff behave as a reasonable businessman? In other words, defendants are entitled to expect to pay only for risks that are strictly commercial, and mitigation gives expression to this expectation by saying that a claimant must not 'abuse' his position. This is, in other words, a question of 'duty'.

10.3.3 Measure of damages

Causation might also be seen as operating, at least in a loose sense, behind all the detailed rules that now govern the measure of damages in contract and tort cases. Such damages rules require a textbook in itself, because the courts and the legislator have had to produce very detailed provisions in respect of personal injury claims, if not property damage cases. One is not talking here, of course, of escaping liability *per se*. The question is one of escaping from part of the liability, for substantial sums of money can still be at stake.

The general rule is simple enough: 'the measure of damages recoverable for the invasion of a legal right, whether by breach of contract or by the commission of a tort, is that damages are compensatory' (Lord Diplock in *The Albazero* (1977), 841). Several difficulties immediately arise even at this general level. Are all damages compensatory? In fact some damages, known as exemplary damages, are not (see *Kuddus v Chief Constable of Leicestershire* (2001)). Does 'compensation' mean the same thing in contract and in tort? If one examines this question from the position of interests, there are differences. In contract the aim of an award of damages is normally to compensate for an *expectation interest* (that is, to put the claimant in the position he would have been in had the contract been performed: see eg PECL, art 9.502). In tort the interest is one of restoration, that is to say to restore the claimant to the position he was in before the damage (see eg PETL, art 10:101). Behaviour may play a role; the defendant found liable in fraud will quite possibly be liable for more extensive damage than had he been held liable in negligence

(PETL, art 10:301(2); *Smith New Court Securities v Scrimgeour Vickers* (1997)). Even the nature of the interest invaded can have a dramatic effect on amounts payable. A claimant whose reputation interest has been invaded may receive as much, perhaps even more, than someone badly injured in a road accident (see *John v MGN Ltd* (1997)).

10.3.3.1 Personal injury

As one descends to lower levels of generality the problems become more detailed but no less difficult. There is the general problem of trying to compensate in money for debilitating personal injury. Clearly non-economic losses such as pain and suffering will by nature be difficult; yet trying to establish the future economic loss is no easier in a once-and-for-all lump sum damages award. 'The aim', as Lord Hope has said, 'is to award such a sum of money as will amount to no more, and at the same time no less, than the net loss' (*Wells v Wells* (1999), 390). However, as Lord Steyn in the same case noted, the system might work well enough in cases where the injuries are relatively minor. 'But', he continued, 'the lump sum system causes acute problems in cases of serious injuries with consequences enduring after the assessment of damages' and in 'such cases the judge must often resort to guesswork about the future' (at 384). The courts try to go beyond guesswork by resorting to tariffs (how much an arm is worth) and discount rates (multiplicand); they aim to be 'fair' and to achieve 'consistency' (*Heil v Rankin* (2001)), although whether they always achieve this depends upon one's view of these terms (see eg Weir, 2002, 197).

Some of the more specific questions are these. What if the claimant is rendered permanently unconscious: should he or she still be compensated for pain and suffering? The answer is that substantial damages can be awarded (*West v Shepard* (1964)). Should money received from public donations or from private accident insurance be taken into account when assessing damages for personal injuries? If such money results only because the claimant is the victim of an accident for which the tortfeasor is liable, there is a clear cause and connection between damage and private compensation. Yet why should the tortfeasor benefit from the public's generosity or from the claimant's own prudence? The PETL state that when 'determining the amount of damages benefits which the injured party gains through the damaging event are to be taken into account unless this cannot be reconciled with the purpose of the benefit' (art 10:103); and this possibly represents English law, although much will depend upon how one interprets 'purpose of the benefit' (*Hussain v New Taplow Paper Mills* (1988); cf *Parry v Cleaver* (1970)). Accidents also impact on the victim's family. If the victim is killed as a result of a tort, the dependants will have their own claim against the tortfeasor independent of any claim by the victim's estate (Fatal Accidents Act 1976). But what if the victim is not killed and a family member gives up his or her job to look after the victim: is this loss recoverable? And, if so, by whom? The law of damages may well have to grant 'rights' by ricochet, and thus the House of Lords has held that carer will receive compensation via damages awarded to the victim but held on trust for the carer (*Hunt v Severs* (1994)).

10.3.3.2 Property

Damage to property may seem very much easier to assess than damage to a human, but it is not without its own problems. Even if one starts out from the idea that property has a market value (PETL, art 10:203(1)), it is not always easy to assess such value. Is the owner of a wrongfully destroyed factory or house entitled to full rebuilding cost, or just to the difference in land value before and after the destruction? Is the owner of a wrongfully destroyed herd of pigs entitled to the replacement value or their sale value? Where the owner has been deprived of the use of a thing, damages may be awarded for this loss of use (PETL, art 10:203(2)), and this could well prove more than the value of the thing itself (*The Mediana* (1900); *The Liesbosch* (1933)). The case law is not entirely consistent and much will depend upon the facts of an individual case together with the choices made by a claimant when faced with a destroyed commercial asset.

10.3.3.3 Mental distress

Mental injury is now a protected interest in certain contract situations where mental well-being is the object of the contract itself. Thus a holiday that turns out to be miserable as a result of a breach of contract will attract damages for mental distress (*Jackson v Horizon Holidays* (1975)), as will a contract with a surveyor specifically asked to report on aircraft nuisance (*Farley v Skinner* (2002)). Aggravated damages awarded in, for example, a defamation case might also be viewed as a form of compensation for mental distress. Equally, damages awarded for the invasion of constitutional rights – for example false imprisonment – can be seen as compensating a mental interest, although awards by juries are now, thanks to legislation, controlled by the judges. This control has been exercised very much in the favour of defendants (*Thompson v Comr of Police for the Metropolis* (1998)). The police have, therefore, not escaped from liability when they wrongfully assault or imprison; but the judges have made their lives easier, perhaps to the detriment of administrative law. The English law of tort has too many masters and is the faithful servant to none of them. But can it ever be otherwise?

10.4 Time and cause

Finally, mention must be made of the 'causal' effects of time on a claim. Put simply, time can act to disentitle a claimant from bringing an action and such a disentitlement is called limitation. This means of escape exists thanks to legislation and it acts only at the level of procedure (and must thus be specifically pleaded); nevertheless it can act, in the law of property, as an indirect means of granting ownership rights to a person who has possessed land belonging to another for more than a certain period of time (Limitation Act 1980, s 15; *Buckinghamshire CC v Moran* (1990)). In the law of obligations the passing of time can prevent a contractor from suing for a debt or for damages and the same limitation is true for claims in tort. The normal limitation period is six years (Limitation Act 1980, ss 2, 5), but there are a number of exceptions of which the most important perhaps is a claim for personal injury. Here the limitation period is three years (s 11), although the court has a discretion to override this limit where it would be equitable to do so having regard to certain statutory conditions (s 33). One might note that in contract time runs from the date of the breach, while in tort it normally runs from the date of the damage.

11 Beyond Contract and Tort

The aim of this last chapter is to move beyond contractual and tortious obligations and to look at liability arising in situations where there is neither promise nor wrong. The need for a category, or categories, of obligation in addition to contract and delict (tort) was recognised even in Roman times. Having divided the law of obligations into contract and delict, the 2nd-century jurist Gaius observed that there were some situations which could not be accommodated within this twofold division (G.3.91). This jurist subsequently added a third category of 'various causes' (D.44.7.1pr). The 6th-century Byzantine lawyers went further and added to contract and delict the two further categories of quasi-contract and quasi-delict (see above, **1.3.5** and **1.3.6**).

11.1 Liability for gain

Delictual (tortious) liability is on the whole concerned with damage and loss incurred by a claimant. The object of the claim is to secure compensation, and this is achieved through a liability to pay damages. It is a question of corrective justice, although in certain situations policy considerations might require an appeal to distributive justice (*McFarlane v Tayside Health Board* (2000), 82). Quasi-contractual (unjust enrichment) liability is different; here the emphasis is not on the claimant's loss or damage (although these may well be relevant) but on the defendant's gain. When viewed through the eyes of a common lawyer, the relevant action is more likely to be debt rather than damages since one is often seeking the repayment of a specific amount of money, although of course other remedies might well be relevant (see Lord Atkin in *United Australia Ltd v Barclays Bank* (1941)). In terms of moral philosophy, the remedy often responds more to distributive rather than corrective justice, and this is one reason why the legislator has intervened (Proceeds of Crime Act 2002).

The general principle governing liability in respect of a gain, since Roman times, is this: no one should be unjustly enriched at the expense of another (D.50.17.206). This principle would appear to contain several essential elements. There must be:

(a) an enrichment;
(b) gained at the expense of another (cf *Cressman v Coys Ltd* (2004), § 22); and
(c) which is unjust (or *sans cause* in French law).

As with delictual liability, two approaches can be discerned. Liability can be approached through a number of specific remedies or causes of action, each of which is governed by its own set of rules. This was the Roman approach, where liability depended on the availability of particular types of *actio*; and it is more or less the Roman approach that is to be found in the *Code civil* (*quasi contrats*: arts 1371–1381; Terré et al, 2002, § 1063).

The use of the word 'contract' in this context comes from the idea that this kind of liability arises out of a situation 'as if' there was a contract between the parties (Terré et al, 2002, § 1026). This 'as if' idea was, however, to be problematic for some later civilians. Either a meeting of the minds existed, or such a meeting did not exist; and if there was no *consensus* there could be no contract. Accordingly a second approach is one where liability rests directly on the unjust enrichment principle itself (cf Terré et al, § 1062, etc). In German law, for example, liability is based on such a general principle (BGB, § 812), though the practical application of this code paragraph has proved difficult.

English law has recently recognised these enrichment claims as falling under a liability that is neither contractual nor tortious. Nevertheless, contract, tort and unjust enrichment can overlap in situations where a defendant has, for example, profited from a breach of contract or a tort. If the claimant has suffered damage equivalent to the gain there is no problem, since the remedy of damages will normally solve the problem (corrective justice). Difficulties occur when the claimant has suffered no damage. In this situation the English judges have turned to equity: a person who profits from a wrong but causes no damage to the victim of a breach of contract or a tort might be held liable in equity thanks to its remedy of account of profits (*Att-Gen v Blake* (2001)) (distributive justice). Some commentators regard this situation as an example of restitutionary damages, but this is an error since account is an equitable debt claim rather than a damages remedy.

The distinction between common law and equity, and between rights and remedies, might seem to make restitution a complex area of law, and to an extent it is. But despite these complexities, the Scottish Law Commission has made a major contribution to the unjust enrichment approach to liability for gain in that it has produced a set of Draft Rules on Unjustified Enrichment (Scottish Law Commission DP No 99) based upon the general principle (see rule 1). In the absence of any other international or European (as opposed to national) code, these draft principles might act as a useful starting point for a general approach which shifts the emphasis off remedies and onto more substantive ideas.

11.2 Enrichment

The Draft Rules deal first of all with enrichment, which they define as an 'economic benefit' (rule 2(1)). They go on to state that a person is enriched 'if his net worth is increased or is prevented from being decreased' (rule 2(2)); and the Rules illustrate this with four examples. These are:

(a) acquiring money or other property;
(b) having value added to property;
(c) being freed in whole or in part from an obligation; or
(d) being saved from loss or expenditure.

These examples can usefully be compared with similar provisions identified in the civil law, but it should not be thought that the notion of enrichment does not present serious problems in either system.

In one English case the purchaser of a motor car discovered six months after the purchase that he had no title to the vehicle, and he thus had to surrender it to the real owner. The purchaser successfully sued the vendor in debt for return of the purchase price, which of course meant that he had had six months' free use of the car (*Rowland v Divall* (1923)). Did this six months amount to an enrichment (cf Draft Rules, rule 3(4))? In another case a householder was held to be justified in refusing to pay for a central system that would not work (*Bolton v Mahadeva* (1972)): did he nevertheless receive an enrichment in respect of the boiler, pipes, radiators and the like? Another problem mentioned by Terré et al is the child who receives private lessons from a teacher who is unable to recover payment because the parents have become bankrupt (2002, § 1067). Has the child been enriched? A further problem is one that has been discussed with respect to the English law of frustration (Law Reform (Frustrated Contracts) Act 1943). A claimant contractor renders services which improve the defendant's house; however, before the services are complete, the house is destroyed by lightning. Has the defendant been enriched, or has the enrichment disappeared with the house? This problem may become more acute where there is no contract to render services but the claimant interferes to protect the house while the owner is absent. Here it could be said that any claim ought to be measured with respect not to the expenditure by the claimant, but to the enrichment of the defendant (D.3.5.6.3; cf D.3.5.10.1; D.3.5.22).

This problem of deciding what amounts to 'enrichment' is as complex as the problem of trying to determine what amounts to 'damage'. The danger with putting too much emphasis on the fact of enrichment is that policy considerations that attach, say, to the law of contract can become undermined if one then introduces a whole new set of rules that attach, independently, to gain. In *Bolton v Mahadeva* (1972), the policy that a non-performer cannot claim the contract price is perfectly coherent with regard both to the law of contract itself and to the law of consumer protection. Suggesting that the victim of the non-performance has gained an unjustified enrichment simply undermines this dual policy factor, a point seemingly recognised in a more recent House of Lords decision (*Wilson v First County Trust Ltd (No 2)* (2003)). Of course, there are situations where focusing on the gain rather than on the apparent policy of contract or tort can be valuable. For example, allowing an insurance company to be subrogated to the rights of a tort party whose liability it has covered, so that it can pursue any other potential defendant, can result in a situation where the loss-spreading aim of tort is undermined by an apparent unjustified enrichment. Thus in one famous case, where a careless employee injured a co-employee, the employer, having been held vicariously liable to the co-employee, was allowed to recoup the damages paid out from the employee at fault (*Lister v Romford Ice & Cold Storage Co* (1957)). Given that the real plaintiff was the employer's insurance company, the point can be made – and was made by several tort specialists – that the loss-spreading aim of tort law (see **6.2.3**, above) was undermined by an insurance company who had in truth been paid to carry this very risk (cf *Morris v Ford Motor Co* (1973)). An independent law of restitution, focusing on unjust enrichment, might well have concluded that the insurance company ought to be denied its remedy of subrogation on the basis that in such a situation other potential defendants of the tort victim have not suffered an *unjust* enrichment by not having to make contribution. The loss should fall uniquely on the insurance company since it had been paid to carry this very risk (damage arising out of accidents caused by employees of the insured). Enrichment, in brief, is a delicate term that often transgresses the frontier between corrective and distributive justice.

11.3 At the expense of another

The second requirement is the impoverishment of another. According to the Draft Rules, there is enrichment at the expense of another 'if it is the direct result of' a payment, grant, transfer, incurring of liability, or rendering of services by another person to the enriched person (rule 3). This transfer may be in fulfilment of an obligation of the enriched person; in adding value to the enriched person's property; in acquiring some other economic benefit for the enriched person; or in any other case where there is an interference with the patrimonial rights of the other person otherwise than by operation of natural forces (rule 3(1)). Such an interference will include, for example, the unauthorised use of property belonging to another; but it will not include a mere breach of contract (rule 3(2)). Thus if D uses C's property while C is away, and unknown to C, it may well be that D will be liable to C for a commercial hire fee (*Strand Electric Co Ltd v Brisford Entertainments Ltd* (1952)).

One possible problem is illustrated by the case of the wine seller who sells as litres of wine bottles that in fact contain only 98 centilitres. The seller after several years makes a huge profit out of this wrongful behaviour, but the loss to each individual consumer is so small as to amount to no loss at all. The benefit is at the expense of the consumers only as a class, but if the wine seller is to be relieved of the profit who should sue? One might note on this the English case of *Att-Gen v Blake* (2001), where the equitable remedy of account of profits was used to deprive a person of a wrongful profit even though the claimant had suffered no damage. However the claimant here was the Government, and thus the extracted profit did not go into a private patrimony. Perhaps all unjust gains made from criminal conduct can now be retrieved by a government agency in criminal and (or) civil proceedings thanks to the Proceeds of Crime Act 2002. This statute has the potential to replace a large part of the private law of restitution for wrongs, thus making the non-statutory remedies of restitutionary damages, account and tracing largely irrelevant (see especially s 240ff of the 2002 Act).

11.4 Unjust (*sans cause*)

The final element of the principle is that the enrichment must be unjust. In civil law this is often rather differently described as being '*sans cause*' (Terré et al, 2002, § 1068), but the Draft Rules indicate that the two terms are seemingly synonymous in that rule 4 states that an 'enrichment is unjustified unless it is justified under rules 5 or 6'. And rule 5 is headed 'Enrichment justified by legal cause'. In French law an enrichment will be *sans cause* 'when there is no legal mechanism, no legal title – statutory, agreement, judicial – which can justify the flow of value from the patrimony of the person impoverished to the person enriched' (Terré et al, 2002, § 1068). Rule 5 of the Draft Rules lists these causes, which are much the same as those in French law, although there is added at the end of the list 'or (g) some other legal cause'. An enrichment is therefore 'justified' if the enriched person is entitled to it by virtue of a statutory provision, rule of law or court decree; or as a result of a contract, will, trust, gift or some other legal cause (rule 5(1)).

The rule makes explicit, also, that the mere acquisition of title does not in itself mean that the enrichment is justified. Rule 6 states that an enrichment can be justified by public policy. This includes incidental benefits enjoyed by another when one person undertakes work and expenditure for himself (cf D.3.5.6.3; Terré et al, 2002, § 1070), together with various other examples of what in English law is often referred to as a voluntary payment. 'Voluntary' and 'policy' in this context have perhaps a moral dimension (Terré et al, § 1069). One interesting situation is where a debtor repays a debt and, having paid, discovers that the debt was in fact statute-barred (see **10.4**); no recovery is possible here if the creditor had himself performed his obligation which created the debt (rule 6(c)). A Roman lawyer might talk here of a 'natural obligation'. Another example in the English case law of a voluntary payment is *Regalian Properties Plc v London Docklands Development Corpn* (1995), where 'pending the conclusion of a binding contract any cost incurred by [a potential party] in preparation for the intended contract will be incurred at his own risk, in the sense that he will have no recompense for those costs if no contract results' (Rattee J, at 231). Things might be different if one party expressly or impliedly requests the other to perform services or supply goods in anticipation of a contract that never actually materialises (*British Steel Corporation v Cleveland Bridge & Engineering Co Ltd* (1984)).

Several difficult cases remain. What if a window-cleaner mistakenly cleans the windows of the wrong house: must the householder who benefits pay? In English law the answer is traditionally, and sensibly, that payment is refused on the basis that liabilities cannot be forced upon people behind their backs. Nevertheless, some have argued that the householder should pay on the basis of an analogy with a mistaken payment; if C by mistake gives D too much change, D is under a clear obligation to return the overpayment. Why should services be different? One answer is that services are different and cannot be valued in the same way as money (cf Terré et al, 2002, § 1071). Another difficult problem is where a contractor only partly performs his contract. The part performance may, even where it does not amount to substantial performance (cf *Ruxley Electronics Ltd v Forsyth* (1996)), nevertheless confer a benefit on the aggrieved party. Should the latter be under an unjust enrichment obligation to repay? English law would appear once again to deny liability (*Bolton v Mahadeva* (1972)).

11.5 Remedies and unjust enrichment

This approach to unjust enrichment liability through the principle itself is, as far as the common law is concerned, rather misleading. The subject is very much remedy-driven, which means that rules attach as much to damages, debt, account, subrogation, tracing and the like as to any substantive law of obligation relationship. In turn these remedies can cut across, say, the frontier between owing and owning, between contract and tort, and between law and equity. Quasi-contract in English law has, for example, traditionally focused on the three non-contractual debt remedies of an action for money had and received; an action for money paid; and an action on a *quantum meruit* (see Samuel, 2001, 391–6). And while these debt actions are clearly *in personam*, they can sometimes be based on an *in rem* (proprietary) substantive right because a debt, as a chose in action, is a form of property (*Lipkin Gorman v Karpnale* (1991); and see Proceeds of Crime Act 2002, s 316(4)(c)). In addition, equity offers its own independent *in rem* claim called tracing; a claimant can reclaim money in another's bank account on the basis not of an obligation, but of ownership (and see Proceeds of Crime Act 2002, ss 304–310). The claimant simply asserts that the money in another's patrimony is his property.

11.5.1 Contribution

The principle of unjust enrichment can cut across, then, such established boundaries as the one between property and obligations (and also, now, between civil and criminal law: Proceeds of Crime Act 2002). Another boundary is the one between tort liability in damages and unjust enrichment liability in debt. Where a victim suffers damage as a result of a breach of contract or a tort by more than one defendant, the victim can sue any particular defendant for all his damage (unless the damage itself is causally apportioned between two or more defendants: see, eg, *Rahman v Arearose Ltd* (2001)). However, the defendant condemned to pay has a statutory right to 'recover contribution from any other person liable in respect of the same damage' (Civil Liability (Contribution) Act 1978, s 1). Thus in the terrible Selby train disaster, where a driver fell asleep at the wheel of his car and his vehicle ended up on a railway line in front of an oncoming train, the driver's insurance company was liable to all the victims. The insurance company attempted, unsuccessfully, to gain contribution from the highway authority on the basis, so it was argued, that the authority's inadequate road barriers contributed to the accident. Had the authority been held to be at fault and a part cause of the train crash, it might well have had to contribute 50% of the final compensation bill.

11.5.2 Subrogation

Another area where restitution and tort come together is subrogation, which has been described as a remedy rather than a cause of action (*Boscawen v Bajwa* (1995)). However, it would be better to see it as an institutional structure rather than as a remedy defined and governed by rules. Subrogation is based on a formal relationship either between two persons or between a person and a thing, and it is a means by which one thing or one person is substituted for another thing or person without the actual form of the relationship changing. There are thus two forms:

(a) real subrogation is where one object is substituted for another object; and
(b) personal subrogation is where one person 'stands in the shoes' of another person.

Take, for example, the situation where D owes C a debt and this debt is secured on D's house. If S pays off C with his own money, the law may on occasions allow S to become subrogated to C's position, with the result that S 'stands in the shoes' of C and takes over the security attached to D's house. The form of the legal structure stays the same, but an individual part changes.

Subrogation plays a central role in the English law of obligations since it is the means by which an insurance company is able to gain access to the courts. Thus in many tort cases the real claimant or defendant is not the named party but an insurance company subrogated to the rights of the insured named party. However, as we have mentioned, this can be problematic because subrogation is not a tort remedy as such but belongs in the law of restitution. It is a device supposedly preventing unjust enrichment. Yet, as we have mentioned, when used by an insurance company to recoup insurance money paid out to a victim of a tort, the principles of fault and unjust enrichment can become confused. The loss-spreading aim of tort can be undermined by the desire, on principles of unjust enrichment, to place final liability on the individual at fault (*Lister v Romford Ice & Cold Storage Co Ltd* (1957)).

11.6 Obligations: concluding observations

The law of restitution both contributes to the idea of a law of obligations and detracts from it. It contributes to such a generic category in as much as it shows that the old dichotomy between contract and tort was simply inadequate as a means of encompassing all the possible types of liability arising in debt, damages, account, rescission and so on. In establishing a sub-category within the law of obligations it became possible to free, for example, quasi-contract from its rather forced inclusion in the law of contract (implied contracts). Certain tort claims for, say, exemplary damages, or in trespass for 'restitutionary damages', can now be seen as belonging elsewhere in the obligations camp.

However, restitution equally reveals some of the problems with attempting to import an obligations category from the civil law tradition. Several types of claim embraced by the principle of unjust enrichment are based on ownership rather than on an *in personam* obligation. A similar situation can be found in tort, where causes of action such as trespass to goods and conversion are designed to remedy interference with possessory or proprietary titles to goods. In other words, part of the English law of property is to be found in the English law of obligations. This rather undermines the whole point of having a law of obligations since this is a category that is supposed to stand in stark contrast to a law of property. Real rights, in other words, are supposed to be sharply distinguished from personal rights. Restitution is also blurring the boundary between obligations and crime. Because it is often difficult to identify particular individuals who have had their patrimonies diminished by criminal wrongs (corrective justice), the state has stepped in to act as the claimant (distributive justice), using either the criminal process itself or statutory versions of account and tracing (Proceeds of Crime Act 2002).

Perhaps the whole idea of a law of obligations belongs to a past era when property rights were less complex, although ironically in the past the term 'obligations' actually had no meaning for the common lawyer (Waddams, 2003, 5–6). No doubt contract will always need, at one level, to be sharply distinguished from possession and from ownership; yet contract and possession do often come together in English law (bailment), and a contract is capable of creating *in rem* rights in respect of both personal (Sale of Goods Act 1979, s 18) and real property (*Manchester Airport v Dutton* (2000)). Indeed contract, or its absence, can determine questions of ownership (*Shogun Finance v Hudson* (2003); cf CC, art 2279). In addition, a contractual debt is, as we have mentioned, a form of property in itself (on which see *Beswick v Beswick* (1966, CA)). When one turns to tort one finds a similar intermixing of property and obligations. Private nuisance, for example, is a tort that attaches to land as much as to a person (*Hunter v Canary Wharf Ltd* (1997)), and the remedies in support of bailment are the torts of trespass and conversion (Torts

(Interference with Goods) Act 1977). Even defamation can be considered as a tort protecting a kind of property right (Ibbetson, 1999, 186).

One conclusion that can be drawn from this is that the expression 'law of obligations' must be treated with great caution by English lawyers. It might seem at first sight an attractive generic category, and might even appear to make the common law more attractive in a rational sort of way to lawyers from other EU countries. However, as a viable idea it is a little like Iraq's supposed Weapons of Mass Destruction; that is to say, a viable idea in the abstract but illusive when one moves to ground level. That contract, tort and restitution should come together to form a generic category of obligations appears in the abstract as a rational idea; but when one gets to examine the individual causes of action all the pieces do not fit into the neat systematic pattern created by those post 16th-century Romanists reworking Gaius' and Justinian's classification schemes (*mos geometricus*) (see Stein, 1999, 79–82).

It would, perhaps, be better to say that English law is based on a spectrum between several conceptual poles. At one pole there is the law of contract; and at another pole, the law of real property. Yet a third pole must now be established which represents the criminal law and criminal procedure. In between these poles there is a law of various causes of action (including statutory orders and the like) and remedies – which can be loosely grouped into categories like tort, family law and so on – reflecting different facets of the individual in society. Some causes of action are patrimonial and reflect the individual as an *economic unit*; other causes of action (eg, defamation, harassment, certain human rights) are framed around the individual as a *social being*. Yet other causes of action (eg, false imprisonment, malicious prosecution, certain human rights) give expression to the idea of the individual as a *political (constitutional) unit*. In addition there are now statutory restitution claims that intermix all of these facets. Such facets give rise to a categorisation that is too weak, of course, to found an inference model from which solutions to cases can be deduced through syllogistic logic. Also, some sets of facts raise at one and the same time social and patrimonial interests (see, eg, *Spring v Guardian Assurance* (1995); and see also Proceeds of Crime Act 2002); other sets of facts intermix the social and the constitutional, or the constitutional and the patrimonial. But then the *mos geometricus* was a European law movement that never crossed the Channel; and anyway, the idea that law is a deductive science is something that most common lawyers find vaguely ridiculous. Law is about judging, not mathematical deduction.

Understanding contractual and non-contractual obligations, in English law at least, requires a subtle and flexible mind that comprehends both legal taxonomy, together with the logic that flows from it, and the limits of such taxonomy in the face of a complex social reality. Categories are the respected employees of legal reasoning, but they are not the masters (see Waddams, 2003). There is no scientific reason why the world needs to be divided into contract, tort and restitution; there is only assertion based on conceptual coherence and consensus amongst the law community. Given that the common law is a system that functions more at the level of fact and argumentation than abstract rule regime (Legrand, 1999, 75–102), the idea of a law of obligations defined within a highly coherent system is alien to its historical and epistemological (knowledge and method) tradition. The common law, in other words, is not an area capable of being reduced to a concise 'map' (see Samuel, 2005). This is a lesson that those learning the law ought never to forget.

Reference Bibliography

Atiyah, P (1979), *The Rise and Fall of Freedom of Contract* (Oxford University Press)

Bell, J (1989), 'The Effects of Changes in Circumstances on Long-term Contracts: English Report', in Harris and Tallon (1989), 195

Bergel, J-L (2001), *Méthodologie juridique* (Presses Universitaires de France)

Birks, P (1996), 'Equity in the Modern Law: An Exercise in Taxonomy' (1996) 26 *University of Western Australia Law Review* 1

Birks, P (ed) (1997), *The Classification of Obligations* (Oxford University Press)

Birks, P (2000), 'Introduction', in P Birks (ed), *English Private Law* (2 vols) (Oxford University Press)

Cane, P (1997), *The Anatomy of Tort Law* (Hart Publishing)

Cane, P and Stapleton, J (eds) (1998), *The Law of Obligations: Essays in Celebration of John Fleming* (Oxford University Press)

Carbasse, J-M (1998), *Introduction historique au droit* (Presses Universitaires de France)

Crépeau, P-A (1998), *The UNIDROIT Principles and the Civil Code of Québec: Shared Values? (Les Principes d'UNIDROIT et le Code civil du Québec: valeurs partagées?)* (Carswell)

Fleming, J (1985), *An Introduction to the Law of Torts* (2nd edn, Oxford University Press)

Goff, R (1983), 'The Search for Principle', reprinted in Swadling and Jones (1999), 313

Gordley, J (1991), *The Philosophical Origins of Modern Contract Doctrine* (Oxford University Press)

Gordley, J (1997), 'Contract in Pre-commercial Societies and in Western History', *International Encyclopedia of Comparative Law*, Vol VII, Ch 2 (JCB Mohr)

Gray, K and Gray, S (2003), 'The Rhetoric of Reality', in J Getzler (ed), *Rationalizing Property, Equity and Trusts* (Butterworths), 204.

Harris, D and Tallon, D (eds) (1989), *Contract Law Today: Anglo-French Comparisons* (Oxford University Press)

Honoré, A (1969), 'Causation and Remoteness of Damage', *International Encyclopedia of Comparative Law*, Vol XI, Ch 7 (JCB Mohr) (completed 1969)

Hudson, A (2001), *Understanding Equity & Trusts* (Cavendish)

Hudson, A (ed) (2003), *New Perspectives on Property Law, Human Rights and the Home* (Cavendish)

Ibbetson, D (1999), *A Historical Introduction to the Law of Obligations* (Oxford University Press)

Jolowicz, H (1957), *Roman Foundations of Modern Law* (Oxford University Press)

Jolowicz, H (1963), *Lectures on Jurisprudence* (Athlone)

Jolowicz, J (1968), 'Liability for Accidents' (1968) *Cambridge Law Journal* 50

Jolowicz, J (1983), 'Protection of Diffuse, Fragmented and Collective Interests in Civil Litigation: English Law' (1983) *Cambridge Law Journal* 222

Jolowicz, J (1985), 'Public Interest and Private Damage' (1985) *Cambridge Law Journal* 370

Jones, J (1940), *Historical Introduction to the Theory of Law* (Oxford University Press)

Kasirer, N (2003), 'Pothier from A to Z', in *Mélanges Jean Pineau* (Thémis, Montreal), 387

Kolbert, C (1979), *Justinian: The Digest of Roman Law* (Penguin)

Lasser, M (1995), 'Judicial (Self-)Portraits: Judicial Discourse in the French Legal System' (1995) 104 *Yale Law Journal* 1325.

Lawson, F (1950), *Negligence in the Civil Law* (Oxford University Press)

Lawson, F (1980), *Remedies of English Law* (2nd edn, Butterworths)

Lawson, F and Rudden, B (2002), *The Law of Property* (3rd edn, Oxford University Press)

Legrand, P (1996), 'European Legal Systems are not Converging' (1996) 45 *International and Comparative Law Quarterly* 52

Legrand, P (1999), *Le droit comparé* (Presses Universitaires de France)

Lévy, J-P and Castaldo, A (2002), *Histoire du droit civil* (Dalloz)

Lewison, K (2003), *The Interpretation of Contracts* (3rd edn, Sweet & Maxwell)

Lobban, M (1991), *The Common Law and English Jurisprudence 1760–1850* (Oxford University Press)

Markesinis, B, Auby J-B, Coester-Waltjen, D and Deakin, S (1999), *Tortious Liability of Statutory Bodies: A Comparative and Economic Analysis of Five English Cases* (Hart Publishing)

Oliver, D (2000), 'The Human Rights Act and Public Law/Private Law Divides' (2000) *European Human Rights Law Review* 343

Ost, F (1990), *Droit et intérêt: volume 2: Entre droit et non-droit: l'intérêt* (Facultés universitaires Saint-Louis, Bruxelles)

Rudden, B (1989), 'The Domain of Contract: English Report', in Harris and Tallon (1989), 81

Rudden, B (1991–92), 'Torticles' (1991–92) 6/7 *Tulane Civil Law Forum* 105

Samuel, G (1998), 'The Impact of European Integration on Private Law – A Comment' (1998) 18 *Legal Studies* 167

Samuel, G (2000), *Sourcebook on Obligations and Legal Remedies* (2nd edn, Cavendish)

Samuel, G (2001), *Law of Obligations and Legal Remedies* (2nd edn, Cavendish)

Samuel, G (2003), 'Property and Obligations: continental and comparative perspectives', in Hudson (2003), 295

Samuel, G (2005), 'Can the Common Law be Mapped?' (2005) 55 *University of Toronto Law Journal* 271

Staudenmeyer, D (2002), 'The Commission Communication on European Contract Law and the Future Prospects' (2002) 51 *International & Comparative Law Quarterly* 673

Stein, P (1984), *Legal Institutions: The Development of Dispute Settlement* (Butterworths)

Stein, P (1999), *Roman Law in European History* (Cambridge University Press)

Stone, R (2002), *The Modern Law of Contract* (5th edn, Cavendish)

Swadling, W and Jones, G (eds) (1999), *The Search for Principle: Essays in Honour of Lord Goff of Chieveley* (Oxford University Press)

Taggart, M (2003), 'The Peculiarities of the English: Resisting the Public/Private Law Distinction', in Craig, P and Rawlings, R (eds), *Law and Administration in Europe: Essays in Honour of Carol Harlow* (Oxford University Press), 108

Terré, F, Simler, P and Lequette, Y (2002), *Droit civil: Les obligations* (8th edn, Dalloz)

Teubner, G (1998), 'Legal Irritants: Good Faith in British Law or How Unifying Law Ends Up in New Divergences' (1998) 61 *Modern Law Review* 11

Turpin, C (2002), *British Government and the Constitution: Text, Cases and Materials* (5th edn, Butterworths)

Van Caenegem, R (1971), 'History of European Civil Procedure', *International Encyclopedia of Comparative Law*, Vol XVI, Ch 2 (JCB Mohr) (completed 1971)

Waddams, S (2003), *Dimensions of Private Law: Categories and Concepts in Anglo-American Legal Reasoning* (Cambridge University Press)

Weir, T (1971), 'The Common Law System', *International Encyclopedia of Comparative Law*, Vol II, Ch 2, Pt III (JCB Mohr) (completed 1971)

Weir, T (1972), 'Complex Liabilities', *International Encyclopedia of Comparative Law*, Vol XI, Ch 12 (JCB Mohr) (completed 1972)

Weir, T (1992), 'Contracts in Rome and England' (1992) 66 *Tulane Law Review* 1615

Weir, T (1998), 'The Staggering March of Negligence', in Cane and Stapleton (1998), 97

Weir, T (1999), 'Non-performance of a Contractual Obligation and its Consequences in English Law', in L Vacca (ed), *Il contratto inadempiuto: Realtà e tradizione del diritto contrattuale europeo* (G Giappichelli), 71

Weir, T (2002), *Tort Law* (Oxford University Press)

Weir, T (2004), *A Casebook on Tort* (10th edn, Sweet & Maxwell)

Weir, T (2005), 'Recent Developments in Causation in English Tort Law', in Fauvarque-Cosson, B, Picard, E and Voinnesson, A (eds), *De tous horizons: Mélanges Xavier Blanc Jouvan* (Société de Législation Comparée, 2005), 883

Williams, G (1951), 'The Aims of the Law of Tort' (1951) 4 *Current Legal Problems* 137

Williams, G and Hepple, B (1984), *Foundations of the Law of Tort* (2nd edn, Butterworths)

Winfield, P (1931), *The Province of the Law of Tort* (Cambridge University Press, 1931)

Zenati, F and Revet, T (1997), *Les biens* (2nd edn, Presses Universitaires de France)

Zimmermann, R (1996), *The Law of Obligations* (Oxford University Press)

Zweigert, K and Kötz, H (1998), *An Introduction to Comparative Law* (3rd edn, Oxford University Press; trans T Weir)

Index